THE SEARCH FOR MIAS

By CHIEF WARRANT OFFICER GARRY L. SMITH
U.S. Army, Retired
Edited by Ed. Y. Hall

THE HONORIBUS PRESS
SPARTANBURG, SOUTH CAROLINA

Published By The Honoribus Press
Post Office Box 4872
Spartanburg, South Carolina 29305

All photographs unless noted are courtesy of
the United States Army or the author.

AN HONORIBUS PRESS WAR SERIES BOOK

ISBN: 0-9622166-3-1

Printed in the United States of America
Altman Printing Company, Inc.

WHERE ARE OUR
MISSING MIAs AND POWs

Chief Warrant Officer Garry L. Smith, US Army, Retired, has written a most remarkable account of his part in the search for America's lost sons of the Vietnam War. As a member of the Joint Casualty Resolution Center (JCRC) staff (See Appendix), Garry participated in eight search trips to Vietnam during the period between 1987 and 1990. As a Vietnamese linguist he was involved in the on the ground "eyeball contact" search in Vietnam for our missing-in-action (MIA) personnel. Garry interviewed hundreds of Vietnamese men, women, and children in the JCRC's exhaustive search for clues – any clues – that would lead the team on a trail of MIA remains, identification and recovery. Garry's interesting and timely story is of vital importance to the questions that emit almost daily from our national media. Where are our MIAs? Where are our missing POWs?

The Search for MIAs will become a classic of Vietnam War literature, and it has been my great pleasure to assist Garry in bringing this important Work to the American people.

Ed. Y. Hall,
Honoribus Press

"There are those inside and outside the government who constantly dig at the Cold War wound to reclaim what they falsely portray as their lost honor in not winning the Vietnam War. What happened in that war happened. The historical events of two decades ago can not be changed. It is also a fact that we can not bring the dead back to life. However, it is honorable and proper that the Joint Casualty Resolution Center continue in its quest for the fullest possible accounting. Our fallen comrades, their next of kin and this Nation demand it."

Senior Government Official
Washington, DC
October 1992

The author by a Jeep Cherokee at the Government Guest House in Hanoi. Eight of these Cherokees were flown to Vietnam on C-141 transport aircraft.

DEDICATION

This book is for Betty, Ross, Carl and Bernice:
a military family that served above and beyond the call of duty.

Chief Warrant Officer Garry L. Smith in the Ashau Valley with former Viet Cong. On the far left is Lieutenant Colonel Cu Pang, who commanded five National Liberation Front military districts.

ACKNOWLEDGEMENTS

I want to make favorable mention of those with whom I served closely at the Joint Casualty Resolution Center between 1987 and 1990. These were: Lieutenant Colonel (US Army) Joe Harvey, Commander; Lieutenant Colonel (US Air Force) Paul Mather; Lieutenant Colonel (US Air Force) James Spurgeon; GS 13 Garnett (Bill) Bell; GS 12 Jim Coyle; GS 12 Bill Gadoury (formerly US Air Force); GS 11 Michael Janitch; Chief Warrant Officer 3 James Webb; Chief Warrant Officer 3 Tom McKay; Master Sergeant David Atherton; and secretary Carol Thrash, whose daughter my son Ross fell in love with.

I want to particularly emphasize the outstanding contributions of Paul Mather, who served overseas resolving the fate of MIAs for thirteen years and Bill Bell, the senior JCRC Vietnamese linguist and investigator. Bill Bell later became Director of the first POW/MIA office in Hanoi.

After you have read this book, you may think it strange that I would offer such lavish praise on Bill Bell. He and I were light years apart on our views about the MIA issue. However, during his tenure at JCRC, Bill provided more information about MIAs than anyone else in the entire federal government. My disagreements with him concerned only the conclusions he reached about the information that JCRC and other governmental agencies obtained. In spite of our differences in this regard, I want to say, Bill, my friend, my confidant, my fellow soldier....I salute you.

Also I want to emphasize the contribution of Colonel Ed. Y. Hall, SCSG, of Honoribus Press. Colonel Hall's editorial expertise in making THE SEARCH FOR MIAs a reality was invaluable. Essentially he took a rough manuscript of personal observations, experiences, and commentaries, and turned it into the attractive and readable book you have in front of you.

And last, but definitely not least, I want to thank from the bottom my heart, Jerry Cook, a military retiree, and his lovely wife Vicki. They believed in this book and made it a reality, long after I had given up hope that it would ever be published.

Garry L. Smith
October 14, 1992

TABLE OF CONTENTS

INTRODUCTION

There are very few books, if any, that have introductions written by an anonymous person. This one does. The reason is that the individual making the introduction is still very much a major player in the MIA issue. Should he publicly lend his name to **THE SEARCH FOR MIAs,** it could be construed by some that his organization, which maintains a neutral stance, is in support of the viewpoints and conclusions of the author. The writer of this introduction has impressive credentials that document his knowledge and expertise concerning all aspects of the POW/MIA issue. His name would be immediately recognizable to those who have had anything to do with resolving the fate of American MIAs. His introduction is in the form of a letter, which is as follows:

Dear Garry,

You have done what many believed was impossible; you've told it like it is. You must now face the slings and arrows from those who do not want the war to end and who will find fault with every fact you have recited. The attacks on your nuances will come later. I salute your courage.

In 1975 you tackled the difficult task of resettling many of our former Vietnamese colleagues from the Republic of Vietnam's Armed Forces. Your job then, and a decade later at the Joint Casualty Resolution Center, as an investigator of MIA cases, was to pick up the pieces of the Vietnam war. You have presented the story of those humanitarian endeavors honestly, factually, and with an eye to detail. You have presented your anecdotes and glimpses of your own two-decade experience in Southeast Asia where the rubber meets the road, to use your own expression. You have done it while it was still fresh in your mind and without malice for those whom we faced on the battlefield. Your anecdotes are topical, without rancor and they accurately reflect many impressions of people in the region, shared by many associates. You have also described the cultural and social differences of those you have met in Vietnam and Thailand which constitute the uniqueness and differences which make us unique as peoples.

I was particularly taken by your description of your latest experiences during Operation DESERT STORM and your finding of the bodies of dead Iraqi soldiers. Your description of what happened to their remains, partially devoured by animals, will not be pleasant for some to read. But, it is a simple fact of war which many in today's world can not comprehend easily. It helps, in a macabre way, to explain why the remains of the wartime dead are frequently not recoverable. Those who reject explanations of witnesses, to include former Viet Cong and North Vietnamese soldiers who can't remember where they buried bodies twenty years ago, need to reflect on these facts. When your experiences in Kuwait are multiplied by a factor of ten, you begin to explain what happened to the remains of our airmen on the Ho Chi Minh Trail in Laos.

Garry, you have seen Vietnam in time of war and time of transition. You have gone where few Americans have ever travelled. Barely two years ago you inched your way along a cliff with your former adversary behind you and a slip away from death, both of you looking for an illusive crash site of an American aircraft which still remains hidden for others to find. You did not flinch. That, more than anything, is the legacy you have bequeathed to those who must rebuild in a time of peace what we tried so valiantly to destroy in time of war.

The Joint Casualty Resolution Center has acquitted itself with dignity in the search for honest answers. Their search, and your own, was not without pitfalls as you coped with political perfectionists demanding a level of accounting and excellence not of this earth. You and others in JCRC were human, made mistakes, learned from them, and moved forward. Such is the reality which we dislike but must accept. Your critics will look to your mistakes and point to them as examples of that they claim is wrong with Washington's efforts. Ignore them.

There are those inside and outside the government who constantly dig at the Cold War wound to reclaim what they falsely portray as their lost honor in not winning the Vietnam War. What happened in that war happened. The historical events of two decades ago can not be changed. It is also a fact that we can not bring the dead back to life. However, it is honorable and proper that the Joint Casualty Resolution Center continue in its quest for the fullest possible accounting. Our fallen comrades, their next of kin and this Nation demand it.

Those who have profited from the MIA issue must be scorned for their perverse use of the dead to enrich their private coffers. Your description of some of the many scams which led to exploitation of some next of kin should be eye opening. The human frailties of Southeast Asian refugees is dealt with in a down-to-earth, straight-forward manner. They are not to be twice-condemned for also being human victims in this tragedy.

You have dealt with your former co-workers of the Joint Casualty Resolution Center as team members who all shared a similar search for truth in a mine field of true believers in cover up and conspiracy theories. It seems that is what makes news these days. Your own writing may languish unread by those who need it the most, but you have done what few ever do – you accepted the challenge and answered the call. For that you are to be commended.

Today, as in the past, the true believers will search for a misplaced comma and botched syntax to accuse you of having a mind set. Most of your soon-to-be critics never saw the war, or its aftermath. They are to be damned for the hypocrisy they have spawned and you need not respond to their childish search for visibility.

Your straight-forward account is part of a process of reintroducing reality to one of the most sordid chapters of American history. I do wish you God's speed. You have more than earned it.

Name withheld by request

Washington D.C., October 1992

PROLOGUE

POSITION VERSUS STRENGTH

During my eight trips back to Vietnam between 1987 and 1990 as a member of the Joint Casualty Resolution Center, I had frequent opportunity to talk to Vietnamese about their war experiences. This was of particular interest to me as a Vietnam veteran, since I wanted to get inside the heads of my former enemies to see what made them tick.

I particularly got a lot of insight from one individual who had not served as a uniformed soldier, but his contribution to the war was as significant as that of any rifleman. He had been a diplomat with duty in the Vietnamese Foreign Service. He said his mission during the latter days of the war was to analyze U.S. newspapers and periodicals in order to follow the mood of the american public. He expressed that in addition to using the information about American war sentiments in developing negotiation strategies to be used in Paris, the information was also used to develop psychological operations to be used against the American government.

The diplomat remarked that the military philosophy of vietnam during the war was something called "Position Versus Strength" (The Chong Luc). He conveyed that the Vietnamese people could never hope to defeat the United States one on one, since it was too powerful to ever be beaten in such an encounter. However, the strategy of the Vietnamese was to look for weaknesses in the American fabric that could be exploited in order to "gain favorable position" from which it could strike the United States at a sore spot. The diplomat told me that he and others during the war constantly studied all aspects of American culture and traditions, looking for inherent contradictions and discontent that could be used against the enemy.

He said the visit by the New York Times correspondent Harrison Salisbury to Vietnam was just such a strategy of influencing American public opinion. And also, allowing American anti-war activists, such as Jane Fonda, to tour Vietnam at the height of the war was an example of "The Chong Luc."

The diplomat maintained that the news media in the United States debated for years the significance of the Viet Cong in South Vietnam. He said the North Vietnamese always controlled the Viet Cong, but deliberately gave it a pluralistic and nationalist image to make it attractive to Vietnamese elements that would not otherwise support a communist revolution. The diplomat asserted that this was a perfect example of carefully studying the political situation and advancing a movement to take in converts who would likely have joined the puppet government in fighting against the North.

At the same time, North Vietnam encouraged the international news media to report that the Viet Cong was a nationalist organization composed of moderate reformers and totally separate in its policy from the North. The diplomat said the result of this deception that was picked up by the international press was that the National Liberation Front became favorably viewed by left-wing elements of American politics.

There is no question that during the war the Vietnamese government exploited American prisoners of war in every way possible. The diplomat with whom I conversed must have seen the POWs as valuable assets in getting the U.S. out of the war and exploited them to the limit. And it worked well: essentially, the terms for ending the war we eventually agreed to was "you give us our prisoners back and we'll go home."

Knowing the Vietnamese policy of looking for weaknesses to exploit, or "The Chong Luc," is it possible that the Vietnamese government could have kept prisoners? Did American soldiers remain behind in Southeast Asia after the U.S. withdrawal from the Indochina War, either as prisoners of war or converts to Marxist ideology? This is a question that has troubled the American public for almost two decades.

The answer for certain is that at least one stayed behind: A Marine by the name of Bobby Garwood did not come out of Vietnam until 1979. He was charged and tried as a deserter by the U.S. Marine Corps. Were there others that we don't know about, either bona fide prisoners of war, deserters, or so-called "progressives"? Many influential Americans, some of whom were or still are in active US. government service, believe without a shadow of doubt that American servicemen, perhaps large numbers of them, were there after the American withdrawal.

Various POW/MIA investigative organizations of the U.S. government, such as the Joint Casualty Resolution Center (see appendix), which I worked for, were created to resolve the fate of the missing. This was the pledge by the Nixon administration that there would be a full accounting of MIAs. These organizations have collected hundreds upon hundreds of reports from refugees alleging living Americans are still being held captive in Southeast Asia. What should we make of such stories? Are these reports proof that the Vietnamese government carried out a clandestine program of holding American prisoners? Were Americans held as some sort of guarantee that the American government would not re-involve itself in the Indochina War? Or perhaps were they held to force the United States to live up to promises of massive aid to North Vietnam that were made by the Nixon administration in the latter days of the war?

Also, if in fact the Vietnamese government did prevent Americans from coming home, other serious questions emerge as to whether the U.S. government knew of the alleged deception and carried out elaborate campaigns to keep the American public from ever finding out that Americans were knowingly left behind. Some influential individuals have made accusations that intelligence activities of the U.S. government conspired to cover-up evidence that Americans stayed behind. Some even have concluded that "hit-squads" were actually given orders to "liquidate" American prisoners who stayed behind to ensure they would never surface to embarrass those who had been in power and were responsible for leaving MIAs to languish in captivity in Southeast Asia.

Also, it has been rumored for years that the Vietnamese government "warehoused" remains of MIAs, pulling a few out here and there for political purposes at opportune times. The question is, has the Vietnamese government used remains as one more psychological weapon in its policy of "The Chong Luc"?

Finally, when I was at the Joint Casualty Resolution Center as an interviewer, we were flooded with thousands of dog tags and bones that refugees brought to us that they claimed pertained to MIAs, which clearly did not . Most were of soldiers who served in Vietnam and returned safely to the U.S. Also refugees told us silly stories about American prisoners who stayed behind, one of whom went by the name of "Bunker Queer". These prisoners had allegedly escaped and were being cared for by local villagers. Was this flood of phony dog tags and silly stories planted by the Vietnamese security apparatus just to confuse MIA investigators and throw us off the track? Was this one more devious plot of "The Chong Luc"?

What is the truth about all of the above? What can we believe about the MIA issue? When I first started to work for the Joint Casualty Resolution Center, I too had serious questions about whether or not our government walked off and left Americans in Southeast Asia. However, I had the good fortune of being able to research significant documents, interview hundreds upon hundreds of eyewitnesses to MIA cases, and travel extensively throughout Vietnam in gathering evidence. I believe you will find in the following pages answers or at least a thoughtful reply to all of the questions that I have addressed in this Prologue.

I want to emphasize that there is no classified information whatsoever in this book. Everything I have used comes from unclassified publications, my own observations, or informal conversations that I had with Vietnamese or knowledgeable Americans. In addition, I have scrupulously followed the guidelines I served under when I was an interviewer assigned to the Joint Casualty Resolution Center, in that I have not addressed specific MIA cases, nor have I disclosed information obtained from investigative sites in Vietnam. I don't think this has hindered what I have set out to accomplish in this book.

I hope this book is meaningful to you. I know that emotions are so heightened over this subject and I pray that if I happen to contradict your theories about the MIA issue, you will not hold this against me. The important point is that I mean no harm whatsoever to MIAs and their families. I would never disparage the memory of an American fighting man who ended his honorable service as an MIA. I dedicated over 20 years of my life to military service and I would do nothing to lessen the supreme sacrifice of others.

Garry L. Smith

Crossing a river in the Ashau Valley.

CHAPTER ONE

THE ADVENTURE BEGINS

I graduated from high school in 1965, just as the American public was slowly learning there was a place called Vietnam. By then, the Vietnamese people had already undergone years of national convulsion, yet few Americans, including myself, were aware that the problems of Vietnam would soon engulf them too. I was one of those Americans swept up in the Vietnam War, and as a result Vietnam has colored just about everything I've done since.

I, like thousands of other Americans, spent years agonizing about Vietnam, before and after I served there in the military. But I was able to experience a healing process that most Americans, particularly Vietnam veterans, have not been able to undergo. I was able to work for three years in an organization that had the mission of resolving the fate of MIAs, a mission which President Reagan stated had the "highest national priority." Because of my job, I was able to go back to Vietnam eight times after the war. These missions gave me a chance to get a lot of venom out of my system and to come to terms with the Vietnamese people.

My involvement with the MIA issue was really a fluke. In December of 1986, as a career Army Chief Warrant Officer Three (CW3), I was attending the Warrant Officer Senior Course at Ft. Rucker, Alabama. My follow-on assignment was to be the 470th Military Intelligence (MI) Brigade in the Republic of Panama. I was a Spanish linguist and the slot I was going to fill required a warrant officer proficient in Spanish. I was qualified, I had orders in hand and I was willing and ready to go.

My wife Betty was not as ready as I, although as an Army wife with years of experience of travelling and moving, she was willing. We had already spent three years in Panama, back when the country was still a very pleasant overseas tour. Betty enjoyed being there immensely, but she didn't care for the idea of going back to a place we had already been. She wanted new adventures somewhere else.

Just before I was to graduate, I got a call out of the blue from my assignment manager in Washington, D.C., CW4 Walt Johnson. Walt asked me if I was interested in going to Bangkok, Thailand.

"Thailand? I didn't even know we had any bases in Thailand," I said.

"Well, we don't, but there's an office of the Joint Casualty Resolution Center located in the American Embassy there."

I was familiar with the JCRC. It had been in the news several times in the past year as the office responsible for resolving MIA cases in Indochina. The Vietnamese government had recently repatriated remains of MIAs, and I remembered reading a newspaper article about

15

the commander of JCRC, Lieutenant Colonel Joe Harvey. He had been interviewed about the turn-over of the remains.

And I also knew a warrant officer named Tom McKay, a Vietnamese linguist, who had told me several years earlier that he was en route to some sort of MIA investigative job in Thailand. However, I was only vaguely aware of the details of his assignment.

Walt asked if I knew Tom, and I replied that he and I were good friends. He told me that Tom wouldn't be extending his tour in Bangkok and he needed to replace him with someone in a hurry. Walt said, "I'm between a rock and a hard place in trying to find a replacement for him. I see you've got Vietnamese language on your records. Are you interested in going to the JCRC Liaison Office in Bangkok?"

Bangkok was one of the last places on earth that I ever thought I would end up in my military career. I said, "Walt, I'd loved to go, but it's been years since I've spoken Vietnamese. Right now I wouldn't even be qualified to order take-out from a Vietnamese restaurant."

I had studied Vietnamese in 1970 and 1971 at a branch of the Defense Language Institute at Ft. Bliss, Texas, but that had been seventeen years before and I had forgotten just about everything I had ever learned there. The last time I had used Vietnamese in an official capacity was in 1975 when I was working with the Vietnamese refugees at Ft. Chaffee, Arkansas. I had not spoken a word of Vietnamese since then.

"Don't worry," Walt said, "I've got it all figured out. I can send you to the Defense Language Institute at Monterey, California, for a twenty week course in refresher Vietnamese. They'll get you up to speed; then you'll be ready for a tour at JCRC. Look, I'm in a real bind. I don't have anyone else I can send. Why don't you talk it over with your wife and see if she likes the idea. If she's for it, call me back in a hurry. I need your answer right away."

I called Betty and told her about the possibility of the new assignment in Bangkok, and she was thrilled. I called Walt back and told him I wanted the job. He said he'd get orders for me ASAP (as soon as possible).

From Ft. Rucker, I drove to my home in Clarksville, Tennessee, took some leave, and spent a lovely Christmas with my family. On January 1, 1987, I headed to the Defense Language Institute in Monterey, California, for twenty weeks of refresher Vietnamese.

No quarters were available for me at the Presidio of Monterey, where DLI is located, so I was eligible to live off post and have the Army pick up the tab. I got a place at Carmel, California for $1,200 a month, coincidentally the exact amount of my per diem. It was a nice, two-bedroom cottage just a few blocks from downtown Carmel. If I hadn't been separated from my family and studying so hard, it would have been truly heaven.

Carmel is a lovely little town with one of the highest per capita incomes in the world. Clint Eastwood, a screen star and film director with immense wealth, ruled as mayor over this feudal domain of stylish shops, expensive art galleries, and upper-crust businesses. And the scenery at Carmel Beach, with seals barking in the distance, is on a par with any beach in the world. However, the water is normally too cold for swimming, even in the summer.

Vietnamese language training was six hours a day, with three or four hours of homework every evening. It was an incredibly intense regimen. Since I wasn't there for a regular class of instruction, and was older than the other students, the head of the Vietnamese Department was flexible in letting me put together a course of instruction that would best fit my needs. I started out by entering a regular class that had been going on for about ten weeks, and when I had caught up and surpassed their level, I moved to a class that had been studying for about twenty-five weeks. I stayed with them until I attained their proficiency and then began one-on-one conversational classes with native instructors. At the end of twenty weeks, I had gotten back my old wartime proficiency, and then some.

Before graduating, I saw a television documentary called "We Can Keep You Forever." The theme of the program was that American POWs were still being held in Southeast Asia, long after the U.S. withdrawal. I was impressed. After watching the television special, I was convinced that Americans were being held in Indochina, and it was going to be my mission at JCRC to find them.

I graduated from the Vietnamese course at DLI, dropped off my car in San Francisco for shipment to Thailand, and flew back to Tennessee for a few days. From there I took a quick trip to Washington, D.C., to meet some of the folks in the POW/MIA business at the Defense Intelligence Agency (DIA). Two of the guys there, Bob Hyp and Sedgewick ("Wick") Tourison, were former prisoner of war interrogators during the Vietnam War. I spent several days getting briefings from them on the MIA issue, as seen through the eyes of DIA. Those two guys were legends in military intelligence circles in the old days, and talking to them face to face was a real thrill for me. (Bob Hyp died of a heart attack about half way through my tour in Bangkok.)

Wick was the senior POW/MIA analyst at DIA and probably the most knowledgeable person in the entire federal government about the MIA issue. I talked to him at length about the television documentary I had seen, about MIAs who allegedly had been kept in Laos and Vietnam. Wick told me it just didn't happen. He said there wasn't a shred of proof any Americans had been held against their will after the war. He said the program was full of inaccuracies and was nothing but a con-job getting people sucked into conspiracy theories. I told him it had certainly convinced me.

Over the next three years I kept in touch with Bob Hyp and Wick primarily by reading the MIA intelligence analyses they wrote; and they read my reports after I interviewed Vietnamese refugees or made investigative trips to Vietnam. After Wick left DIA, I read his definitive history of military intelligence interrogation in Vietnam in a book entitled TALKING WITH VICTOR CHARLIE.

Before leaving Washington, I visited the Vietnam War Memorial. I had been there several times before, but this time I went with a little more purpose because of the type of job I was going to be involved in for the next three years. I got up early, just before sunup, and jogged over to the memorial. When I arrived I was the only person there; not even park attendants were present. I found the engraved names of the men I had known. Two of them, only youths at the time of their deaths, had been classmates of mine in high school. I found the name of my roommate from Vietnamese language school, Stanley Tillotson. I found the names of four officers killed during the battle of An Loc. And finally, I located the name of the very last casualty of the Vietnam War, an Army colonel, who frequently visited the B-52 targeting office where I worked in Bien Hoa, Vietnam.

I stood in silence for a few minutes and then started to exit the memorial. On the way out I stopped to admire the disarmingly beautiful statue of the three soldiers. For the first time since I had been coming to the wall some years back, I noticed they appeared to have paused momentarily in mid-stride and were gazing at something in the distance. I instinctively turned to see what they were looking at and was overwhelmed. They were staring at the names on the wall. As only great art can do, the sculptor had captured the true essence of a national emotion.

From Washington, D.C., I returned to Tennessee, and my family and I tied up all of the dangling ends and headed for Bangkok. The first stop on the way was Honolulu, Hawaii, for inprocessing and to talk to Lieutenant Colonel Joe Harvey, the Joint Casualty Resolution Center commander, about my job. I drove a rental car out to Barber's Point Naval Air Station to JCRC Headquarters to meet LTC Harvey. Harvey, a short, hefty guy, unquestionably gives off the aura of being the person in charge. After visiting with him a while, there was no question in my mind that he was more than qualified to be the senior MIA hunter in the U.S. government.

Harvey spoke pointedly about "standards and conduct" and how important it was for me to maintain a high degree of professionalism while working at the Liaison Office in the American Embassy in Bangkok. He emphasized this was particularly critical since I would not only be representing JCRC, but the American Embassy as well. Also, in my travels I frequently would be the primary representative of the U.S. government regarding MIA matters.

Harvey said I would be interviewing Vietnamese refugees at camps in Hong Kong and Macau. I would be required to make a trip to those countries every ten to twelve weeks. At that time Tom Mckay had responsibility for the route, and I was to make the trip with him once to learn the ropes before he left Bangkok and returned to the states. At the conclusion of the interview trips, I would return to Bangkok and write reports, which would be sent for analysis at JCRC headquarters in Honolulu and the Defense Intelligence Agency in Washington, D.C. Harvey also told me that I would be attending technical meetings in Hanoi with him, in which JCRC and Vietnamese officials would engage in dialogue and exchange information about selected MIA cases.

MIA investigative teams were not going into Vietnam then, as they eventually would be on a routine basis before my tour at JCRC was up. Consequently, what was to become the major portion of my job, MIA investigative team leader, was not even mentioned. Harvey himself was not aware of the dramatic opportunities that were on the horizon concerning the search for MIAs.

When I was meeting with Harvey at that time, I didn't know that he was in such a politically sensitive job. I found out later that the POW/MIA issue had created power blocs in and out of the federal government, and Harvey, as chief MIA hunter, constantly had to walk a tightrope among outspoken rivals who would love to see him thrown to the wolves. There were a number of individuals and groups that were unhappy about the way the MIA issue had been handled, and many of them thought JCRC had done very little to resolve the fate of the missing. They wouldn't have been happy with anyone who was sitting in Harvey's chair.

I later learned that Harvey, as a result of back door political machinations by a disgruntled MIA group with high- level contacts in Washington, D.C., had once been hired, fired, and re-hired, all in the course of a few hours. The story was that he showed up to work one morning and there was a note on his desk to call his boss in the Pacific Command headquarters. He made the call and his boss told him that a lieutenant colonel named Bill Jordan would be immediately assuming command of JCRC.

Dumbfounded, Harvey asked if he had been fired. Harvey's boss, just as shocked as Harvey at the sudden call from Washington said, "I don't know, but I'll call some friends and find out."

Harvey's boss called back a short time later with the answer. Yes, he had been fired and he was to clear out as soon as possible.

Then a couple of hours later, his boss called again. No, he hadn't been fired, but Lieutenant Colonel Jordan would be assigned to JCRC as Harvey's deputy and understudy, and in an undetermined period of time would assume command of JCRC.

Harvey learned later that another influential group got wind that he was about to get the axe. They intervened on his behalf by making a few well placed telephone calls themselves and got Harvey reinstated.

Jordan did become Harvey's deputy, but eventually moved on to another assignment. Years after the incident, Harvey, as proof of his own political adeptness, was still very much in command of JCRC. Harvey later retired from the military and got a high-level civilian job at Pacific Command headquarters (PACOM) in Honolulu as an action officer dealing with the MIA issue.

Having worked with Harvey closely for several years, I can attest to his competence and his genuine concern over the MIA issue. I can't think of anyone better suited to have been commander during the difficult and volatile period he was in charge of JCRC.

While at JCRC headquarters in Honolulu, I also spent some time meeting and talking to the MIA case analysts, one of whom was an old friend, Master Sergeant (Army) David Atherton. In upcoming years, Dave was to be my team NCOIC (Noncommissioned Officer in Charge) on several MIA investigations in northern and central Vietnam. Dave and I had been NCOs together years earlier at the 519th Military Intelligence Battalion in the mid-1970s, my last assignment as an enlisted man before I was appointed as a warrant officer.

Dave had been a missionary kid who grew up in the Philippines. His parents worked for Wycliffe, an organization that translates the Bible into tribal languages. As a result of living in remote areas of the Philippines, he was quite adept at austere conditions and had no problem in travelling around Vietnam when we started the in-country MIA investigations.

Dave was stocky and short, wore glasses, and was extremely witty. His forte was telling corny jokes, and he could roll them off one after another. Also, when others were telling jokes, he could inevitably figure out the punch lines before they got to them and would usually top whatever had been told. Dave could have been a stand-up comedian, but the Army found him first.

Dave had occasion to use his fast wit once during an MIA investigation, in the Ashau Valley at a town called A-Loui. All around A-Loui were battlefields, including the infamous Hamburger Hill where vicious and bitter fighting occurred between American and North Vietnamese forces. One evening Dave and I were leisurely walking around sightseeing in the little town, when a group of Vietnamese gathered around and started asking us questions. A woman in the crowd asked Dave where he was from, and he replied in Vietnamese, "Hoa Ky (America)."

Suddenly her friendly tone changed and she heatedly asked, "Are you from the same America that bombed all of the villages around here?"

Quick as a flash Dave answered, "No, I'm not from that America. I'm from the other one!"

Also, I met LTC (Army) Tom Hodge for the fist time. He and I would eventually work together on a daily basis in Saudi Arabia during Desert Shield/Storm. Hodge was a fireball Special Forces infantry officer and Vietnam combat veteran whose training and skills were oriented toward leading combat troops, not serving as a paper pusher. Unfortunately that was his basic function at JCRC.

Hodge's writing skills, though quite adequate for anything he would ever need to do in combat, did not match the quality required for a paperwork organization like JCRC. The production of reports, analytical research, and negotiation material were most of what JCRC did in Honolulu. A female Naval lieutenant at JCRC headquarters used to go through reports Hodge had written and rewrite them. This infuriated him no end and he was still mad about it when I worked with him years later at Special Operations Command Central in Saudi Arabia.

After several days of inprocessing and getting acquainted with the JCRC staff, my family and I travelled onward by air to Don Muong International Airport in Bangkok.

We landed about midnight, which seems to be the time most international flights arrive in Bangkok. My new boss, Lieutenant Colonel Mather (U.S. Air Force), the OIC (Officer in Charge) of the Liaison Office, was waiting for us at the airport. He had brought along an embassy van and the Liaison Office driver, Mr. Sataporn. (I got to know Sataporn well during the next three years. He and I travelled frequently to refugee camps in and around Bangkok, and twice up to northeastern Thailand to look for a crash site on the Mekong River.)

My family and I were filled with both anticipation and excitement as we drove from the airport through the darkened city that was going to be our home for the next three years. Mather took us to the Imperial Hotel, which is right next door to the Vietnamese Embassy, for the night.

He told us to get as much rest as we could, and then come to the American Embassy the next day to get I.D. cards and start inprocessing.

We didn't know it, as our jet-lagged bodies dropped off to sleep about two o'clock in the morning, but the next day would start a whirlwind three-year adventure for me and my family that was above and beyond anything we could have possibly imagined.

The American Embassy in Bangkok is down the street from the Imperial Hotel. The hotel, the Vietnamese Embassy, and the American Embassy are all located in the same block. Before walking to the embassy the next morning to start inprocessing, my family and I strolled around the block just to take in the sights and smells of Bangkok for the first time in daylight. While walking, Betty held onto her purse tightly, just like she used to do in Panama years ago. I walked on the outside of my wife and kids to protect them from would-be muggers. It all seems kind of silly now, knowing as we do that Bangkok is one of the safest cities in the world as far as street crime. But we didn't know that then and we were taking the same precautions that we used to take in Central America.

One of the reasons I believe Farangs (Thai word for foreigners) become victims of crime in Bangkok is that they are lured into a false sense of security by how safe everything seems to be. They stop being careful and something happens to them.

My family and I stayed at the Imperial Hotel in Bangkok for a couple of days, then moved into embassy quarters less than a mile from the American Embassy. The quarters, which were leased by the State Department, were absolutely beautiful. We lived on the eighth floor overlooking the lush greenery of Lumpini Park, located in the middle of the city. We had four bedrooms, a maid's quarters, and five bathrooms. One recommendation: if anyone ever offers you a job with the State Department overseas—take it!. Unquestionably, embassy personnel live better, at times even lavishly, than most other employees in the federal government.

Shortly after our arrival, we enrolled our three kids, Ross, Bernice, and Carl, in the International School of Bangkok (ISB), which cost the U.S. taxpayer a solid $6,000 for each kid every year for the three years we were there. The education they received at the school was superb. All of the classes were conducted in English, and the students came from all over the world to include Japan, Arab countries, Israel, the People's Republic of China, and Taiwan. With such varied backgrounds and from countries that were even antagonistic toward each other, it's amazing that there was any cohesion among the students at all. But there didn't appear to be any significant hostility expressed by any of the students against one another, at least as far as my family and I could see.

My wife, who had over the years given up good jobs to follow me around in the military, was now unemployed. As with most military families, there are hidden costs involved in serving, and interruption of spousal employment is probably the most notable disadvantages. Betty had just resigned a good teaching job in Clarksville, Tennessee, a town where good jobs were at a premium. However, everything worked out well. She managed to get a job teaching at the International School of Bangkok, the same school our kids were attending. Betty ended up with a better paying job than at any other school where she had taught. With both of our salaries, we lived very well in Bangkok.

Another benefit to living in Bangkok was the sightseeing opportunities. We were never bored. On the weekends, when I was not travelling, we frequently would visit special places of interest and then have a nice meal. Also during our tour our family was able to take trips to China, Hong Kong, Burma, Singapore, Malaysia, Indonesia, and all over Thailand. And I travelled to Vietnam and the Philippines as a result of my job.

When I first arrived in Bangkok, my duty section in the American Embassy, the JCRC Liaison Office, gave me a couple of days to get settled, then I started going into work regularly. As I was getting into the swing of things, I got acquainted with the guys, and one gal, in the liaison office: Garnett (Bill) E. Bell; Jim Coyle; Tom McKay; William Gadoury; LtCol Mather, the boss of the JCRC liaison Office; and Mrs. Iris Stansfield, the secretary. Iris probably should have been paid twice the salary she was making. Her job title was secretary, but in reality she was a senior administrative assistant, and the place would probably have fallen apart without her.

Iris eventually left Bangkok and was replaced by Mrs. Carol Thrash. Her daughter Cindi and my son Ross carried on a romance during the last few months of our tour in Bangkok.

Garnett E. Bell, a GS-13 Department of Defense civilian employee, was Mather's deputy. I had known Bell before I arrived at JCRC when we worked together at Ft. Chaffee,

Arkansas, in 1975. There we were involved in the processing of 50,000 Vietnamese refugees. Although his first name and middle initial appears as "Garnett E." in national news about Congressional MIA hearings and investigations in Vietnam, informally he goes by "Bill." I asked him how "Garnett" ever became "Bill," since he didn't have "Bill" or "William" in his name. He told me he didn't know. He had been called that ever since he was a little kid.

Bill first came to the Liaison Office in Bangkok in the late seventies as an Army Vietnamese linguist when the Boat People first started fleeing Vietnam. He was career military, but as soon as JCRC started getting civilian slots he retired and took a job as a GS-13. After I left JCRC he moved up another notch and for a period of time was the Director of the POW/MIA Office in Hanoi. This was quite significant and historical in that this was the first official U.S. government office to open in Vietnam since the fall of the South in 1975.

Bill is remarkably fluent in Vietnamese and one of the best non-native Vietnamese speakers in the entire federal government. I suppose Wick Tourison at the Defense Intelligence Agency speaks Vietnamese as well as Bill, but I haven't met anyone else who does.

Bill is one hundred percent positive American POWs were held in Southeast Asia against their will after the American withdrawal. Bill's viewpoint was shared by another individual in the MIA investigative system, Colonel Millard Peck, who eventually resigned in protest as Director of the POW/MIA office in the Defense Intelligence Agency.

Bill has been interviewed a number of times by the press over the years about the MIA issue, but his most memorable comments to the American public came in late 1991 before a senate subcommittee investigating the MIA issue. Bill was asked, as the senior American official assigned in Hanoi, whether or not he believed Americans were held in Indochina after the U.S. withdrawal. Bill answered in the affirmative, and stated at least ten remained behind. Bill's comments made national news.

In spite of Bill's many talents as an investigator and writer, he had a personality trait that I believe was a hindrance in his position as an MIA investigator at JCRC: he was incredibly suspicious and invariably suspected the worst motives in people, particularly the Vietnamese. Anything they did was subject to great skepticism. Bill never accepted what they told him at face value or first impression, which is the mark of a good investigator, but I believe he carried his skepticism to extreme.

I felt Bill's suspicious nature got in the way of his objectivity. He often refused to be persuaded by seemingly clear evidence about MIA cases we were investigating. As a result, he frequently left an element of doubt in his reports that clouded and even sometimes stopped the resolution of cases. In my opinion, a number of MIA incidents he worked on should have been categorically resolved, and the reason they were not was because of his constant wariness that the Vietnamese had manipulated the evidence.

Bill Bell had strong allies in certain elements of the Defense Intelligence Agency and the federal government who shared his dark suspicion of the Vietnamese. Therefore his investigative reports received a lot of attention and praise from those quarters, and in my opinion, made it hard for the reports to be objectively analyzed.

I particularly enjoyed the times I had with Bill Bell in Hanoi during the negotiation session with the Vietnamese. Every couple of months, LTC Harvey would lead a delegation to Hanoi to meet with Vietnamese officials to discuss the status of MIA cases in Vietnam. When no meetings were going on, we were free to wander around Hanoi, and Bill Bell and I usually took off together to explore the city. Bill had been there dozens of times before and knew the city better than any American I know.

We used to go to night clubs in Hanoi, and more often than not, Vietnamese would come over to our table to talk to us and find out where we were from. As a joke, Bill would pretend he couldn't speak Vietnamese and I would interpret for him. Then, gradually, Bill would start using a few words of Vietnamese, and our Vietnamese guests at the table were always impressed that he was making such an effort to learn a few words of their language. Then

Bill would start speaking more and more Vietnamese until he was carrying on a fluent dialogue. The effect of the illusion, which was always hilarious, was that he had learned Vietnamese in the course of the conversation.

One funny thing happened one night when Bill and I left a French restaurant and travelled by three-wheeled bicycle across Hanoi (the passengers sit up front in a seat across two wheels, and the driver peddles in the back). The two drivers, neither of whom knew that Bill and I spoke Vietnamese, were talking back and forth about us as we drove along. One of them said in Vietnamese about me, "This guy's really heavy (I'm 6' 4" and weigh 215 pounds)." The bicycle driver who was hauling Bill said, "You think that one's heavy, you ought to try peddling the fat guy here!"

Bill Bell was great at telling jokes in Vietnamese and could make a Vietnamese audience roll with laughter. One evening in Hanoi, Bill told a joke to a Vietnamese official while I listened on. Bill said that it seems Ho Chi Minh died and went to heaven, and shortly afterward, Le Duan, a protege of Ho Chi Minh died also. Ho met Le Duan at the Pearly Gates and said, "Before I let you in I want to know how you carried out the mandate I gave you before I passed on. That mandate consisted of nine words: 'There is nothing more precious than independence and freedom (Khong Co Gi Quy Hon Doc Lap Tu Do).' I want to know how you carried out my mandate."

In Vietnam, every Vietnamese knows those nine words; they appear on walls and billboards all across the country. Ho Chi Minh electrified Vietnam with them in a speech at the height of the American bombing. The context of the speech was "They can bomb us five, ten, fifteen, or even twenty years—it doesn't matter how long—There is nothing more precious than independence and freedom!"

The punch line of the joke was, Le Duan answered, "I carried out one third of it: 'There is nothing (Khong Co Gi).'"

In refugee camps when Bill would tell that joke, laughter would erupt. But on this occasion the Vietnamese official was silent, though Bill and I both could see in his eyes he was trying his best to keep from bursting out laughing.

Jim Coyle, GS-12, was another Vietnamese interviewer in the Liaison Office in Bangkok. Prior to coming to JCRC, he had been a Ph.D candidate at Cornell University. His graduate specialty was Vietnamese history and he spoke Vietnamese extremely well, though not as well as Bill Bell (Jim and I used to sit together at meetings in Hanoi and marvel how well Bill would carry off difficult interpretations). Jim's educational program was sidetracked when he came to JCRC, and, according to him, it's doubtful if he'll ever go back. He seems perfectly content to continue doing what he's doing at JCRC. Jim was the best writer, and his investigative reports had a prose quality that was excellent. He was the Ernest Hemingway of JCRC. Jim was the epitome of the absent-minded professor. Also, he was a self-admitted, world-class procrastinator.

Harvey told me one time that it was probably a good thing Jim was such a procrastinator. Had he been more efficient in his educational goals, he undoubtedly would have gotten his Ph.D and JCRC would never have had him. Harvey thought the world of Jim Coyle and considered him to be one of JCRC's most valuable assets. I agree with Harvey's assessment.

Jim is physically a big man, but in spite of his large size, he comes across as being gentle-natured. The appearance, however, is deceptive. Jim can be very forceful when necessary and he has a temper that can go off like a grenade, particularly if he feels he has been jerked around on an investigation. But in comparison to Bill Bell, Jim was content to leave the leadership role to others while he stayed in the background and pontificated on the issues. Jim was a great pontificator.

Jim's method of operation on investigations in Vietnam was to delegate almost everything to his team members who came from JCRC headquarters and the Army remains identification laboratory in Honolulu. Jim acted as an interpreter during the investigations, while his team members took notes, performed analyses, and wrote draft reports at the end. Jim then took their draft products and turned out masterpieces in investigative reporting. Since he constantly used his team members and expected them to do so much, they became expert at what they did.

Tom McKay, whom I was replacing, was still at the JCRC Liaison Office when I arrived in Bangkok. Fortunately for me, we had an overlap of about a month. I had known Tom years before when we were E-6s together in the 519th MI Battalion, Ft. Bragg, North Carolina. (Dave Atherton had served with us, but in a different company in the 519th.) Tom was a smart guy and had many unusual talents: he was an outstanding Spanish guitarist, a computer whiz, a stage-performance magician, a skilled locksmith, and was fluent in Vietnamese. He also had some strange quirks. He believed in astrology, including the Chinese version, and he would frequently analyze people as to their Sun Signs.

The guys in the office used to tell a funny story about Tom. Supposedly, a refugee coordinator at one of the camps in the Philippines sent word to Bangkok that he had obtained a bone and a dog tag of an MIA from a refugee. Such incidents are almost invariably a refugee scam to make money or obtain resettlement, and they very seldom ever amount to anything, but JCRC interviewers still have to go through the motions and conduct a serious investigation. Tom duly showed up at the refugee camp to get the bone and dog tag of the alleged MIA. The refugee coordinator, who was incredibly disorganized, started searching his cluttered office looking for the items. He eventually told Tom he had lost them. Tom pulled out a pad and started writing a statement, reading it aloud as he wrote: "Mr. ___________ stated to the JCRC interviewer that he lost a dog tag and remains of an MIA."

The refugee coordinator, turning pale as he had visions of his career going down the tubes, got excited and said: "It wasn't remains, it was just a bone!"

Tom corrected his statement and read out loud: "Mr. ___________ stated to JCRC interviewer that he lost a dog tag and a 'partial' remains of an MIA."

Bill Gadoury, an Air Force Senior Master Sergeant, was the Thai and Laotian linguist at the Liaison Office in the embassy. During any investigations in Laos he was the interpreter and senior investigator. Bill later retired and went to work for JCRC as a GS-12 doing the same job he was doing as a senior non-commissioned officer. Bill was a stabilizing force in JCRC and I can't say enough about how good he was as an investigator and a linguist. I am going to talk about Bill quite a bit more in another chapter.

Paul Mather, an engineer, which is a strange profession for an MIA hunter, had been in JCRC since its inception. He had served a total of 13 years in JCRC, which has to be a record for spending time in one job in the military. He was originally with JCRC in Vietnam, and after the fall of Saigon he moved with JCRC to a base on the Thai-Laotian border. Mather was an easy-going guy to work for and one of the better bosses I've ever had. He would have loved to have stayed on at JCRC for the rest of his life but was nearing 30 years of military service and facing mandatory retirement.

Mather had been a member of the Leonard Woodcock Commission that had gone to Vietnam during the Carter presidency. The purpose of the commission was to look into the normalization of relations with Vietnam and to get the Vietnamese to increase cooperation in the resolution of MIA cases. During one of the one-on-one sessions with a senior Vietnamese official, Woodcock made a personal request to the Vietnamese to allow Mather's fiance, Luan, to leave Vietnam so she could marry Mather. The North Vietnamese victory in 1975 had totally disrupted their marriage plans. The Vietnamese agreed and Luan left Vietnam. Shortly afterward she and Mather were married.

This ended up causing unforeseen problems for Mather.

A number of people were suspicious of the marriage of a woman from a communist country. This was particularly true since Mather was in charge of the JCRC Liaison Office in Bangkok, the primary office responsible for investigating MIA cases in Southeast Asia. Many people believed JCRC was conducting a whitewash of the MIA issue already, and Mather's marriage with the full permission of a communist regime opened him up to a great deal of criticism.

Mather was at a National League of Families conference once in Washington, D.C., when he overheard one of the attendees complaining about "that guy Mather with his 'commie' wife." That hurt him deeply.

In July of 1988, Mather returned to the United States and was eventually hired by DIA as a POW/MIA analyst in Washington, D.C. No one could have possibly been more qualified for the job. Mather's contribution to the MIA issue and the resolution of active cases has been immeasurable. The country owes Paul Mather a debt of gratitude for his service and dedication to a most troubling issue.

Mather was replaced by LtCol James Spurgeon, an Air Force Academy graduate and navigator. Spurgeon was outstanding. He was efficient, smart, and fully capable of running a complicated organization like the JCRC Liaison Office. Although Spurgeon was happy to have been selected to come to JCRC, he was determined not to get stuck there for the rest of his career as Harvey and Mather had done. He was definitely career-minded and intended to move to the higher ranks, whereas Mather and Harvey had shot themselves in the foot, promotion-wise, long ago. Mather and Harvey were fully aware that when they left JCRC, their military careers were essentially over. Spurgeon wanted to be a full colonel, and he had realistic hopes of going beyond that.

When I retired from the Army in August 1991, I was complaining about how much money I had lost by not being able to stay in one place and build equity in a house and have possessions like some of my relatives and friends had done. My oldest son Ross told me, "Yeah, that's all true, Dad, but think of all the places you've been, the things you've done, and the friends you have had. That has to even things out." He was absolutely right.

The author discussing an upcoming mountain climb with counterpart Ngo Hoang.

CHAPTER TWO

INTERVIEWING IN THE REFUGEE CAMPS

One of the missions of the JCRC Liaison Office in Bangkok was to send interviewers to Vietnamese and Laotian refugee camps throughout Southeast Asia to talk to refugees about MIAs they may have seen or known about. In order to do this, the interviewers in Bangkok were assigned routes that had to be covered every 10 to 12 weeks. Jim Coyle had the southern route, which was made up of the Vietnamese refugee camps in Singapore, Indonesia, and Malaysia; Bill Bell was responsible for all of the Vietnamese camps in Thailand; Bill Gadoury took care of the Laotian refugee camps on the Thai border; and I was the primary interviewer in the camps in Hong Kong and Macau.

There were two camps in the Philippines covered by JCRC, but several of the guys back at JCRC headquarters in Honolulu usually made that run. Occasionally the JCRC Liaison Office in Bangkok sent interviewers there; I made the trip once and Bill Bell and Tom McKay made it a number of times.

There were Khmer Rouge camps in Thailand on the Thai-Cambodian border, but we were prohibited from entering those by the American Embassy in Bangkok. U.S. government policy was that we were to have nothing to do with anything in which the Khmer Rouge was involved. But from time to time we did interview Cambodians who lived in a non-Khmer Rouge section of one Vietnamese camp located near a little Thai town called Aranyaphatet.

Bill Bell and I took a trip once to the camp at Aranyaphatet to interview some Vietnamese and Cambodian refugees. The Vietnamese there were all southerners who had fled Vietnam through Cambodia. We got some fairly good information from a couple of the refugees, but mostly they had bogus dog tags and pieces of bone they claimed had come from MIA remains. Bill also talked to a Cambodian who wanted money for a dog tag that he had. He said his family was hiding the remains in Cambodia. We checked all of the names of the dog tags with an MIA list we always carried with us, but none of the names were good.

We stayed at a motel in the town of Aranyaphatet and in the evenings after interviewing, Bill, Sataporn, and I would wander around sightseeing. To me the town was interesting because being a border town, it has both a Thai and Cambodian flavor. One thing I remember about Aranyaphatet was the strange food the vendors sold on the streets from their culinary push carts. One of their specialties was fried grasshopper, which they would fry in pans of oil. I bought a small bag of the crispy critters, thinking I would try just one to see what a fried grasshopper tasted like. I enjoyed it so much I ended up eating all of them and even bought a second bag. I tried to get Bill Bell to try one, but he looked at me like I was crazy. Sataporn would eat them though.

Eating salty grasshoppers works up a thirst, so I went into a little Thai store to buy a soft drink. I thought the cute little Thai girl minding the store was going to throw up when she saw me munching on grasshoppers. She put her hand over her mouth and turned away. I learned then that not all Thais liked all of the food that is sold on their streets.

We completed our interview trip and drove back to Bangkok, where we read in the paper that Cambodian troops had shelled Khmer Rouge forces located between them and the refugee camp at Aranyaphatet. Several Vietnamese refugees were killed in the shelling that had occurred shortly after Bill Bell and I left the camp.

When I first arrived in Thailand, Tom McKay had the Hong Kong and Macau refugee interview route, and Mather told Tom to break me in on the route before leaving JCRC. So Tom and I went together on my first trip to Hong Kong and Macau in August of 1987, and LtCol Mather went along too.

I thought I would never learn the route. It all seemed so incredibly complicated. We constantly took taxis, subways, and ferries. We travelled by a Hong Kong police boat to two of the camps, Hei Ling Chau and Chi Ma Wan, which were located on islands in Hong Kong Harbour. Then we went by subway and hovercraft to a camp called Tuen Mun, which was located in the New Territories. Two camps, Argyle and Kai Tak, were located in the city on the Kowloon side of Hong Kong, and we went there by subway and taxi. (Argyle had been a Japanese camp for British officer POWs during World War Two.) To interview in Macau we had to travel by jetfoil to Macau, a distance of sixty miles, then take a taxi to a Catholic relief organization, and from there catch a ride with the organization's driver out to the camp.

Tom gave me the idea of using three by five inch cards to record how to get to all of the camps, which helped. Whenever I would leave my hotel en route to a camp, I'd pull out a card with the directions and fares conveniently recorded. But after I started travelling on my own and got familiar with where everything was, I didn't need the cards anymore. Even though it's been a long time since I was last in Hong Kong or Macau, I think I could get to all of the camps almost in my sleep.

When I first started working for JCRC, I could cover the five refugee camps in Hong Kong and the one in Macau in less than a week. By the time I left JCRC in mid-1990, it took a full twenty days to cover the Hong Kong and Macau route. The number of camps had grown to nineteen camps in Hong Kong as the Vietnamese economy worsened in 1988 and 1989 and refugees began leaving in droves.

As the refugee population started to grow dramatically in 1988, several "super camps" that housed thousands of refugees were built in more remote parts of Hong Kong. The older camps were quaint and laid-back, but the new ones were impersonal and massive monuments of concrete, steel, and barbed wire.

During my three years at JCRC, I made a total of sixteen trips to Hong Kong and twelve to Macau. Each trip I normally interviewed thirty or forty refugees, and toward the end of my tour as many eighty or ninety refugees, all without the aid of an interpreter. My tactics in getting refugees to talk to me about MIAs evolved over a three year period. Initially I'd visit the camps and get a refugee to make a camp call-out on the public address system. The announcement would say something like, "Attention in the camp...An American official is here seeking information about U.S. MIAs. If you know anything about the circumstances of the capture or death of an American, or know the location of a crash site, please come visit the American official immediately."

To some extent this was successful, but as I grew more proficient in Vietnamese and more knowledgeable of how the Vietnamese mind worked, I started going into the camps to press the flesh. This was in addition to the camp call-outs. In no time I'd attract a crowd because of my Vietnamese language ability. Later, after I started making MIA investigative trips to Vietnam, I had pictures to show of villages where I had been.

The pictures had an even greater attraction for drawing a crowd than my Vietnamese proficiency. I would show up at a camp with a batch of pictures and in a few minutes be surrounded by dozens of Vietnamese. As I became more knowledgeable about where refugees were from, I would try to include a few pictures of villages familiar to them. Occasionally they would recognize people in the photographs, which would create even more of a stir.

The photographs and my walking through the camps were really bait to meet people and get them to open up about what they knew about MIA incidents. The way it would frequently work was that after I had engaged a group in conversation, one of them would say something like "Mr. Thu in building such-and-such knows about the grave of an American," or "I saw an American taken prisoner when I was a little boy." Whereupon I would take down the details and call out the refugee later to undertake a complete interview.

When I first started walking through the camps to find sources, I made the mistake of trying to interview refugees on the spot. But that didn't work because I suddenly would find myself and the source surrounded by dozens and dozens of refugees trying to get close to hear what was going on. Vietnamese are some of the nosiest people in the world and when something is going on, everyone becomes a self-proclaimed expert on whatever is happening.

The camps were miserable places, though they were relatively clean and safe and the inhabitants seemed to have sufficient rice. In spite of the fairly good conditions, living in a refugee camp day after day created a tremendous amount of stress, particularly among the men. The women usually adjusted relatively well, but the men did poorly. My guess is the women were able to do better because they were able to keep busy doing traditional Vietnamese feminine chores such as cleaning and rearing children. Vietnamese males are very chauvinistic and in most instances will not do "women's work", and as a result have little to do but languish and brood in their own self pity, day after day, year after year.

But as stressful as the camps were, I only met a handful of people who told me they wanted to go back to Vietnam. During a trip to the two refugee camps in the Philippines, a Vietnamese refugee told me the reason he would rather be in the camps than back in Vietnam was that in Vietnam, every night before going to bed he wondered if sometime in the night he'd hear the dreaded knock at the door that would take him away. He had already spent time in a re-education camp and always had the fear that someday he would have to go through that terrible ordeal again.

He said life in Vietnam got so miserable for him that he made arrangements to leave Vietnam by boat, but the boat was totally packed and he knew it wasn't going to make the voyage without sinking. Consequently, he didn't board and the boat left without him—and was never heard from again. Evidently it sank on the high seas and everyone perished. He said several months later through clandestine contacts, he made arrangements to catch another boat, and it too was overcrowded. But this time he was desperate. He just couldn't take another day of being in Vietnam. He jumped on the boat, which was already in danger of sinking before it was even launched, and sailed all the way to Subic Bay in the Philippines in the most congested conditions imaginable.

The boat trip to Hong Kong was generally safe. The navigation was easy since the boats followed the coast all the way to Macau, and then on into Hong Kong Harbour. But the route to Malaysia, Indonesia, Singapore, and the Philippines was not an easy trip at all. The boats had to travel over the high seas and sometimes ran into bad weather. But certain months traditionally have good weather, and these were the months in which more boats were launched. The refugee camps always grew in population at these times.

Also, the boats travelled through the Thai fishing fleet, where frequently they fell easy victim to Thai pirates. Thailand has one of the largest fishing fleets in the world—some 30,000 thousand boats on the water at any one time—and a lot of these are manned by criminals. A refugee boat passing by is a tempting target to those who make their living on the other side of the law. Some of the crimes against Vietnamese boat people committed by Thai pirates were hideous beyond belief. Rape and sadism were common. The level of criminality reached a peak during one attack in 1990 when pirates threw over one hundred refugees overboard. All died, and many of the bodies were found mutilated.

One refugee told me he was on a boat robbed by pirates, but the women among the passengers were able to escape rape by covering themselves in engine oil and grease.

I've looked closely at a lot of refugee boats and it's amazing to me how thirty and forty, and even sometimes as many as seventy and eighty people, could possibly fit on them. And most of the boats don't appear to be seaworthy; it's almost miraculous there have been as many successful boat escapes as there have been since 1979.

One refugee, a former South Vietnamese Army captain, told me that all of the passengers on his boat had never been on a boat before, including himself. The boat captain deserted at the last minute and he was drafted to be the pilot and navigator. The passengers reasoned that since he had been a military officer, he surely would know how to use a compass and a crude map. He told me that he pointed the boat in the general direction of the Philippines, and off they went.

I frequently asked refugees why they left Vietnam. A lot of them said they left because they fell into disfavor with the government and as a result couldn't get employment, since the government is the primary employer. When a person is black-balled in such a way, not only does he have difficulties getting work, but he is closely watched by the security police.

But the vast majority of the refugees told me they just couldn't make ends meet. When I was making trips to Vietnam with JCRC, the average Vietnamese would tell me he made about fifty cents a day (1,000 Dong in 1990), and it cost about twice that to live. A chicken cost about a dollar (4,000 Dong), and a kilo of rice cost about seventy-five cents (1,500 Dong). When they reached the point where they could no longer survive, they loaded up the kids, along with grandmother and grandfather, and headed for a new life, much like the so-called "Okies" who left Oklahoma during the dust bowl days and headed for the promised land in California.

The Vietnamese government instituted severe penalties for fleeing the country illegally, but as one Vietnamese official once told me, there is little the government could really do about it. He said they locked them up, but as soon as they got out they tried it again. He expressed to me that because of the potential outcry of the world press, it would be impossible for the government to take stronger measures, such as shooting would-be escapees.

Back before JCRC was allowed into Vietnam, refugee interviewing produced the majority of the information about MIAs. Since JCRC has been going into Vietnam, the percentage has shifted dramatically and now more information comes from the in-country investigations. But at one time, interviewing refugees was about the only way to get any information at all. And there was a lot of information to get; the large population of boat people contained many witnesses to MIA cases.

In Hong Kong I once interviewed a boat pilot who had brought over a large number of refugees in his fishing boat several week before. He told me about an incident he said he had witnessed years before in which an American pilot had been killed. He searched the pilot's body and had recovered documents that the pilot had been carrying on his person. These included a green military I.D. card, photographs of family members, and some other official-looking documents that the refugee was unable to identify.

I pulled out my green Army I.D. card and the refugee got excited and exclaimed that was the same kind of card he found on the pilot.

The refugee conveyed to me that he kept the documents for years and had brought them with him to Hong Kong. He expressed that he had hidden them in the roof of the cabin of his fishing boat, and to the best of his knowledge they were still there. He stated that when the Hong Kong police took him and his passengers off his boat at Green Island, a refugee processing facility in Hong Kong Harbour, he didn't realize he would not be seeing his boat again and didn't take the documents from the hiding place.

I had high hopes of getting the documents from the boat. If I could get them, the chances of resolving a case would be almost assured. I immediately called the Hong Kong Harbour Authority and after explaining who I was and what I wanted for the umpteenth time, I finally reached a senior official who could help me. I told him the story the refugee had related to me.

The official said he was sorry but he doubted if he could help me. He remarked that refugee boats are usually burned shortly after they are intercepted by the harbour police and towed to Hong Kong. He said the boats are frequently infested with vermin and also present a hazard to shipping, thus the need to get rid of them as quickly as possible. I told him the boat had arrived just a few weeks before and asked him to check to see if the boat had been torched yet. The official took my information, including the boat number and the date of arrival. He told me he would call me back as soon as he had an answer. A couple of hours later I got a call at my hotel from the official, and he told me that the boat had been burned a few days ago. I was too late. So near and yet so far.

I was disappointed about not getting the documents, since they would have clearly identified the pilot and would likely have allowed a case to be resolved. Even without the documents, the refugee's information was still important, but something tangible to have gone along with it would have been so much more convincing.

Although refugee interviewing has been extremely successful, there are problems with it. Occasionally, refugees with time on their hands—lots of time—will dream up wild stories that interviewers and analysts have to run down. Their motive is to gain resettlement or money, neither of which they ever get for their efforts. The U.S. government does not pay or give special resettlement consideration for remains or information, regardless of how good it is. And refugees are told that right up front. However, some refugees will deliberately test the system and fabricate stories, which gets them nothing and causes JCRC and DIA to expend countless hours in sorting out their scams.

Most of the fabricated stories refugees invent are fairly easy to weed out by analysts, but some refugees are very creative and they are able to elaborate stories that are very difficult to get through.

But strangely some of the stories I thought were fabrications turned out to be true. Once a refugee in Hong Kong told me about a pilot who ejected from an F-4 in Hai Phong Province and then said the aircraft landed by itself in a rice field. That sounded totally bogus to me, but I duly reported it, just as I was required to do. We didn't have the option of choosing what we reported, even if we knew the refugee had made up the information. We wrote it up word for word just as it was given to us. This particular refugee claimed that an F-4 landed by itself after the crew bailed out, and that's exactly what I wrote and sent by message to JCRC and DIA.

The report came back correlated to an actual case. I was surprised. I pulled out our file on the case to which the analyst said the report had correlated, and sure enough, the refugee was telling the truth. The pilot said in an interview after he returned during Operation HOME-COMING that the last thing he saw before being blindfolded and led off to years of captivity was his aircraft in an upright position in a rice field, like it had landed by itself!

Whenever I would interview refugees, just taking the required administrative data—name, place of birth, education, etc.—was time-consuming. To speed up the process, I made a fill-in-the-blanks interview sheet, written in Vietnamese, for the refugees to fill out before I talked to them. If I had a number of refugees in a camp I wanted to talk to, I'd call several of them out and get them to fill out my interview sheet while I was interviewing someone else. Then by the time they were finished with my sheet, I'd be ready to interview them. The sheet had all of the personal data that I would have to submit in my eventual report, and I would ask them in Vietnamese to describe the incident they allegedly witnessed or knew about.

Once a comical event happened as a result of one of my fill-in-the-blank questions. The question asked for the refugee's sex: male or female (nam hay nu). A fisherman from Hai Phong Province had written "nu (female)", and I corrected him. I said, no, you should have written "nam (male)". The fisherman, who was a real basic kind of guy with very little education, was adamant that he meant to have checked "nu." We went back and forth on this for a while and as I was scratching my head wondering what he was talking about, he finally blurted out, "The pilot was female!"

"What?" I said, still not comprehending what he was trying to tell me.

"The dead pilot was a woman!"

Then I understood: he answered the question about sex, based not on himself, but on what he believed was the sex of the pilot.

He then told me he and several other fishermen had found the body of a Caucasian woman with long black hair floating in Hai Phong harbor. She was wearing only white panties and a wristwatch. The fishermen assumed she was a dead American pilot who had bailed out over the harbor, since attacks and overflights by U.S. aircraft were numerous at that time. The story was too unusual for the fisherman to have made up, so I believed he was telling the truth. But there were unquestionably no American female pilots lost over Hai Phong Harbor.

My explanation of the story was that perhaps the body had come from international shipping that was in the harbor. Bill Bell said that the body probably was a dead pilot, but that exposure in the water may have deformed the physical features of the deceased to make the body look female. I don't know what the answer to the mystery is; I just know that the refugee sincerely believed the story he told me about the female pilot.

One thing I learned about interviewing over the years: concocted lies usually follow a very pat format with a clear, concise, almost stereotyped, chain of events. The truth, however, often has murky or missing details, and frequently the time line is distorted. And a true story often has strange things in it that people normally don't make up, such as an aircraft that landed by itself or a dead woman pilot.

It's difficult to talk about some subjects when it comes to racial or ethnic characteristics, because it often leads to remarks that are stereotypical and unfair. When I talk about the traits or mind set the Vietnamese have, I don't believe I am being prejudiced, and I certainly don't want anyone to think I dislike the Vietnamese. I dedicated a number of years of my life to learning their language and culture, and the friendships I've formed with Vietnamese, inside and out of Vietnam, are the warmest I've had with any national group, including my own.

But I think as a whole, groups of people do tend to have certain behavioral characteristics, and to ignore them totally may be politically correct, but in the real world, impractical.

I believe that an example of a Vietnamese cultural characteristic is their treatment of truth. In this regard, I've seen some merit in Tom McKay's theory that even if a Vietnamese has told you the truth on most matters during an interview, he or she will still lie to you at least once. Tom said it's just part of their culture and a "face" thing with them. If a Vietnamese is totally truthful with a westerner, that means he or she is not in control, and, therefore, has lost face. When Tom first told me that, I chuckled, but over the years as I had more and more experience in interviewing Vietnamese, I began to think maybe he was right.

I told Jim Coyle what Tom told me and Jim agreed, at least in part. Jim is married to a lovely Vietnamese lady and had considerably more knowledge than most people about how Vietnamese think. He said that he had caught his wife in "white" lies for years, particularly in talking with people she had just met. When he would admonish her about stretching the truth or coming up with an outright falsehood when there was absolutely no reason to do so, she would merely shrug and say in Vietnamese, "He's not my grandfather." Jim said the saying conveys a meaning that a Vietnamese does not have to be truthful to those outside of the family.

LtCol Mather essentially said the same thing. He told me that sometimes his wife Luan would say things to casual acquaintances that would be made of whole cloth. Later when he would ask her about why she had deceived the person, she'd say something to the effect that, it didn't matter; the person in question was not a family member.

Bill Bell was always suspicious of anything the Vietnamese told him, and even in casual matters he took what they told him with a grain of salt. Once Bill asked me about a road I had been on in Vietnam. I told Bill the road was terrible and it would be much better to take another route that was longer, but would save time. I wondered why Bill had asked me that question since he had no intention of travelling on that particular road, and as far as I knew really had no need at all for that piece of information. Bill said, no reason; he was just checking the veracity of something a Vietnamese had told him.

I've come to the conclusion that in the refugee camps and in Vietnam, truth is not the same as truth in the West. Truth is very general and can be restated to one's advantage or to fit the Asian concept of "face." The family is truth and anything outside of that is really secondary in importance.

As a strategy in getting around the problem of refugees or witnesses lying, I would stress that their information was important, not to me, but to the families of the missing Americans. The Vietnamese revere the concept of the extended family, and getting them to think in family terms when answering questions turned out to be the key in getting more truthful responses.

But this didn't always work because there is some real scum in the refugee camps who could care less about family or the feelings of others. If they saw the opportunity to realize some personal gain, they would do it instantly regardless of whether or not some one else would be hurt in the process. Criminals are the same the world over. They crossed that thin line between right and wrong years ago and never looked back.

I estimate that in a three year period I interviewed well over 1,500 refugees and wrote perhaps 2,000 reports. For a while, I kept close track of the numbers of people I talked to and the reports that I had written, but after a while this became a bookkeeping chore that took too much time.

The only thing I ever did toward the end of my tour to keep track of the refugees who had been interviewed was to maintain a list of who had provided information in the camps in Hong Kong and Macau. Sometimes, in those camps I would interview a refugee about an incident, and then I'd discover that the refugee had been interviewed by Bill Bell or Tom McKay several years before. And it didn't necessarily help to ask the refugee if he had ever given anyone his information. Half of the time he would say, "No," even if he had been interviewed extensively in the past. So I usually carried an up-dated computerized list with names that I could check quickly to see if the individual had been talked to before.

One problems I had in interviewing refugees was getting them to nail down a date on which an incident occurred. They were usually pretty good about the time of day: morning, afternoon, evening, night, but the year was often in error. The months were usually off too, though the refugees could often recall the weather: cool, cold, hot, rainy, cloudy, etc. And particularly incidents that had occurred in rural areas could be associated with the rice growing and harvesting seasons. But even with this information it was often difficult to determine the time of the year because certain areas of the country have several rice seasons.

In the early years of the Vietnamese exodus, all of the boat people were considered "refugees" in the legal sense of the word. Because of their status, they were eligible for resettlement in a third country, such as the United States, Australia or Canada. But when the refugee problem got worse in 1988 and vast numbers began streaming out of Vietnam, Hong

Kong realized it could not continue as a country of first asylum.

Hong Kong announced it would still take the boat people, but only temporarily, until arrangements could be made with Vietnam to send them back. All of the newcomers were screened, and those who were determined to be "economic migrants," which eventually amounted to ninety percent or more of the refugee population, were placed in detention camps awaiting their return to Vietnam. About ten percent were determined to be genuine refugees, and these were placed in special camps for eventual resettlement to a third country.

Hong Kong made a financial deal with Vietnam that would allow a number of "economic migrants" to be sent back to Vietnam. But the 50 or so who were rounded up in the middle of the night and forcibly sent back created such a negative backlash in world opinion that both Vietnam and Hong Kong backed off from the deal. The United States was highly critical of sending them back, which to me was strange logic considering it sends back thousands of Mexicans and other illegal immigrants every year.

The Hong Kong government started a voluntary repatriation program which had some success, but only a fraction of the camp inhabitants have volunteered to return to Vietnam. The Hong Kong government put a lot of emphasis on the program. One of the means of enticing the refugees to sign up was to show them a very slick video that played on every emotional Vietnamese heartstring imaginable. The film deserved an academy award.

But one time a refugee out-slicked the Hong Kong propagandists. The refugee contacted the Hong Kong authorities and said that he was convinced and ready to go back. He went through the interview process with humanitarian assistance workers and even was interviewed by representatives of the Vietnamese government. He got on the aircraft, smiling and happy, and every bit the repentant prodigal looking forward to returning to the workers paradise of Uncle Ho Chi Minh.

One month later he entered Hong Kong Harbor on a boat with his wife and children. He had just taken advantage of the opportunity to return to get his family out.

For years refugee interviewing was the "bread and butter" of agencies such as JCRC that have been in the business of investigating MIA cases. When JCRC started going into Vietnam to investigate cases, I asked LTC Harvey if he thought it was still necessary to send interviewers to the camps, since we were having so much more success in resolving cases inside of Vietnam. Harvey expressed that it was still necessary because the Vietnamese could cut us off in Vietnam tomorrow. If that happened where would JCRC be as an investigative organization? He said, bureaucratically, JCRC continually had to fight for its turf and should it release its grip on the camps, even briefly, it would get pushed out.

I'm sure Harvey's analysis of refugee interviewing is the correct one. He's an expert in political survival who has outlasted his peers in the MIA business year after year. In any event, refugee interviewing is here to stay.

Author and team members conducting field excavation of a grave site.

An official banquet in Hanoi. From left to right: Major Pham Theo, Bill Bell, Ngo Hoang, LTC Joe Harvey, the author, and Dr. Nguyen Thu. LTC Johnnie Webb, CILHI commander, is sitting on the opposite side of the table.

CHAPTER THREE

RELUCTANT WARRIOR

The ghost of Vietnam has haunted me for much of my life and seems like it has always been with me. My earliest memories of hearing about the country were in junior high school. I vaguely remember news stories then about attacks by the Viet Cong and the fear of the country falling to the communists. Where I was a high school student, the news about Vietnam intensified as the United States became more and more involved. But it all still seemed so far away.

One of the first decisions that I had to make after graduating from high school in 1965 was what to do about military service. The selective service machinery was gearing up to support the military machine that was slowly coming to life. Incredibly, few Americans, including myself, knew that by 1966 the national leadership had already irrevocably committed a generation of Americans to a war. But in spite of strong public denials from the Johnson administration that America was going to war, the signs of war were unmistakable as young men began to receive draft notices and more and more troops were sent to Vietnam.

For most of the Vietnam War, the U.S. government had a blatantly unfair policy that draft-age students could avoid military service by going to college. For most young men at that time, it was a matter of enrolling in college or being drafted. If you didn't or couldn't come up with the bucks to go to college, you got a draft notice. It was as simple as that. I was able to get the money so I went to college for four years while a lot of guys my same age got drafted and went to Vietnam. Fair or not, that's the way the system was. I don't condone the fact that I was willing to let others serve while I sat out the war; I'm just saying the system gave me a choice—and I chose.

In September 1969, after completing college, I got a job as a high school English and Spanish teacher in a little Texas town called Orange Grove. The draft was hot on my tail, and shortly after I was hired, I received a draft notice. But the school district superintendent contacted my local draft board and requested that I be given a deferment on the basis of being employed in a shortage public service field. My draft board informed me that I could elect to finish out the school year, but immediately afterward I would be inducted into military service. I thought that would eventually work out fine since in a year I'd surely be able to find a way to beat the draft again as I had done for four years as a college student.

As I drifted through the school year as a mediocre teacher, the national news was that the Congress of the United States had legislated the creation of a national lottery that would determine eligibility for induction into military service. I was sure the lottery was going to be the answer to my draft problem. In fact, my birthday, January 13, 1947, corresponded to one of the highest lottery numbers and made the chance for induction just about nil. Or so I thought.

Promptly at the end of an enjoyable year, at least for me, but a largely unproductive school year for my students, I got a letter from the selective service with an ominous first line saying: "Greetings from the President," followed by "...your friends and neighbors have selected you for induction into military service." Surely there had been a mistake! I had an incredibly high draft number. But, as a letter from my congressman explained, after I had complained of an "injustice" being committed against me, I was not eligible for the national lottery. I had already been drafted a year previously. Remember?

The handwriting was now on the wall and the question was not if I would be going into military service, but when. I made the rounds of the service recruiters to see what they had to offer. I reasoned that since I had to go into military service anyway, I might as well do something I liked. I was not adverse to military service per se; I was just confused as most Americans were as to what was happening in Vietnam. Vietnam was a quagmire, and now I was involuntarily caught up in something I didn't understand.

I took a number of tests and talked to recruiters from the various services but nothing clicked. The training they offered just wasn't me. And then the Army recruiter said, How about learning a foreign language? It'll only cost you one extra year tacked on to the two years you have to serve anyway. Learn a foreign language? Yeah, that's it! I love studying foreign languages. But which language? He had five openings: Thai, Laotian, Cambodian, Korean...and Vietnamese. The choice was mine.

And then I did a strange thing. Within a split second, I sealed my fate for years to come. "I'll take Vietnamese," I said, knowing full well that the other four languages would likely keep me out of the war, and the fifth would almost guarantee that I would in some way be involved in it. In essence, I was volunteering to go to Vietnam.

After taking the oath of enlistment with ten or twenty other young men, some of whom had voluntarily joined, and others who had obviously been coerced into enlisting by the legal system, I was off to Ft. Ord, California, to attend eight weeks of basic training. Vietnamese language school would come after I successfully completed the initial military training that millions of Americans have undergone and seemed to have survived, no worse for wear.

My recruiter told me I was joining a "new" Army, as evidenced by the fact that the skinhead haircuts were now out. According to him, troops could now wear their hair in basic training almost in civilian style. So confident was I that the Army had changed, at the Reception Station at Ft. Ord I told the barber that I wanted a nice little trim on top and not too close on the sides. Hey, this might not be too bad after all. Even the buck sergeants assigned to lead us around and assist us in inprocessing were nice guys. Some of them were even draftees and were finishing up their two year tours of duty. They leisurely took us to get our shots, eat at the mess hall, and they even gave us tips on how to survive basic training.

Then came the drill sergeants from hell. "You guys that got them sissy haircuts...get 'em fixed!" And we did, in spite of our belief in so-called rights to longer hair. These guys were so intimidating. They looked like they came right off the screen from the "The Good, The Bad, and The Ugly." I could almost hear the movie's theme song, but no Clint Eastwood was going to come to our rescue. Even our newly found sergeant buddies who had initially been in charge of us were obeisant to these overpowering aliens.

I still remember my drill sergeant's name: Becker. One doesn't easily forget personalities like that. Even now I'd probably brace against the wall if he walked by. At the time I was an out-of-shape wimp who couldn't run a mile, and Staff Sergeant Becker didn't like wimps. And worse, SSG Becker didn't like college boys who had the potential of screwing up his basic training platoon. I realized right from the start that guys like Becker could make life miserable for privates who didn't or wouldn't fit into his concept of order in the universe, so I immediately took to heart his admonishment to "cooperate and graduate."

Years later I lived at Ft. Ord with my family, and I frequently would jog miles (this time in shape) through training areas where I had frequently done pushup for one infraction or another under Becker's or some other drill sergeant's sadistic gaze. The ghosts from the past were still there after all that time. I could hear Becker yelling at some kid who turned right when everybody else turned left: "Not that left, Trainee! Your other left!" And there was Hew Lin, a drill sergeant from Hawaii, singing "Tiny Bubbles..." Then we'd answer in refrain, "Tinnny Bubbles..." And Hew Lin would continue in song, "...in the wine." And we'd complete, while marching, a moving melody that would do old Don Ho proud.

Up until that time Hew Lin was the toughest and vilest-talking human being I'd ever seen. He looked and sounded like some evil being the "Warriors of the Universe" would battle on Saturday morning television. One day in a theater he dressed us down in the coarsest speech imaginable just before the chaplain was to give us a talk. After concluding his diatribe about how we lower life forms were privileged to have someone like his majestic self guide us through the darkness of our ignorance, Hew Lin did a sharp military about-face, saluted smartly, and said, "They're all yours, Chaplain!" He walked off the stage leaving us to an obviously befuddled man of the cloth.

Hew Lin was in incredibly good physical condition and could run for miles. Also, anytime he put our basic training company in the "front-leaning-rest" position, a euphemistic Army word for pushup, we knew we were in trouble. The rule was one of the drill sergeants had to do the exercise too, which with Becker and some of the other drill sergeants wasn't too terribly threatening. But with Hew Lin we knew we were in for a rough session. He easily could do a hundred at a time.

One day Hew Lin perceived we were slow running out to his formation. He ordered all 160 or so of us basic trainees to run back into the barracks and move our loaded footlockers outside. After we drug all 160 footlockers downstairs, banging against the steps all the way, we all formed up adequately to his critical eye. Then he ordered us to drag the footlockers back upstairs. He threatened that next time, should we again decide to move slowly to his formation, we would be bringing down our wall lockers. Needless to say when we knew Hew Lin was in charge of the company, we moved like mad men.

Among our ranks was a hippy-looking guy named "Rader," who had a glassy-eyed appearance about him that I'm sure came from an undetermined amount of substance abuse over the years. The day we were issued our M-16 rifles, he announced that he was a conscientious objector and refused to sign for his rifle. Becker was furious and threatened him, but Rader stood firm. Several days later I saw Becker slug Rader in the face—and Rader stood there and took it but still refused to give in. During the next couple of weeks we ran everywhere, always carrying our rifles, and Rader was always right there with us...empty handed. The rest of us grudgingly admired Rader because he stood up for what he believed in and refused to cave into Becker.

One day Becker saw me chewing gum in class. "What's that in your mouth, Smith?" He pronounced the word "Smith" as if he were describing something stuck to the bottom of his shoe.

"Gum, Drill Sergeant" said I stupidly, knowing full well that he already knew what was in my mouth.

And justice followed swiftly. For the rest of the day I walked around with a wad of chewing gum sticking out of my nose.

And the most dreaded sound of all was the noise of a rifle carelessly falling on the ground. The words that followed from omniscient drill sergeants were always the same: "Go on down with it!" The guilty soldier would inevitably follow instruction to "Do pushups until I get tired!" Only then did the felon atone for his hideous sin.

Becker had a mean streak and would drop little comments that a certain soldier needed a "blanket party" to straighten him out. This is a nighttime form of barracks justice where soldiers throw a blanket over a sleeping soldier who is constantly screwing up and pound him. It must have been a frightening and humiliating experience for someone to undergo. I woke up several times during basic to the sound of a half dozen vigilantes slugging someone under a blanket.

Undoubtedly, should I or anyone else have decided to have done so, we could have easily nailed Becker to a wall for slugging and threatening troops and his encouragement of blanket parties. He was flagrant in the way he did things and a complaint would have started an investigation and gotten a lot of sworn statements. But I wasn't interested in bringing Becker down; I wanted only to get through basic with the least amount of personal discomfort and stress as possible. Basic was only eight weeks long, and I would never see Becker again. If I kept my nose clean, basic training would be just a brief interlude in what was to amount to a three-year Army career. The guys who made waves or didn't conform were the ones who had problems.

And then one day hell was all over. I graduated from basic training. After graduation, I travelled to Ft. Bliss, Texas, to attend Vietnamese language training at the Defense Language Institute, Southwest Branch. At that time there were several thousand soldiers studying Vietnamese in classrooms at Biggs Field, an airfield in the immediate vicinity of Ft. Bliss. The courses varied from several weeks of very basic vocabulary and conversation, usually for military policemen and infantrymen who only needed the rudiments of the language to do their jobs, to the long 47-week course in which I was enrolled. Most but not all of the long-course graduates were going to end up in military intelligence, but I didn't know that at the time because I didn't even know what military intelligence was. There were two dialects being taught: North and South Vietnamese. I took the southern dialect course.

The duty was great: classes were six hours a day, five days a week, with about an hour of homework at night. The rest of the time was our own. In addition to goofing off and running around, which I did plenty of, I occasionally did something socially useful, such as volunteering to teach English in the evening in the barrios of El Paso to newly arrived Mexican immigrants. I worked for free in a federally funded program called "Project Ser."

In the course of my duties at Project Ser, I met a long-haired Army lieutenant from an artillery unit at Ft. Bliss who was involved in an anti-war group in El Paso. He eventually was thrown out of the Army and given the worst efficiency report I've ever seen: zeros in every area. He returned to his home in Pennsylvania and became involved with an anti-war groups there. On one occasion he and others broke into an office of a U.S. senator and poured chicken blood on his records. Had it not been for some very serious high-level string pulling by some influential people, the former lieutenant would likely have done serious jail time.

During my year of language school, I even had a love affair with a Vietnamese instructor, something that was totally prohibited by school regulations. She could have been fired and I could have been severely disciplined. But, such is youth.

I presume she was peripherally involved in some kind of criminal activity, though I'm not exactly sure what. One day at her apartment I came across dozens of canceled Swiss bank checks. The amounts of the checks were for incredible sums of money: $10,000 and $20,000 were typical. I asked her what the checks were for and got only a vague response. I'm not totally convinced that she knew what they were for.

One day she said she had to go to New York to see "Mr._________." "Who's that?" I asked. She explained that he was a businessman who did business with her family in Saigon.

"Why do you need to see him?" I pressed. Vague answer.

By this time we were well progressed in our relationship and I said, "He should come see you. Besides you'd have to take off from your job if you went there."

I thought that would be the end of it, but lo and behold one afternoon a week later, Mr. __________ flew to El Paso from New York. My girlfriend and I picked him up at the airport, and then later in the evening the three of us went to eat Chinese food in El Paso.

During that particular time the news was full of stories of corruption in the PX systems in Vietnam, and while we were eating he complained bitterly that the U.S. government was on a witch hunt and was out to get some former PX employees who had done nothing wrong. Also during the meal, I could never quite pin down exactly why Mr. _________ was in El Paso or anything substantial about him other than that his wife was Vietnamese and that my girlfriend seemed to know her well.

We finished our meal and the three of us drove to the local Ramada Inn in El Paso to drop Mr. _________ off. I pulled into a parking slot and suddenly Mr. __________ and my girlfriend jumped out of the car, dashed into his room, and left me sitting in the car. I just sat there. I was too stunned by their actions to do anything else. In less than a couple of minutes my girlfriend came out alone and said, "I have to go to Western Union." I took her there and she wrote out a telegram that said cryptically in Vietnamese: "Mr. _________ was here." ("Ong ________ da o day.")

To this day I don't know what that was all about. She never gave me a hint, even though I asked her about it a number of times.

Toward the end of my Vietnamese course, my girlfriend decided she wanted to go to college. So one day a college president, who she said was a friend of her family in Vietnam, flew down from Nebraska in a small plane, picked her up and took her out of my life. I never saw her again. I got a few letters from her, and a friend of mine dropped by the college once to see her, but our relationship died. We lost touch and I don't have a clue what happened to her.

From Ft. Bliss, I travelled in my newly purchased yellow Volkswagen to Ft. Huachuca, Arizona, to attend the Army's Interrogation of Prisoners of War Course. It was slowly dawning on me that the U.S. Army would soon expect something in return for a fun year of learning Vietnamese.

The class was filled with about forty or so Defense Language Institute graduates, most of whom had attended language courses at the school in Presidio of Monterey, California. Only a handful of us were Vietnamese linguists. The rest had studied Korean, German, Russian, Hungarian, Spanish, or Arabic. I think with the exception of one or two students we all had attended a minimum of four years of college.

One requirement of the course was that we had to sign a statement saying that we understood that there might be times in our military intelligence assignments that we might have to lie or do things that conventional American society might consider to be wrong and unethical. It was worded cleverly in such a way that it sounded innocuous, but there was no question in our minds as to what we were being told to agree to. Everyone in the class eventually signed it. The alternative would have been cook or infantry school.

Years later the Army got into "ethics" and that was the big "buzz" word that was supposed to be in officer efficiency reports. By then I was a senior warrant officer, and sometime during that period I attended a military ethics class taught by a chaplain. He was explaining the importance of ethics in the Army and how our word as officers had to be our bond. As an off-hand comment during discussion time, I related that the U.S. Army had once made me sign a statement saying that, in effect, I would agree to lie, cheat, and steal in the course of my official military duties. I recall that he couldn't quite pull his lecture together after that.

I shouldn't have set the chaplain up like that, but I could see a clear distinction between falsehoods told within one's own system of laws and regulations, and falsehoods told with an intention to deceive a foreign country that is a potential adversary of the U.S. government. I had no ethical problem in carrying out a ruse or deception against a foreign power in the service of my country.

We are told in the Bible that we shouldn't kill, yet exceptions were made by God Himself for a just war. And on one occasion God even commanded David, someone whom God said was a man after his own heart, to be deceptive. David feared to go to a certain place because his archenemy Saul would find out where he was through informants and kill him. God told David that if anyone asked why he was present at the place, David was to say that he was there to sacrifice to the Lord. David also lied to the Philistine kings about military operations. He told them that he was conducting raids against Saul, when in fact he was attacking garrisons belonging to the leaders he was lying to. Also there is the passage in the Bible where God actually put a "lying spirit" in the mouths of false prophets to deceive a wicked king.

So I had no ethical qualms at all about agreeing to participate in military intelligence activities that potentially might use tactics that in normal circumstances could be considered to be "unethical" or wrong.

For eight weeks we studied military intelligence subjects that included "approved" psychological interrogation techniques that were in accordance with the Geneva Conventions. We conducted mock interrogations with role players, some of whom had been interrogators in Vietnam, and spent hours writing reports. The course was excellent.

I graduated from interrogation school and was now a full-fledged "MI puke." In the Army helicopter pilots are "rotor heads"; infantry troops are "grunts"; special forces soldiers are "snake eaters"; mechanics are "grease monkeys"; and all military intelligence specialists are "pukes."

Since I was en route to Vietnam, I was authorized to take 30 days of leave, which I took in Texas. During my leave, I met a beautiful red-haired woman who was an elementary school teacher in Ft. Worth, Texas. I fell head over heals in love and knew I had something to come back to. In December 1971 I said goodbye to the new and final woman in my life and headed to Oakland, California, for preparation to go to Vietnam. Oakland Army Depot was the first stop on the journey that I had spent years trying to avoid.

Scenes from hell: a hundred toilets were lined up in rows with no partitions between them; hundreds of sinks; hundreds of bunks; and the lights were on twenty-four hours a day. Every couple of hours there were formations where menial details were assigned just to keep people busy. Also, at the Army "gulag" in Oakland, all of us going to the "Nam" were issued jungle fatigues and boots. And then at one of the many formations, one by one we got departure times and boarded buses that would take us to Travis Air Force Base. There we waited hours before finally climbing up metal stairs to a civilian aircraft that would take us to Vietnam. For me the ordeal only lasted three days. I was lucky. Some of the guys had been there for weeks.

It was night when we approached Bien Hoa Air Base. From the air we could see thousands of lights in the concertina wire that was a measure to ward off "Victor Charlie." Upon landing, we off-loaded from the aircraft and boarded military buses with screened windows—to keep Charlie from lobbing grenades into the bus—and headed through downtown Bien Hoa. MP gun jeeps, with an M-60 machine gun mounted in the center of the jeeps, were at the front and back of our bus convoy.

The first thing one notices when landing in South Vietnam is the sickly sweet odor of rice. Or at least that's what everyone said it was; and then in a day or so you wouldn't notice it anymore, until you had left the country and come back...and you'd smell it all over again.

On the edge of Long Binh post, across town from Bien Hoa Air Base, we entered a military compound called a "replacement center." It was surrounded by rows of concertina, was filthy, and generally smelled like urine. The compound was overflowing with soldiers from the 101st Airborne division, combat veterans recently arrived from I Corps. Bien Hoa was in III Corps.

If you ask a Vietnam Vet where he was during the war, chances are he'll say, "I was in I Corps," "II Corps," "III Corps," or "IV Corps (pronounced "eye-core," "two-core," "three-core," and "four-core," respectively). The Vietnamese Army was organized into four military corps, and under each corps headquarters were South Vietnamese Army (ARVN) combat units. The southern half of Vietnam was divided into four corps areas or zones: the uppermost corps was bordered on the north by the Demilitarized Zone and the lowermost corps was the Delta region, through which the Mekong River flowed. How U.S. soldiers ever picked up a Vietnamese military regional term to describe where they were located during the war is beyond me, but it worked well and was, and still is, universally used by Vietnam vets to describe where they were assigned.

The 101st soldiers called us "newbies" which was the term for the brand new guys just coming in country. We newbies were intimidated by the grunts from the 101st. With their weathered uniforms and cocky demeanor, they looked at us with the air of superiority that high school seniors look at brand-new freshmen. It was obvious they had spent some time in the boonies, because several of them didn't even bother to find bunks in the ramshackle wood and screen barracks. They just lay on the ground wherever it suited them.

Early the next morning we were all rudely awakened by replacement center "cadre." In the Army, sleeping-in is frowned on for some reason. It's perfectly acceptable to have absolutely nothing to do—but doing nothing will not be done lying down. And you better not put your hands in your pocket while you're doing nothing.

Since we couldn't sleep, rather than totally waste my time standing around doing nothing, I wandered around the replacement center getting my bearings and carrying on conversations with Vietnamese workers who were employed doing menial work. At one point in my meandering stroll, I spent some time gazing across a field at another nearby military compound. I remember as I stood there thinking, "I wonder where I'll end up?" I never would have guessed that at least for part of the time, I was going to end up in the very compound across the field at which I was staring.

Several times a day we'd have formations, and one-by-one our names would eventually be called and we would disappear into the gigantic personnel system. When our names were called, we lined up behind signs that corresponded to regional replacement activities within Vietnam. I remember one sign had the words "Bien Hoa" and another had "Phu Bai." There were other signs, but I don't recall the destinations written on them. I specifically remember the two signs because I lined up behind the "Bien Hoa" sign when my name was called, and the grunts from the 101st would laugh nervously when anyone was called to stand behind the "Phu Bai" sign. I didn't have any idea where Phu Bai was, but I knew without a doubt from the reaction of the grunts that I didn't want to go there. And strangely, seventeen years later, during MIA investigations in Vietnam, I got to know Phu Bai well.

From the replacement center my group went by truck to an Army personnel facility at Long Binh base. I don't remember too much about the place except I recall sitting in a room next to a hoodlum wearing glasses with cracked lenses. He wasn't going where we were going, thank goodness. He was getting a dishonorable discharge and was being shipped back to the states. The rest of us weren't there very long when jeeps drove up to pick us up. We drove by the replacement center from where we had come, and turned in at the next gate at the compound I had observed earlier.

The compound was known as Plantation, but it obviously wasn't a plantation. There wasn't a tree in sight. Some of the old timers who had been at Plantation back before "Tet" of '68 told me that it had in fact once been a lush rubber plantation. But the whole area had been cleared by the famous Rome plows, a remarkable piece of American ingenuity manufactured in Rome, Georgia. In the coming weeks while driving in and Around Bien Hoa, Long Binh, and Plantation, one Plantation resident from the old days showed me where the rubber trees had been along the barren roads. Now nothing was evident except for red dirt. The trees had all been cleared to keep the elusive Viet Cong from ambushing American and ARVN (Army of the Republic of Vietnam) vehicles. The only trees that remained were in a patch on nearby Long Binh post. I got the feeling that maybe someone left them just to show what they were like.

At Plantation I was assigned to the 219th Military Intelligence Detachment, which was a thirty-two man unit that supported the Third Regional Assistance Command, or TRAC (pronounced "track"). TRAC had previously been named "Second Field Force," but underwent a name change after so many combat troops left Vietnam after President Nixon started the withdrawals. I suppose that since there was no longer a "field force" there was no reason to keep the name. The Second Field Force had been an incredibly huge, corps-sized combat unit that contained legendary units such as the 1st Infantry Division (the Big Red One) and the 25th Infantry Division (Tropic Lightning). In reality Second Field Force was an Army corps, but General Westmoreland thought calling large American organizations "corps" would be confusing with the four Vietnamese corps: I, II, III, and IV.

The major headquarters in Vietnam to which most combat unit belonged were the Third Marine Amphibious Force (III MAF), which operated in the Vietnamese I Corps area, the First Field Force, which was in II Corps, and the Second Field Force, later known as TRAC, which operated primarily in III Corps. The Second Field Force also had combat units that deployed in IV Corps, or the Delta area, a number of which engaged in "riverine" warfare. American order of battle in Vietnam was complicated and it took me years to get sorted out what units belonged to whom.

The 219th MI had four sections, in addition to a headquarters section with maintenance and administrative personnel. The sections were Interrogation, Order of Battle (intelligence analysis), Imagery Interpretation (air photography analysis; guys in this section were called "squints"), and Counter-Intelligence. I was in the interrogation section.

I didn't stay at Plantation for more than a few days. As soon as I got there I was informed by the detachment sergeant that I would be travelling by Huey (UH-1 helicopter) to a town on the Cambodian border called Tay Ninh. I would be joining some other MI soldiers from the 219th MI Detachment who were at Tay Ninh providing intelligence support to the forward headquarters of TRAC. TRAC had the mission of monitoring and supporting an ARVN cross-border operation into Cambodia. The purpose of the operation was to clean out sanctuaries controlled by North Vietnamese forces in Cambodia.

The next morning one of the detachment NCOs, an interrogator named Sergeant Doering, picked me up in a jeep at my "hootch" (pre-fabricated metal buildings with a concrete floor) and took me to the "Red Carpet" to catch a Huey to Tay Ninh. Right away he started talking about the rocket attack that had occurred the previous night at Bien Hoa Air Base, which was on the other side of Bien Hoa City from where we were. (The three big American bases at Bien Hoa were Long Binh, Plantation, Bien Hoa Air Base, and Bien Hoa Army Post.) He looked incredulous at me when I told him I hadn't heard a thing. He said, "How could you not have heard it?. Bien Hoa was hit by eighty or ninety rockets!" I had slept through the whole thing.

Sergeant Doering dropped me off at the Red Carpet and I caught a Huey going to Tay Ninh. This was the first time I had been in a helicopter, and my first good air view of Vietnam. I guess what surprised me the most about the view were the myriad of shell craters that were literally everywhere over the countryside.

And then the second thing that caught my attention was the majestic Nui Ba Den, or Black Virgin Mountain, that rises out of the rice paddies and overlooks Tay Ninh City. Viet Cong and American forces existed in an uneasy truce on the battle-scarred mountain. The Americans had a base at the very top and the Viet Cong lived in caves at the side. But some months later, during the so-called "Spring Offensive" or Nguyen Hue Campaign, as it was known to the enemy, the American base on top was eventually overrun.

There were two bases at Tay Ninh: Tay Ninh East and Tay Ninh West. The chopper landed at Tay Ninh East, which was a Vietnamese base surrounded by a mud wall and concertina. On the edge of the base was an airfield with dozens of helicopters belonging to a U.S. Cavalry unit. A number of the aircraft were Cobra gun ships that brandished fearsome teeth and eyes. The pilots and aircraft crews wore the distinctive "Cav" hats, made famous later by the movie "Apocalypse Now." A soldier from the unit I was going to be assigned to for an unknown period, the forward headquarters of the III Military Assistance Command, picked me up in a jeep. The rest of the headquarters was back at Plantation where I had come from, but a forward element, including the commander, Major General James Hollingsworth, was here in Tay Ninh.

The driver dropped me and my gear off at the forward TRAC headquarters, which was located in a wooden bunker covered with sandbags. I met the intelligence officer, Major Beagle, who explained to me that I would be doing interrogations and translations of Vietnamese documents. I was to get experience with an interrogation "go-team" of three soldiers from the 525th MI Group in Saigon. The individuals on the team were an ARVN sergeant and two Americans: an enlisted interrogator and a lieutenant. Although they were from the 525th MI Group, they would be working out of the forward TRAC headquarters for the immediate future.

The mission of the "go-team" in Tay Ninh was to interrogate prisoners ARVN units had taken in the cross border operation. The team members were writing reports called "knowledgeability" briefs to send back to their unit in Saigon. The purpose of the reports were to identify prisoners with information that could answer specific intelligence requirements levied on their unit by the senior command their intelligence unit supported.

For the next couple of days I went around with the go-team doing interrogations. The first interrogation that we did was of a Viet Cong (South Vietnamese Communist) who had been captured nearby by ARVN troops. Although the other enlisted interrogator and I were Vietnamese linguists, at that time we really were not good enough to interrogate in Vietnamese without assistance. Consequently, the ARVN sergeant assigned to the go-team interpreted the questions and answers. Later in the tour, just before it was time to rotate back to the states, our proficiency was at the level where we could do things like that fairly easily.

At one point during the interrogation, the other enlisted interrogator became convinced that the prisoner was lying and said so. I remember vividly the look of terror on the prisoner's face as he was confronted with the alleged falsehood by an angry American looking down at him. We were prohibited by Army regulations from doing anything physical to the prisoner, but he didn't know that. The fact that political officers in his own unit had undoubtedly fed him propaganda that Americans were murderers who would torture him to death actually aided us in the interrogation. The fear that he had of us eventually induced him to cooperate.

Another interrogation was a little more complex. Two Khmer Rouge (Cambodian communists) had been captured in Cambodia and flown out by American Cav aviation units operating in support of ARVN units. The two prisoners, both wearing only black shorts, were brought blindfolded to our location. Brought in with them were their two bicycles reinforced with wood that could carry several hundred pound bags of rice or military equipment. The prisoners were part of a Khmer Rouge transportation unit.

We couldn't communicate with the prisoners since they didn't speak English or Vietnamese. However, a Cambodian captain was present who spoke French in addition to his native language of Khmer. And we also were able to use the linguistic services of a Vietnamese colonel who could speak French and English in addition to Vietnamese. We set up a chain in which we asked questions in Vietnamese and English, which the colonel then translated into French, and the Cambodian captain translated into Khmer. And then the answers came back to us the same way. I'm not sure how successful the interrogation was, but it was extremely interesting to participate in.

Paul Rester, an interrogator from the 219th MI, was also at Tay Ninh. We had been Vietnamese students together in El Paso and students at the interrogation course at Ft. Huachuca. He and I became good friends in Tay Ninh and kept up our friendship even after we left Vietnam. We followed each other around the Army for years.

One day Paul and I took a break from our duties in Tay Ninh and travelled by jeep to the famous Cao Dai Temple and gardens located near the city. The temple complex was absolutely lovely, but unquestionably one of the strangest places I've ever visited. A gigantic eye dominated the center of the main temple, within which also were huge supporting columns with carvings of serpent dragons entwined around them. The Cao Dai religion, which is a mixture of Christianity, Buddhism, and the occult, had its headquarters on the grounds. In addition to Jesus, Buddha, and Moses, all part of the Cao Dai litany of deities, Victor Hugo somehow was included too. The adherents to the faith communicate with the supernatural by means of automatic handwriting.

When Paul and I were about to enter the temple area, a Cao Dai priest would not let me go in armed. Paul did not have a weapon but I was carrying a .45 automatic. I gave the pistol to the priest for safekeeping and then felt like a total fool giving away our only means of defense to a total stranger and a member of a exotic cult to boot. Besides that, just a few miles from where we were walking around were enemy base camps with real North Vietnamese and Viet Cong soldiers. But all's well that ends well and I retrieved my pistol in good order as we exited the grounds. Can you imagine if I had never seen the guy and my weapon again? "Well, sir, I gave my gun to a funny-looking, bald- headed guy in a yellow robe and..."

All of the Americans working at Tay Ninh East base camp lived in an old French hotel on the edge of Tay Ninh, which was in walking distance of the base camp. We weren't supposed to walk back and forth because of the danger from attack, but I did anyway. In fact, one of the most obnoxious NCOs I've ever known in the Army chewed me out once for doing so. I thought he was an idiot so I continued doing it anyway, but that was probably one of the few times in his Army career he was right about something. Tay Ninh did have a lot of Viet Cong and it wasn't safe to go willy-nilly wandering around. And just before I had arrived in Tay Ninh, a soldier had been shot somewhere in the city.

The hotel was surrounded by a high wall on which there were watch positions at various strategic places. Cambodians were our hired guards, and on Christmas Eve of 1971 I took duty for Paul, which consisted of keeping the guards awake. Paul had been invited by some Vietnamese soldiers to attend a special party, so I agreed to pull guard for him. I had a nice time, too. The Cambodians were all good troops and needed no special attention. I spent the night communicating with them as best I could—a few could speak a little Vietnamese. I walked from guard post to guard post talking with the guards and watching the lovely roman candles that the Catholic faithful were setting off in and around the city. I've always wondered what happened to those guys when Pol Pot took over.

The next day, Christmas, I slept for a few hours and then reported to work at Tay Ninh East. There I saw, for the first time, our boss, Major General James Hollingsworth, commander of TRAC. He was walking around to all of the work sections with a female reporter and wishing everyone a merry Christmas. I didn't know it at the time but I was meeting a legend in the U.S. Army. He had been an armor officer in Patton's army during World War II and had extensive combat experience in tank warfare in Europe. Cornelius Ryan, a prominent author known for his writings about the allied thrust through France and Germany, described in detail combat incidents involving Hollingsworth. Also, S.L.A. Marshall, one of the better known writers of Vietnam War history, wrote about Hollingsworth in a book called, BATTLES IN THE MICHLIN.

In the coming months I would see a lot of Major General Hollingsworth. He was a profane, chain-smoking Texas A and M graduate who loved to shock people with his comments. The general, who carried a pearl-handled .357 magnum revolver, once said: "When you kill a communist, it makes you feel good deep down inside your heart." (He was later made to apologize for that remark by General Creighton Abrams.) Hollingsworth also occasionally used bad grammar in the midst of his profanities. Now I know perfectly well that General Hollingsworth, who was one of the more eloquent orators I've ever heard, was quite capable of correctly using the English language. But he was an actor and he had a Pattonic destiny to be the Texas Warrior King, a role he played to the hilt.

Once during the Battle of An Loc, which was still several months in the future, General Hollingsworth was flying around in his helicopter when he saw a North Vietnamese tank on the edge of the jungle. The two door gunners on the sides of the Huey opened up, and Hollingsworth followed suit with his .357 magnum. According to reliable witnesses he had the time of his life, firing and yelling like a cowboy, although history doesn't record what happened to the tank.

It was in Tay Ninh that I saw my first war dead. In walking back and forth from Tay Ninh East to our quarters in the French hotel, I would pass an asphalt helicopter landing area on which Vietnamese helicopters were usually sitting. One evening about dusk, I observed bags being taken off the helicopters. Casually, I walked over to see what was being unloaded, and I saw that the grisly cargo was bodies wrapped in ponchos and tied to long poles. The dead warriors, all Vietnamese, were being placed in rows along the ground. As I watched, Vietnamese soldiers cut the bodies free and tossed them unceremoniously into awaiting ambulances. They threw the poles in a pile on the edge of the asphalt. Over the next few days I watched as the piles of blood-stained poles grew larger and larger, evidence that the Vietnamese were taking heavy casualties in Cambodia.

Some time in January 1972, after having been at Tay Ninh for a month, the forward elements of TRAC returned to Plantation. Paul Rester went back by vehicle convoy and I flew by helicopter. When I was in Vietnam doing MIA investigations, I always wanted to go back to Tay Ninh for a visit. I thought I'd get the chance during one particular investigation that was conducted in Tay Ninh Province, but by the luck of the draw another MIA investigative team ended up there and I went somewhere else. I was glad to have had the opportunity to have gone there during the war. It was a good place to get broken in and to get prepared for the next phase of my Vietnam tour.

When Paul Rester and I returned from Tay Ninh and started working at the Vietnamese III Corps Headquarters, we had interesting jobs. However, we had no idea that the most exciting part of our Vietnam careers was only a few short months in the future: The Battle of An Loc.

A Vietnamese transport helicopter that carried a joint team to the Ashau Valley.

CHAPTER FOUR

SCAMS, DOG TAGS, AND STRANGE STORIES

One of the jobs interviewers had at the Liaison Office in the American Embassy in Bangkok was greeting people who called up from the front gate and requested to talk to an American official about MIAs. There wasn't a week that went by that we didn't have at least one visitor, and sometimes many more.

The visitors often had information to give us that they had obtained during a trip somewhere in Southeast Asia. Frequently they were stopping in Bangkok on the way back from Vietnam where they had been tourists or were visiting family members. Generally the information was dog tag information or rumors about American POWs still in Vietnam. Most of the people who came to see us were honest citizens who felt they were doing their patriotic duty, but from time to time, we'd receive visits by scam artists. These individual had the morality of kidnappers, whose only intention was to obtain money. I met some real scum during my three years in Bangkok.

The first day I started to work at JCRC, a "Mr. Tony" called Mather and said he knew where the American POWs were being held and he wanted to cut a deal for $50,000 that afternoon to get them out. I listened to Mather's end of the conversation as he told Mr. Tony that the U.S. government does not pay for information about MIAs, but that should he have something he wanted to tell us he'd be happy to send an interviewer over to talk to him. Click.

Most of the scams were pretty standard and easy to see through. Sometimes they consisted of photographs of bones of an alleged American or grainy pictures of a supposed living POW. Of course, the persons with the information and photos were always totally altruistic themselves, but for some cash he or she would be able to get in contact with sources in Vietnam, Laos, or Cambodia who would be able to strike a deal to get the remains or live Americans out. The money was never for the people who were holding the remains or live Americans, but to pay bribes to the corrupt officials of the various governments involved. The person delivering the message was just an intermediary who was not involved in any way in the transaction.

In my mind, one scam stands out more than the others. The perpetrator of this particular scam should be nominated for an Academy Award. This was the case of the geographic surveyor who allegedly discovered remains at a B-52 crash site in Hai Phong Province.

The head of the American Chamber of Commerce in Bangkok called up one day and said he had been approached by an American claiming to be an engineer working for a foreign geographical survey corporation. He said the engineer told him that he had just arrived in Bangkok from Vietnam where he had spent two months conducting extensive geographical surveys under a contract with the Vietnamese government. The individual claimed that during the surveys, he and his party had come upon the crash site of a B-52 and in the wreckage had recovered American remains.

The engineer asked the American Chamber of Commerce representative what he should do with the information he had. The representative, who is an extremely nice guy and honest as the day is long, wrote a letter to the American Embassy, which was forwarded to the Liaison Office for action. LtCol Spurgeon called the Chamber of Commerce representative and requested he contact the engineer and invite him up to the Liaison Office.

The alleged engineer showed up at the embassy several days later, and he looked and sounded genuine. Spurgeon invited him to sit down and have a cup of coffee while we chatted. For once our guard was down. Normally when we had visitors who wanted to talk about remains, our antenna went up and we were prepared for just about anything. But this time we believed we were talking to a real engineer who was who and what he said he was. And on top of that, the scams we usually dealt with were not prefaced with a letter from the American Chamber of Commerce in Bangkok and forwarded to us from the office of the ambassador.

The engineer told us his story about a surveying contract his engineering company had been undertaking in Vietnam, when he and one of his teams found a crash site of a B-52 and recovered remains. He said the remains were being kept at a local village in Hai Phong Province on the Laotian border.

Hai Phong Province is not on the Laotian border. As a matter of fact it is on the other side of the country from Laos. But I let the remark go right over my head because I just assumed he misspoke or I hadn't heard him correctly. Then he said it again. The village where the remains were being held was on the Laotian border in Hai Phong Province. Suddenly I realized that this was just a run-of-the-mill scam artist who had shown a little more ingenuity than usual in getting in to see us. As the engineer talked, I wrote Spurgeon a one-word note: "Scam!" I saw the light go on in his eyes as he caught the drift of what was going on.

Then the other shoe dropped as it always does. A certain amount of money was needed to bribe government officials in Hai Phong Province to get the remains out of the country. He and his village contacts in Hai Phong were only acting under humanitarian principles, you understand, and wanted nothing for themselves.

Then the engineer showed us a dog tag that had supposedly come from one of the remains in the B-52. I looked up the name but it didn't pertain to any MIA case. Was this guy stupid or what? Didn't he think we would check to see if the name he gave us was any good? Maybe someone had scammed him into thinking the dog tag belonged to an MIA, and he in turn spun his own scam around the dog tag. Who knows. The dog tag had "USMC" stamped on it, which meant that it had once belonged to a proud member of the U.S. Marine Corps.

To play the game out, I said: "You know, it's kind of funny; this is a Marine Corps dog tag, and the aircraft it came out of was a B-52, which is a U.S. Air Force strategic bomber. I wonder what a marine was doing flying in a B-52?"

The engineer, looking at me with a straight-face and without batting an eye, said, "Maybe the guy was just catching a ride."

Why sure, that makes sense. Why didn't I think of that? Gee, I think I'll catch a ride over Hanoi tonight on a B-52 and have a little fun watching the SAMs come up at supersonic speed. Did this yahoo sitting in front of us think we were dumber than rocks?

I pulled out a map of Hai Phong and asked if he would mind locating the village where the remains were being held. He searched the map intently for a few minutes and then said he was sorry, but he wasn't familiar with military maps. But, he had his maps back at the hotel. Tell you what: I'll go get them and be right back after lunch. Why, that's a great idea. Handshakes all the way around. Let me walk you out.

I went with the scam artist out to the main gate of the embassy and just before he signed out with the guard, I said, "Say, you don't mind if I run an FBI check on you, do you? We really have to be careful about whom we are dealing with."

With a smile on his face that betrayed no fear whatsoever, he said, "Why no, of course not." In parting he calmly said, "I'll be back this afternoon with the maps." And he disappeared, never to be seen again.

There has to be a special place in Hell reserved for people like that.

Another scam that all of the interviewers used to get from time to time were the Bunker Queer stories. I'm serious! The stories were that Bunker Queer and two other Americans were American prisoners of war still living in Vietnam. One version that I once got from an American Vietnamese visitor to the embassy was that Bunker Queer and his two compatriots had somehow ended up in the custody of a local villager. The villager, the close relative of the American Vietnamese lady who was visiting our office, said that her relative had been feeding the three men, but one of them was deathly ill and about to die. The villager needed money—a lot of money—in order to buy medicine to save the life of the Americans.

The first time I heard a Bunker Queer story, I almost laughed. But it wasn't our job to laugh. Our mission was to take the information verbatim, as if every word were the gospel truth, write a report, and send it on up the chain. We did not analyze reports at our level. That was what the analysts at JCRC headquarters in Honolulu and the Defense Intelligence Agency in Washington got paid to do.

The two individuals who usually were reported to be with Bunker Queer turned out to be American soldiers who served their year in Vietnam and were alive and well in the U.S., living mundane, middle-class lives, and never having the slightest inkling they were the subject of intense analytical discussions taking place at DIA, deep in the bowels of the Pentagon. Neither of the former Vietnam vets had ever been prisoners of war. But analysts could never figure out who Bunker Queer was. They speculated that perhaps the name was a corruption of the name of a soldier who had also returned to the states. The names of all three likely came from dog tags that had been lost by American soldiers during the war, and which somehow some ingenious Vietnamese was able to use.

Occasionally at the Liaison Office, we would get letters from Bunker Queer and others, mailed directly from Vietnam. A typical letter, which I have included without all of the usual misspellings, would be as follows:

"My name Bunker Queer. I American MIA shot down July 23, 1966 Hai Phong. I being helped by Vietnamese friend. I very sick. Please send $5,000.00 U.S. money so I buy medicine or I die. Thank you."

I really enjoyed the photographs that I would get from time to time of Bunker Queer and his compatriots. Usually the subjects of the photographs were emaciated-looking people with obvious Asian features, but once the picture was of a rotund Caucasian male with a white goatee. The individual looked like Burl Ives and must have weighed at least 300 pounds. We chuckled for days about the "fat" Bunker Queer. We reasoned that his life as a prisoner of war had suited him well over the years.

Once scam artists mailed a color photograph to the American Embassy of a skinny Caucasian wearing black pajamas, the typical garb of peasants in Vietnam. The message in the accompanying letter was that the individual in the photograph was a prisoner of war who could be brought out of Vietnam with a cash payment by the United States government. Everybody in the MIA investigative community in Bangkok, Honolulu, and the Defense Intelligence Agency in Washington, D.C., recognized immediately that the photograph and message had all the makings of a typical scam, but that didn't matter: the system was being put into full gear to investigate the alleged surfacing of a living American MIA.

A few days later, the individual in the photograph showed up at the embassy. He told us that he believed he had been part of a scam of some kind involving MIAs. He said that a few days before he had met two Americans in a bar who asked him if he wanted to make an easy seventy-five bucks. He agreed and they took him out to a rice paddy where they had him don black pajamas and then took his picture. He said he'd had a few drinks at the time and was willing to go along with the photograph session, but after he sobered up, his conscience started bothering him and he decided he should report the incident to the American Embassy.

He was an interesting guy. He had been in Thailand for years and had originally come there as an American airman back during the war. During that time thousands of American airmen were stationed at five Air Force bases in the northeastern region of the country. At the end of his tour of duty, he married a Thai girl and they moved in with his wife's parents on a rice farm. He had been in Thailand ever since living like a rural Thai and working in the fields. By the time we met him, his Thai was better than his English.

After World War I, a number of famous American writers were part of the "Lost Generation" that remained behind in France after the war. In the same way, Thailand is the home of hundreds of American expatriates who in some way had been connected with the Vietnam War and never went home. Several of the bars even cater to Americans who served in particular organizations like Air America and Special Forces. The main English language newspaper in Bangkok has a weekly column called "Trink's Page," which is written by an American journalist named Bernard Trink, who keeps up with the nighttime activities at watering holes frequented by American expatriates. Many of these Americans dwell in the glorious days of the past, the present visited only in the protective wrapping of an alcoholic haze.

Southeast Asia is filled with shady characters who are always looking for well-meaning people to prey upon. Once I advised close friends of mine not to take a certain action because I knew that they would be setting themselves up for a scam. What they planned to do had nothing to do with MIAs. Their adopted teenage son, who was Vietnamese, was interested in finding out who his birth mother and father were. In 1975, his Vietnamese parents put him on an aircraft that was flying out of Vietnam and he never saw them again.

My friends wanted my advice as to whether they should attempt to locate their son's parents. I immediately told them to forget it. I said as soon as they made known what they wanted to do, a couple would come forward with a scam saying they were the boy's parents. Undoubtedly, they would even come up with something that looked legitimate, like photographs and a birth certificate. Wading through all of the lies would be impossible. They agreed and did not pursue the idea.

One scam we used to hear about that was occurring in Vietnam was being carried out by an individual who called himself "Johnny King." Refugees coming out of Vietnam would tell us about a B-52 pilot by the name of Johnny King who was living in a certain village in Vietnam. One refugee told us that his sister had married Johnny King and local people were supporting the couple with food and shelter. And, eventually, Jim Coyle interviewed Johnny King, who had come out in the refugee traffic. Johnny King turned out to be an Amerasian who supported himself with the scam that he was a B-52 pilot who had escaped. Local people cared for him, gave him money, shelter, and portions of their meager rations.

Jim said he had a hard time believing Vietnamese villagers would have fallen for Johnny King's scam. He was much too young to have been a B-52 pilot, and his features were more Asian than Caucasian. Also, Johnny King spoke Vietnamese with no accent. Surely the Vietnamese would have suspected that someone speaking perfect Vietnamese was likely not an American. Jim really scratched his head over that one.

One scam that former South Vietnamese draft dodgers frequently engaged in was to claim they had served in the South Vietnamese military during the war. In this way they would be eligible for resettlement in the United States. Many refugees from the South had indeed served honorably, but there were a lot of refugees who avoided military service and were now trying to get the benefits of those who had served.

Former Vietnamese servicemen would arrive in the refugee camps without any documentation that they had seen military service in the South. This happened frequently since many of them had been able to escape with only the clothes on their backs. American official with military experience in Vietnam were charged with investigating these cases and making assessments as to whether they were genuine former South Vietnamese soldiers or not. In several cases, former Viet Cong were caught claiming service in the South Vietnamese Army.

Leave it to the Vietnamese mind to come up with documentation to fool the dumb Americans, and more times than not it actually worked. In the camps classes were held on various military subjects for those who hadn't been in the military. The classes included the assembly and the disassembly of the M-16 combat assault rifle, military terminology, wear of the military uniform, and unit history. Grainy pictures of soldiers in wartime uniform proliferated, as evidence of service, until a sharp observer noticed the so-called veterans were all wearing the same uniform.

For a while it was popular for refugees from southern Vietnam to tell American resettlement officials they had served with the resistance after the fall of South Vietnam in 1975. But word got around that American refugee coordinators believed that story was bogus, so those stories stopped. But occasionally we'd run into someone who hadn't gotten the word and would try to spring the story on us.

Once a refugee told Bill Bell he had fought in the resistance after 1975. Bill happened to be an expert on the subject. When he and I were together at Ft. Chaffee years before working with the Vietnamese refugees, his job was to determine the state of any stay-behind resistance movement. With a straight face, Bill asked him, "Gee, how many Cong An (public security officers) did you kill?"

Taken aback by the question, the refugee said, "I didn't kill any Cong An."

Bill said, "Oh. Well, how many bridges did you blow up? Surely if you were in the resistance, you must have blown up some bridges."

The refugee's face dropped: "No, I didn't blow up any bridges."

"Well, how about rumors? Did you start any rumors?"

Bill Bell had finally hit on something the refugee could talk about that he had done. Yes, he had started all kinds of rumors.

We got involved in a lot of mini-scams involving dog tags and bone chips. Whenever JCRC interviewers travelled around to visit the refugee camps, they would invariably pick up dozens of dog tags allegedly pertaining to MIAs. Refugees would bring out dog tags and pieces of bone for which they wanted money or resettlement assistance. We always told the refugees that we couldn't give them anything for their dog tags and bones, but they could hand them over to us in a spirit of humanitarian cooperation if they wished. They usually did when they found out the items weren't worth anything. And we wanted them so we could get them out of the refugee camps where they did nothing but fuel bogus stories about Americans still living in Vietnam.

Over the years we collected literally thousands of dog tags and bone fragments, but only a tiny percentage were ever correlated to MIAs. Frequently the refugees didn't have a metal dog tag, but had pencil rubbings made from a dog tag. Some of the names on the rubbings appeared over and over.

I once asked LTC Johnnie Webb, the Commander of the Central Identification Laboratory, Honolulu, what his organization did with all of the hundreds of alleged MIA bone chips and remains that JCRC packaged up, which someone eventually had to carry by hand to Honolulu. Webb told me that the U.S. government had very specific procedures to follow regarding remains, and each one of those little bone chips had to be recorded and then eventually disposed of in a very precise format.

Remains, even if they did not pertain to MIAs, had to be hand-carried and not mailed or put in luggage that was to be stored in the hold of an aircraft. Many times passengers have sat next to JCRC travellers without realizing that in the overhead compartment above them were human remains. JCRC interviewers all had official passports and orders stating we were authorized to transport human remains, so there were no problems going through customs with human bones. We had full authorization to be doing what we were doing, but it did lead to some humorous incidents. Once when I was leaving Hong Kong with remains, an X-Ray operator zeroed in on a bag filled with almost a complete skeleton. The individual bones were clearly visible on the security monitor. I thought the Hong Kong security police were going to pounce on me in a heartbeat, and I had all my documentation in order ready for the interrogation. But the female operator merely shuddered and started the conveyor belt on her machine that gave me back my bag of bones. She never even looked at me.

In most cases, the dog tags and the remains proved not to relate to MIAs, but every now and then they did. Once Jim Coyle got lucky on an interview trip and brought back a complete set of remains that were later determined to be MIA. The Central Identification Laboratory, Hawaii (CILHI) did a thorough examination of the remains, to include checking dental X-Rays. The examination, which was one hundred percent conclusive, proved the remains were MIA.

Once a Vietnamese refugee arrived in the Philippines by boat with hundreds of dog tags and a barrel completely filled with human remains, none of which were MIA. I have no idea how those were eventually shipped to Honolulu.

The stories of how refugees got the dog tags and remains were as varied as the names on the dog tags themselves. Some of them claimed to have been out looking for Sandalwood in the forest when they happened upon a crash site. Many others said that just before they left Vietnam, a relative or friend came to their home and gave them a dog tag and a piece of bone.

Some good DIA analysts have concluded that the Vietnamese Ministry of the Interior was responsible for interjecting dog tags, bones, and silly stories about Bunker Queer and others into the refugee system. The motive would have been to defuse and manipulate the MIA issue. However, in spite of this theory, I believe the primary motivating factor for the bogus reporting was that many Vietnamese think absolutely nothing about scamming each other. If they can sell a dog tag or a piece of bone, they will do it. There are thousands of dog tags all over Vietnam waiting for a sucker and a story.

Montagnards were heavily into the business of selling remains. They frequently sold entire skeletons complete with dog tags and I.D. cards to buyers. Sometimes they accepted only gold or American currency in the transaction. The Vietnamese would buy the remains and then flee the country with the intention of getting a huge reward from the U.S. government and resettlement for themselves and their family members.

Once a refugee broke down and cried when I told him the name on the dog tag was not an MIA, and the remains he brought were likely Asian (nguoi vang). And then I had to tell him that even if the name and the remains turned out to be MIA, the U.S. government could give him nothing for them.

Frequently the owner of the remains spent their life savings to buy bones and dog tags, then risked a hazardous boat trip through storms and pirates to the Philippines, or wherever, only to be told they couldn't be compensated or helped in any way for their efforts.

One guy in the Philippines turned pale when I told him the name on the dog tag was not MIA. He said, "I could have gone to prison for nothing." Holding remains is highly illegal in Vietnam and carries a jail sentence. He and his family had bought remains and his wife was still hiding them at home in Vietnam. She and the kids stayed back while he fled with proof of their purchase. His plan was that in exchange for the remains, the U.S. government would assist him in getting his family out of Vietnam. He immediately wrote his wife and told her to get rid of the remains.

I've been asked why the United States government doesn't pay for information and remains of MIAs. I can categorically say that if the government ever agreed to do something like that, JCRC would be deluged with phony stories, remains, photographs, and who knows what else. The scams are bad enough as it is, but with rewards the floodgates would be opened.

One time LtCol Mather and I were given an almost complete set of remains, and strangely they turned out to be American—but not MIA. A well-known reporter called Mather and said that he had just come out of Ho Chi Minh City with a brown paper bag full of bones. He asked if we could come by his hotel and pick them up, which we did. His story was that a Vietnamese came up to him in Ho Chi Minh City, shoved the bag into his arms, and walked off. The reporter, thinking the remains might be MIA, put them in his luggage and brought them to Bangkok. He called the American Embassy, explained his predicament, and was advised that the JCRC Liaison Office was the official agency in Bangkok responsible for taking custody of remains alleged to be MIA.

Back at the embassy, Mather and I laid the bones out on the floor. Also in the bag were dog tags, a green I.D. card, chits from an NCO club at Tan Son Nhut Air Base in Saigon, a driver's license, and some coins. We checked records, but the name on the dog tags and I.D. documents clearly did not pertain to any known MIA case. But then the individual's name that was engraved on the dog tag popped up on my computer screen as a non-MIA casualty in Vietnam. The skeleton lying on the floor looking up at us was an Air Force NCO who had died in a C-130 crash in Vietnam. It was eerie staring into the airman's eyes in the photographs of the military I.D. and driver's license, and at the same time seeing his eyeless skull looking up at us. I felt like I was watching a modern version of Shakespeare's HAMLET.

But if we had remains of an American casualty in front of us, then why was he not on our list of MIAs? After some investigation, we learned that the C-130 had crashed in a remote, enemy-infested area, and American graves registration specialists went to the crash site and determined the entire crew aboard the aircraft to be dead. Because of the danger of attack, they had to withdraw and were able to conduct only a partial recovery. Although remains had been left behind, the dead crew members were not MIAs since their fate had been verified by American graves registration personnel.

Evidently, some time after the crash, scavengers entered the crash site, recovered the remains, and they ended up in the arms of an American reporter in Ho Chi Minh City. A strange, strange story indeed.

The author takes a break with Vietnamese province officials in the Ashau Valley.

CHAPTER FIVE

IN THE REALM OF THE TEXAS WARRIOR KING

Plantation, where I spent most of the Vietnam War, was the royal realm of Major General James F. Hollingsworth, the Texas Warrior King. The base was a sprawling labyrinth ringed with dense tangles of concertina wire. Inside the razor-sharp jungle of steel, lit up at night like a Christmas tree, were deadly Claymore mines and trip flares. Behind the wire, every hundred feet or so, were guard towers manned by GIs with machine guns. The guards, who were perpetually bored out of their minds, swatted insects hour after hour, often smoked marijuana, and listened to AFVN, the American armed forces radio station in Vietnam. I pulled guard duty several times before I made E-5, which exempted me from the disagreeable duty, and I can tell you it was a miserable experience.

In addition to the reinforced, underground concrete bunkers of TRAC headquarters, where Hollingsworth held court, was a huge GI city divided up by rank. General Hollingsworth lived in a house, his senior staff (brigadier generals and full colonels) lived in cabins, field-grade officers (majors and lieutenant colonels) lived in trailers, company-grade officers (lieutenants, warrant officers, and captains) lived in two-story barracks; and NCOs and lower enlisted men lived segregated from each other in a gigantic ghetto of pre-fabricated, metal "hootches". Inside the hot buildings, which had been erected over rough concrete floors, GIs built plywood partitions to separate the bunks and give some privacy. At night as one walked through the enlisted slums of Plantation, the pungent odor of marijuana was perpetually evident. Also the laughter of Vietnamese girls, who had been checked into the compound by GIs through an MP checkpoint, could clearly be heard.

Allowing prostitutes into Plantation was vintage Hollingsworth. Hollingsworth once said in defense of his libertine fraternization policy that troops who weren't sexually interested in girls wouldn't fight when the chips were down. (He said it much more explicitly than this.) I'm sure the Amerasian kids conceived at Plantation have no inkling that they owe their existence to the strange military philosophy of an eccentric American general.

Drug use at Plantation, as at most American military bases toward the end of the war, was rampant. So many things about the Vietnam War were erroneously reported in the press, but one thing conveyed accurately was the extensive drug use. Marijuana was used daily by thousands of soldiers, and toward the end of the war heroin, called "Smack" by GIs, became a big problem. I personally knew several MI soldiers, some of whom had sensitive intelligence jobs in TRAC headquarters, who were addicts.

One addicted soldier in my unit, who was going through unassisted withdrawal, told me that he felt like someone had beat him up. He was trying to get "clean" for the mandatory urinalysis he would have to undergo before he could get on the "Freedom Bird" that would take him back to the states. He did not want to embarrass his family by being detained for drug rehabilitation at the end of his Vietnam tour. I hope to God he was able to free himself from that hideous scourge.

On one occasion I learned that a tough-looking soldier who lived in the plywood cubicle next to me in the hootch was selling Smack. Secretly, I went to the commander and made a complaint about him and three weeks later the commander ordered everyone in the unit to provide a urine sample for drug testing (yes, it took three weeks for him to get around to doing something about the information I provided).

The soldier, as expected, turned up positive and was sent to LBJ (Long Binh Jail) for drug rehabilitation. At the end of thirty days he was sent back to the unit—to the same cubicle next to mine. Now, no longer did I have to worry only about heroin being sold from the next cubicle, I had to be concerned with the fact that it might leak that I was the guy who had gotten him picked up for drug abuse in the first place. But all's well that ends well. He was arrested by CID (Criminal Investigation Division) for some other offense shortly after his return and was taken out of the unit for good.

A couple of days before he was carried off in handcuffs, I did have an altercation with him that could have caused me serious legal problems. He used to play loud music on his stereo in the early evenings and throughout the night, and I had trouble sleeping, even with earplugs. I asked him a number of times to turn the music down, and he would a little, but finally one evening he told me, "It is down, man."

I went into a blind rage. I'd had enough. In addition to seeing a constant parade of glassy-eyed soldiers wandering through the hootch, I had to listen to music I couldn't stand, day in and day out, at noise levels above safety for the human ear. I stormed into my cubicle and got my M-16. I had in mind that I wasn't going to shoot the guy, but I was definitely going to fire a few rounds and get his attention. I probably would have ended up making a mess of my own life in the process, but I wasn't concerned about that at the moment. Paul Rester, who was visiting me in my cubicle, watched in wild-eyed horror as I loaded a clip and chambered a round in my weapon.

Paul blurted out, "What are you going to do, Garry?"

In fury I yelled, "I've had enough! I'm not going to take any more of that jerk! I've asked him nicely for days to turn that garbage music down and he has totally ignored me!"

As I headed out into the narrow hall that ran between the cubicles, suddenly there was silence. The music stopped completely. The soldier, who had been listening to everything that was going on, knew that I meant business. And from then on he turned off his music any time I came around.

It's a shame that in this world are scum whose only motivation to get along with others is through the use of force.

As at most American bases in Vietnam, we had to use outhouses for latrines. Human waste ended up in discarded fuel drums that had been cut in half by a blowtorch. The barrels, placed under a row of wooden toilet seats in smelly, hot, wooden shacks, had to be emptied and the refuse burned every couple of days. If not, the stench quickly became intolerable and the refuse filled with maggots. In some units, lower ranking GIs had the undistinguished task of refuse-burning (GIs had a less polite term for it), but fortunately for us at TRAC, our unit contracted with local laborers to do this job. That was one indignity I never had to endure during my tour in Vietnam.

One day one of our hootch-maids (Vietnamese girls we hired to do our laundry) came running into my room to tell me something. Since I spoke Vietnamese, they usually came to see me if they wanted to communicate anything to the American GIs. She excitedly was saying in Vietnamese, "Come quick! Something has happened to Papa-San!" Papa-san was an old man we had hired to burn our refuse. (Papa-San and Mama-San were the names given by GIs to older Vietnamese men and women. Strangely, the words are not in the Vietnamese language but came from another war in which Americans fought.)

I ran outside with her to a field behind our row of hootches where the old man usually worked burning waste, and I found him collapsed. I checked his pulse but could feel nothing. However, I detected that he was still faintly breathing because I could see saliva bubbles coming from his mouth. I got another soldier to help me and together we loaded him into a truck and drove to a Vietnamese hospital in downtown Bien Hoa. I sat in the back of the truck holding the tiny body of the old man. As we drove along I looked into the lines of his old, weathered face and wondered about all that he had done and seen during what must have been a very hard life. I saw that he was wearing a tiny gold crucifix around his neck, which indicated he was part of the large Catholic community that lived in and around the Bien Hoa area. During the trip through the city, the old man died in my arms. I felt him breathe his last and grow very still. Vietnamese medical personnel confirmed that he was dead when we reached the hospital.

When I first started working at CTAP, for a while I had an additional duty that took about an hour out of my day. I attended Hollingsworth's briefings and assisted officers in their presentations. My job was to stand with the briefing officer in front of Hollingsworth and his royal court and put charts up and down for the briefers. I was the only enlisted man present. I never said anything and the task was totally menial, but it was extremely interesting to be in such close contact with Hollingsworth and hear firsthand what was going on in III Corps. I wouldn't have missed doing it for the world.

Hollingsworth and his deputy, a brigadier general, usually came to the briefings together and sat in leather chairs in front of whomever was briefing. The members of the audience sat behind them in a mini-auditorium in theater-type chairs. The first row was reserved for senior staff, which was composed of six full-bird colonels, one of whom was the boss of the MI pukes, Colonel Arthur Belknap, the TRAC G-2 (senior intelligence officer).

Belknap, who was a huge man, almost to the point of being obese, frequently took barbs from Hollingsworth. Hollingsworth would turn to him from time to time and say, "Well, King Arthur, what does your department of bull-shit have to say about that?" Belknap was a brilliant man and always had a respectful, intelligent comment to make in return, but you could tell by his reply that he didn't like Hollingsworth's sarcasm that was directed toward him and his intelligence soldiers.

The briefings always began with: "Gentlemen, the commanding general!" We'd all rise and wait for Hollingsworth and his deputy to be seated before the TRAC chief of staff, Colonel Tallman, would tell us to take our seats. Immediately after sitting down, Hollingsworth would light the first of a half-dozen cigarettes and nod for the briefing to begin.

A short, skinny Air Force weather officer (captain) would start off by saying, "General, the weather in Sanger, Texas (Hollingsworth's hometown), this morning is..." The captain was extremely witty and could hold his own against Hollingsworth's off-the-wall comments. In fact, watching the two of them engage each other every morning in a battle of wits was the highlight of my day. The captain would say something funny, and Hollingsworth, who was extremely witty himself, would invariably end up with the best punch line. I'm sure the captain could have bested Hollingsworth a time or two more than he did, but in the presence of the Texas Warrior King, one did need to remember his place.

One morning, Hollingsworth was late in coming to the briefing. When he finally arrived he told us that he had been talking with President Richard Nixon on the telephone. This was during the Spring Offensive of 1972 and Nixon was personally calling senior commanders to get their assessment of the ability of the South Vietnamese to stand firm in the face of the North Vietnamese onslaught. Hollingsworth said he had personally assured the president that South Vietnamese forces in the III Corps area were more than a match for the invading enemy and would hold their own.

Also, during the enemy offensive there were a number of senior VIPs from Washington who were making personal visits to bring back impressions of the "Vietnamization" of the war effort. Several of these individuals, who had ambassadorial and senior cabinet rank, stopped in to visit Hollingsworth at TRAC. Right before one of these visits, Hollingsworth determined that the General Officers' Mess, which was the dining facility for senior officers at TRAC, needed painting before the arrival of the VIPs. The paint was peeling off in large chunks and the building really looked bad. Hollingsworth called up the TRAC Command Sergeant Major and told him he wanted a detail to paint and do some much-needed repair work to the facility.

As a result, in the middle of plotting B-52 strikes during the Spring Offensive in 1972, my boss told me that the command sergeant major had selected me to be part of the group that would paint Hollingsworth's mess facility. As best I could, I read him into what I was doing so he could pick of the ball and put the final touches on the targets that would be struck that evening.

I went over to Plantation and with about twenty other soldiers, all under the supervision of a fat captain, mixed paint. We had an assortment of different colors from which we were trying to make a dark brown, but we ended up with the most horrible color of purple you can imagine. We didn't deliberately screw it up. We just didn't have enough of one color to do the whole job, so we had to mix other colors. The more we tried to tone it down the worse it got. At lunch time, Hollingsworth came to the dining area and I thought he was going to fall over when he saw the hideous mess we had made. The face of cold steel that had looked unflinchingly at death and disaster a hundred times suddenly betrayed a feeble emotion of not knowing what to do. He didn't say a word to us, but I know his staff heard about the botched paint job. Undoubtedly, Hollingsworth's important guests got a kick out of eating in a purple dining facility when they came to dinner that evening.

About once a month enemy units would launch 122mm Soviet-made rockets against American bases from their sanctuaries in the Bien Hoa "Rocket Belt." The belt was a wide strip of jungle north of Bien Hoa Air Force Base, which was located across town from where we were at Plantation. North Vietnamese and Viet Cong would set up eight to ten rocket launchers in the jungle strip from which they would fire a barrage of seventy to eighty rockets at the base. The attacks usually came at dawn. The rockets would hit less than a second apart and in a minute the awful racket was over, yet the emotional trauma from the sudden shock lasted for days. A number of times I jumped out of my bunk and watched as flashes from the explosion walked back and forth at Bien Hoa Air Force Base, just a few kilometers away. Minutes after the attack, helicopters would vainly take off from Bien Hoa in search of the elusive foe.

As I said, I lived at Plantation but worked in downtown Bien Hoa at the South Vietnamese III Corps Headquarters. The headquarters, which bordered Bien Hoa Air Force Base, usually caught several rockets when the base was hit. Once, several rockets struck next to the entrance of the underground concrete building where I worked, and I walked around to look at the destruction. Trees were felled like they had been cut with a chain saw and brick buildings were peppered with holes. Inside one of the buildings, razor-sharp pieces of rocket had come through the wall, passed through the body of a South Vietnamese colonel, splattering pieces of flesh and internal organs against the wall behind him. Outside, a South Vietnamese soldier had been killed. He dove for cover, but while still in the air, caught the full force of a blast and was cut to shreds.

Paul Rester lived on the Vietnamese compound in a mobile home, and I went over one morning after a dawn attack to see how close he had come to becoming a casualty of the war. A rocket had exploded next to the trailer sending tiny pieces of shrapnel just inches above his sleeping body.

Years later when I was investigating MIA cases in Vietnam, one of my Vietnamese team members asked me where I had been during the war. I told him I spent the war in Tay Ninh and Bien Hoa Provinces. He told me in return that he had conducted missions in Bien Hoa Province during the same period of time I was there. He told me his unit frequently had the mission of launching rocket attacks against the Air Force base at Bien Hoa. Small world indeed.

Plantation was next to Long Binh Post, which had a huge ammo dump. One night Viet Cong sappers slipped through the concertina and placed charges in and around cases of ordnance stored in the dump. How they could have possibly gotten through the lighted concertina without being seen by guards is a mystery to me. The guards must have been asleep or high on drugs.

The resulting blasts, which continued in salvos, one after another for twenty-four hours, caused us all to have a rude awakening. I wasn't jarred awake like that again until years later in Saudi Arabia during Desert Storm when a SCUD landed in the desert several kilometers away from where I was sleeping.

But even as brilliant a military maneuver as the Viet Cong attack was, part of the plan went awry, as even the best military plans often do. One of the four sappers participating in the attack was separated from his comrades during the exfiltration and didn't make it back through the concertina. He got lost and wandered around Long Binh Post until sunup. An MP patrol picked him up and Paul Rester interrogated him.

At Plantation I ran into my former roommate from Vietnamese language school, Stanley Tillotson. Stanley ended up not needing his expensive year-long language school training. He was assigned to a halfway house as a counselor for alcoholics and heroin users. The halfway house was in a trailer compound located on Plantation, not too far from where I was living. Stanley was responsible for monitoring substance abusers from the time they began their treatment until their release several weeks later. The therapy consisted, as far as I could see, of sitting around in groups and talking with counselors like Stanley.

One day Stanley and several other counselors at the halfway house were moving wall lockers somewhere. They loaded the lockers on a truck and were accompanying them to their destination. A couple of the guys with Stanley told me he was sitting on the back of the truck holding onto the wall lockers. On the highway in front of Plantation, and at a speed of about thirty miles per hour, Stanley fell off the truck, hit his head, and died instantly. A tragic and needless death.

I had known fellow students from high school who had died in Vietnam, but I hadn't been close friends with any of them, as I had been with Stanley. He and I had been roommates and were in the same Vietnamese class for a solid year. And I had talked with him several times a week at Plantation up until a day before he was killed. The shock of his death was physically sickening to me, made worse by knowing he had died in a stupid, preventable accident.

A few days later, I almost became a casualty from an accident myself. One day as I was returning to Plantation from the South Vietnamese III Corps Headquarters, the steering wheel came off in the hands of our Vietnamese driver, Mr. Tam. He turned around to look at the three Americans in the jeep with that silly Vietnamese smile that always appears at the worst possible moment. We were yelling at him to stop as the vehicle wobbled uncontrollably down the road. We barely missed hitting an oncoming truck by a hair before we ran off the road into a ditch. The whole thing looked like it was right out of a Laurel and Hardy movie.

When I think of the war, my thoughts don't go back to Vietnamese language school or the time I was in Tay Ninh as an interrogator, although those experiences will always be with me. But my mind turns almost instinctively to the months I spent living in Hollingsworth's kingdom targeting B-52 strikes.

The experience at CTAP left me with mental cobwebs that I had to clean up after I got back home, since in that job I had been responsible for the deaths of hundreds, possibly even thousands, of enemy soldiers and civilians. The job was partially responsible for creating the ghost of Vietnam that haunted me for years.

Initially my job at CTAP was to read hundreds of classified intelligence documents that came in daily through the message center, extract intelligence information that indicated locations of enemy units, and plot the information on maps.

The senior officer in charge of the targeting office in CTAP was called the "Mad Bomber." When I started working in CTAP, the Mad Bomber was a West Point graduate by the name of Major Munch. Munch would take my maps with the intelligence information I had plotted and develop B-52 targets. He would move a little plastic rectangle, the scale model of a B-52 strike, or Arclight, around on a map until he felt he had adequately covered the data. Then he would record the coordinates of each of the four rectangle points of the plastic scale model where they were located on the map. The coordinates and the list of what was in the proposed target were sent through the TRAC Air Force liaison office to the Air Force command responsible for flying the B-52 missions from Guam and Thailand. Within twelve hours the targets would be hit, and sometimes much sooner, should aircraft already be in the air on the way over to Vietnam when the target message was passed up to them.

The B-52 was an awesome weapon of war. Three B-52s, each carrying approximately thirty tons of ordnance, flew one Arclight mission. The aircraft dropped strings of 500 pound bombs into an area two kilometers long and one kilometer wide. We experimented getting the proper length of the Arclight. When I first started working for CTAP, the Arclights were all three kilometers long, but reconnaissance showed there was too much space between bombs. We even went to one kilometer by one kilometer Arclight strikes for a while, but the strike was too condensed and the bomb craters overlapped, wasting firepower. We finally settled on the two kilometer by one kilometer formula which continued for the remainder of the Vietnam War.

After Munch left, a new Mad Bomber came on board by the name of Captain Henry (Hank) M. Robertson. Robertson and I and six Vietnamese became CTAP. Since Munch and several other CTAP officers had ended their tours of duty and gone home, I found my duties greatly expanded from extracting target data to actually creating target boxes for strikes. I was a "speedy-five" (Specialist Fifth Class) by this time and unquestionably the most powerful E-5 in the U.S. Army. I could bomb just about anything I wanted, within reason, of course. I drew target boxes all day long, gave them to Robertson for approval, he'd brief General Hollingsworth in the evenings, and the targets would be struck that night or the next day. Seldom did Robertson ever turn down a target that I had developed, and I personally targeted hundreds of Arclights during my tour of duty at CTAP. Sometimes I targeted as many as thirty a day.

Our Vietnamese soldiers who worked with us, six in all, commanded by Captain (Dai Uy) Tam, were extremely helpful. He and his team would assist us in extracting target material from American intelligence documents that we were authorized to give him and his team. Also they shared intelligence information with us that they obtained from intelligence reports produced by South Vietnamese intelligence agencies.

Even though twenty years have passed, I'm not at liberty to go into details about some of our sources of intelligence information, but as you can guess, a lot of it came from HUMINT (human intelligence) and SIGINT (signals intelligence) sources. Because of the dense forest that covered so much of the area we were targeting, IMINT (imagery intelligence, or overhead photography, etc.) wasn't very helpful.

Some intelligence information sources, such as "Sniffer," were totally useless to us. Someone got the bright idea that airborne, whiz-bang gadgetry could be engineered to "smell" ammonia concentrations from urine. This would enable American units to pinpoint enemy locations hidden in the forest. It's possible other units had success with Sniffer, but I don't think CTAP ever targeted a single Arclight based on this type of data. Although we got vast quantities of readings, we just couldn't get the information to correlate with other intelligence, leading us to believe we were being given the locations of water buffalo and monkeys, as well as Viet Cong.

Most Arclights that we developed were based on multi- intelligence information sources. For example, a helicopter crew would radio in that they were receiving ground-to-air fire from a certain location. Then perhaps an Air Force FAC (forward air controller) would report seeing enemy personnel or equipment in an area. Or a prisoner of war or defector would divulge his unit's location. These are unclassified examples. Our intelligence sources were much more extensive and often provided a wide variety of information. In any event, after a few days our intelligence maps at CTAP would show silver-dollar-size areas of plotted information. At this point I would take a rectangular plastic scale replica of an Arclight, place it over the data, and then go through the administrative process of getting the target struck.

In the late afternoons, Major General Hollingsworth would fly to the South Vietnamese III Corps Headquarters for his targets briefing. The "Mad Bomber" would brief the Texas Warrior King, and eventually his successors, concerning targets that we had developed during the day. The general often knew how many strikes were going to be allotted to him, which was usually a smaller number of targets than we had developed. Therefore, he invariably made the ultimate choice as to which of our targets were going to be hit. However, he usually accepted the Mad Bomber's recommendation as to which targets would likely have the best results, but occasionally he didn't. Every now and then the general wasn't happy with the targets we had developed, and we would literally have to go back to the drawing board and come up with a new list.

Much of our information was "time-sensitive," meaning that the longer the time interval between obtaining the information and getting "steel on target," the greater the chance that the target box would turn "cold" and nothing would be hit, hence the need for speed in the developing and selection process.

Enemy units frequently moved around, which made targeting difficult, but they tended to return to the same areas over and over again. This was particularly true in Cambodia where a lot of the enemy structures were heavily fortified and more permanent in nature (some of the bunkers were made of concrete). A piece of new intelligence information in an area where there had been little activity for a while often meant the enemy had moved back in.

Frequently when I was developing a target on one of our intelligence maps, I was quite cognizant of the fact that human lives depended on how I laid that little piece of plastic across the target information plotted on the map. The final position of that little rectangular piece of plastic often determined who was going to live and who died.

Our Vietnamese team members were allowed to read intelligence reports classified up to "Secret" that were "uncaveated." "Caveat" is a term that means an additional restriction in dissemination applies. One caveat was "NOFORN," meaning no dissemination allowed to foreign nationals. From time to time Robertson and I would get documents that would say the "NOFORN" caveat could be removed should certain items in the document be excised. In those cases he'd take a heavy black pen and mark out the sensitive areas so our Vietnamese counterparts could still have access to the information.

One day one of the ARVN soldiers showed me a CHICOM (Chinese communist) pistol that he'd obtained in a cross-border operation somewhere in Cambodia. He kept it in a safe in an ARVN office next to CTAP. He invited me to his office to look at the pistol. I noticed that the safe was filled with U.S. classified documents, most of which bore "NOFORN" markings. I asked the ARVN soldier where the documents had come from and he said the office had previously been American back before the ARVNs took it over, and they must have belonged to them. So much for security of your government's secrets.

My favorite target of all time was the one I got from a library book. Remember the book, BATTLES IN THE MICHLIN, in which I said Hollingsworth was a major player? Well, I took a target verbatim out of that book. When I read the book, I was struck by the fact American soldiers from the 1st Infantry Division, better known to Vietnam vets as the "Big Red One," stumbled onto concrete bunkers in the jungle. A six-digit coordinate was provided in the book as to its location. I looked the coordinates up on a map and the location was definitely "Indian country." I decided that a base camp made of concrete would likely still be in use. I plotted the coordinates of the North Vietnamese base camp, which came from the library book, on one of my maps, but didn't develop a target on it right away.

I waited until I got recent intelligence in the area, and I didn't have to wait long. At the first indication that enemy troops were in the area, I dropped the inevitable piece of plastic onto the map to cover the library-book data and the new intelligence. I worked up the target request, Hollingsworth approved it, and it got hit that very night. Something was definitely in there because immediately after the strike we received all kinds of intelligence information that enemy units were moving toward that location. But exactly what was there I never knew.

Years later, Robertson ran into the author of BATTLES IN THE MICHLIN, Brigadier General (retired) S.L.A. Marshall. Robertson told him about the target we had put together from information we had gotten from his book. Robertson said Marshall laughed and laughed.

General Marshall then told him, "One of the big problems in the war was American soldiers would spend a year learning their jobs, and then just when they had become expert in what they were doing, it was time for them to go home. Consequently, they were replaced by 'newbies' who had to start learning from the beginning. Essentially we fought one war a dozen times." That was certainly true of CTAP. There was a definite learning curve in targeting effective Arclight strikes. You had to pretty much be on the maps day after day in order to catch the subtle nuances of troop movements that would lead to targeting successful strikes. The experience factor in targeting Arclights in the jungle was crucial.

Sometimes mistakes were made in plotting B-52 strikes. Once a Army captain in the staff section of TRAC that handled air operations (G3 Air) caused a B-52 strike to hit 100 kilometers away from where it was intended. Grid coordinates for targets were alpha numerical combinations like XT 867543. A coordinate such as XU 867543 has all of the numbers that the first coordinate has, but differs by one being "XT" and the other "XU." The two letters in the military grid system represent boxes that are 100 square kilometers. Consequently "XT" and "XU" are exactly 100 kilometers, or about sixty miles apart. Somehow "XT" had erroneously become "XU," and the strike landed exactly 100 kilometers away from where it should have struck. Fortunately the strike landed deep in the jungle and no friendly troops or civilians were wounded or killed.

Making an error in drawing a B-52 strike was extremely easy to do. That's why it was so necessary to plot carefully and to constantly check our work. Once we had a wall map tear loose from the plastic acetate that was covering it. The map dropped down several inches inside the acetate, causing target data plotted on the acetate to be several kilometers off. However, the mistake wasn't all that significant since the targets were all in the infamous Iron Triangle; a couple of kilometers or so wouldn't make much difference since it was all "bad guy" territory anyway. Our six ARVNs were responsible for that one.

But there was another strike that killed eighty-eight Cambodian civilians that was my fault. It happened like this:

A senior officer in Saigon got the idea that we should go back and start bombing all of the old sanctuary areas in Cambodia that we had bombed the previous year but had not hit with Arclights for some time. The reasoning was the North Vietnamese likely had moved back into those areas since we had ignored them for a while.

But the MACV target office in Saigon didn't have any of the old target data that had been used the previous year. I had it all. Not only did I have the original intelligence that had been used then to make the Arclights, I still had a set of maps on which the old Mad Bomber, Major Munch, had plotted the strikes.

A lieutenant came down from MACV headquarters with the instructions to get targets in each of the major sanctuaries that had been hit during the days of Major Munch, for a total of 100 Arclights (flown by 300 B-52s). I spent the next couple of days rearranging Munch's target boxes to get more area coverage. In order to avoid the possibility of an enemy agent alerting the enemy of the impending air attacks, I was instructed that our Vietnamese allies were not to be told what we were doing. The ARVNs in our office saw me plotting targets but did not realize anything out of the ordinary was happening since I was always plotting something.

One of the sanctuary areas that the MACV target office wanted to hit was the "Dog's Head" area of Cambodia. (American GIs gave names such as Angel's Wing, Parrot's Beak, and the Hairpin to the different areas on the Vietnamese-Cambodian Border. On a military map the squiggly line that indicated the border often had unusual shapes that resembled the names they were given.) We had targeted the Dog's Head months before and had unbelievably good luck hitting lucrative targets. So for this new round that MACV wanted to initiate, not only did I have access to the old intelligence that we used in developing the targets, but ARVN units had conducted an incursion into the Dog's Head some months before and had provided us with hard target locations of bunker complexes before withdrawing. We knew that in several areas there were over 1,000 concrete bunkers. The Dog's Head had been a major staging area for North Vietnamese troops for years, and they had built it up extensively to support their operations. Drawing targets around all of the ample data that we had was a very simple thing to do.

But obtaining targets in another area that MACV wanted to hit again, the Chup Rubber Plantation in Cambodia, wasn't so easy. Major Munch had targeted scores of Arclights in the Chup back in December 1971 and January 1972, but his targets had been "area" targets. Munch had ample intelligence that the North Vietnamese were in the Chup in force, but he didn't have the type of intelligence that would pinpoint exactly where they were. Since he didn't have hard data, Munch covered the Chup with Arclights, which was "carpet bombing" in every sense of the word. Munch theorized that thirty Arclights (ninety B-52s; roughly 2,700 tons of bombs) would cover a vast area and would get the enemy sooner or later.

During Desert Storm, reporters asked General Schwarzkoph if the allies were using the B-52 for carpet bombing. Schwarzkoph answered that he didn't know what that was. The Mad Bomber knew exactly what carpet bombing was in the Chup Rubber Plantation in January 1972.

Since MACV was requiring us to develop targets in the Chup, we had to come up with intelligence there. CTAP didn't have any recent intelligence in the Chup, and I wasn't keen on using Munch's carpet-bombing strategy. In looking for information, I went to the OB (Order of Battle) Section of TRAC to visit my good friend SP5 Jim MacMillan to see if he had anything current. He didn't. But in doing his analytical work, he noted there was a particular Cambodian village that every Chieu Hoi (returnee) and North Vietnamese prisoner of war passed through during their infiltration into III Corps. I took the coordinates of the village, made it into the center of a B-52 strike, gave it to the lieutenant for him to pass back to MACV, and the target got hit a few days later.

Shortly afterward in the Stars and Stripes newspaper, an article appeared saying the Cambodian government had complained to the U.S. government that American B-52s had killed eighty-eight Cambodian civilians in a village in the Chup Rubber Plantation. The village where the Cambodian were killed was the target that I had turned in as part of the strikes targeted in the Chup Rubber Plantation. I showed Robertson the article and his comment was, "Looks like those guys in Saigon really screwed up!" Then I told him that the strike was CTAP's. He turned pale and said, "We don't need to bring this up again." And we didn't, and no one ever questioned us about the incident. We continued business as usual.

I had problems for years about that particular strike. There were moments of reflection when I would dwell on the fact that with very little thought or concern, I had written down on a piece of paper the coordinates of a Cambodian village, and eighty-eight people died. I finally was able to convince myself that we were at war and war is ugly. When you're targeting hundreds of Arclights, sometimes thirty a day, and thousands of tons of bombs are falling, occasionally you're going to make a mistake. The amazing thing was that we made so few mistakes. Under such circumstances, the potential for a tragedy is ever present. I'm sorry those people died, but they did and there's nothing I can do to bring them back.

There was one thing about the Vietnam War that always was strange to me and that was the incongruous fact that a war was going on in the midst of affluence. On the larger bases were P.X.s that sold an amazing array of civilian goods, to include refrigerators, televisions, radios, stereos, fans, alcoholic beverages, cigarettes, and all kinds of food items. Also at places like Long Binh post and Bien Hoa there were swimming pools, bowling alleys, and even a nice Chinese restaurant. There seemed to be truth in the saying that absolutely anything was available in Vietnam if you had the money—except victory.

Another thing strange about the war was the ability of troops to take R and R (rest and recuperation) for a week or two back to the states or to several neighboring countries. It was a weird feeling for me to be plotting Arclights one day, and then the next to be on a civilian airliner in civilian clothes en route to Honolulu. There I met my fiance and we married at Ft. DeRussy chapel on Waikiki Beach. Both sets of parents attended the wedding. After two weeks of wedded bliss, I returned to five more months of targeting B-52 strikes.

In April, three North Vietnamese divisions and two regiments of one Viet Cong (National Liberation Front) division, supported by tanks, had entered the III Corps area where TRAC was the senior American headquarters. The North Vietnamese division were the 5th, the 7th, and the 9th. The Viet Cong division was the Binh Long Division.

The 5th North Vietnamese Division had launched out of Cambodia and taken the town of Loc Ninh and captured a TRAC soldier, Captain Mark Smith. The Texas Warrior King stayed on the radio with Captain Smith until he finally was overrun by the enemy and captured. The conversation that occurred between Hollingsworth and Smith was recorded and printed verbatim in LIFE magazine the week Loc Ninh fell. Captain Smith was eventually released in January 1973. Later in San Francisco, after his release, he had a restaurant debate with Jane Fonda. Captain Smith, later promoted to major, became active in MIA groups that believe U.S. servicemen were held in Laos and Vietnam after the U.S. pulled out. Mark Smith in later years lived in Bangkok working for MIA groups as a private POW/MIA investigator.

After taking Loc Ninh, the 5th NVA division moved on toward the town of An Loc. Lead North Vietnamese tanks actually entered the city before units from the defending Vietnamese division stationed in the city, the 5th Infantry Division (ARVN), finally figured out what was going on and started resisting. The 5th Infantry Division (NVA) was going head-to-head with the Infantry Division (ARVN). The 5th ARVN held firm and stopped the momentum of the offensive, although An Loc continued to be surrounded for months.

My good friend James M. Webb, who years later took my place as a MIA investigator at JCRC in Bangkok, happened to be at An Loc at the time on a military intelligence mission. He took part in hand-to-hand fighting in the city. He told me that the battle was so confusing, especially for someone who had never been in hand-to-hand combat before. Once he threw a grenade and didn't pull the pin. At one point in the battle he was bayoneted in the back by a North Vietnamese infantryman. His attacker was killed, but Jim was lying on the ground with a bayonet, still attached to the dead man's rifle, sticking in his back. Guys who were with Jim had a difficult time pulling the bayonet out. They finally stood on his back and were able to extract the wicked weapon, but blood was spurting everywhere. Jim was patched up and lived to tell me the story at the Liaison Office in Bangkok in June 1990.

The night Loc Ninh fell, General Hollingsworth flew to the ARVN III Corps headquarters in Bien Hoa City, where TRAC elements were co-located with the ARVN headquarters. Hollingsworth came in bellowing curse words in his Sanger-Texas accent at the top of his lungs. He said he knew where the enemy was located and he wanted Arclights yesterday! Officers drew target boxes around the coordinates Hollingsworth gave them and passed the boxes to the Air Force liaison officer. The targets were electronically transmitted to B-52s already en route, which struck Hollingsworth's targets. The strikes were extremely accurate and decimated enemy units located between Loc Ninh and An Loc. Also, one fortuitous strike stopped tanks and infantry dead in their tracks as they were entering the city. Unquestionably, the B-52s stopped the advance into An Loc and saved the city, and possibly even South Vietnam.

The only significant ground forces that stood between the enemy and Saigon was the 5th ARVN division. The enemy's intention was to knock out the 5th ARVN division, make a mad dash toward Saigon, and knock the South Vietnamese and Americans out of the war.

With the momentum of the North Vietnamese assault stalled at An Loc, the 18th and the 25th ARVN divisions were moved from IV Corps to III Corps and placed between the 5th ARVN division's rear and Saigon. In effect, the enemy offensive was now over, even though North Vietnamese and Viet Cong units would continue their pressure on An Loc for months to come.

During this time, the cover of TIME magazine had a picture of fearful looking Vietnamese in retreat, and the caption: "The Specter of Defeat." The liberal press was getting geared up to do its usual Vietnamese bashing.

The enemy offensive was a gamble by the world's best gambler himself, General Giap. The general for years had been known to raise the stakes to the limit, betting the farm, and he always won. Even during the Tet Offensive, a total tactical failure, he won. He lost thousands of soldiers, but Tet was the beginning of the end for American involvement in Vietnam.

But this one time Giap lost. North Vietnamese and Viet Cong troops died like flies around An Loc as enemy units were decimated. Toward the end of 1972, the North Vietnamese Army in the South, largely as a result of American air power, was in shambles. In addition, the mining of Hai Phong Harbor had been extremely effective and critical supplies had been reduced to a trickle. Added to all of this was the severe pounding by B-52s the Vietnamese took in the North during President Nixon's Christmas Bombing. The North Vietnamese government was desperate. It had to do something to get the United States out of the war to have any chance of winning. It opted to agree to a peace treaty, which exchanged time for the American withdrawal of forces from Vietnam and the return of American prisoners of war.

After several spectacularly successful B-52 strikes against North Vietnamese forces during the Battle of An Loc, Robertson and I, were instructed to appear at TRAC headquarters for a ceremony in which Bronze Star Medals would be awarded to us by Brigadier General Tallman, the TRAC Commander. Brigadier General Tallman, who was the spitting image of NBC News' Edward Newman, had recently assumed command from the outgoing TRAC commander Major General James F. Hollingsworth. Hollingsworth had returned to the states for treatment of medical problems, undoubtedly related to having been on dozens of battlefields.

Robertson and I, with two other officers from another section, marched into General Tallman's office and stood at attention as he awarded us Bronze Stars for actions related to the Battle of An Loc that had raged for months.

The next morning, Brigadier General Tallman and three other officers, the TRAC Chief of Staff, the G3 air officer, and General Tallman's aide, a second lieutenant, all flew to An Loc, which had been under siege for months by three North Vietnamese infantry divisions. Upon landing at the airfield, North Vietnamese artillery rounds began falling all around their helicopter and the four were killed instantly.

All of us were in a state of shock at TRAC. The war was brought home to us in a real way. One by one the ARVNs in our office came over to Robertson and me and expressed their regrets, as if the dead men had been members of our family.

Upon receiving the news of the deaths, Major General Hollingsworth immediately flew back to Vietnam and travelled directly to the chapel at TRAC where the command was gathered for a eulogy service for Brigadier General Tallman and the other three officers. Robertson and I were sitting together. Hollingsworth with other senior officers, took his place in the front row of the chapel.

A senior officer gave the order: "Sergeant Major, present the colors!" The drums beat, and the colors of the unit and the nation were marched in the presence of a guard of honor.

In the midst of an awesome silence, The Texas Warrior King rose and addressed those assembled. His theme was the profession of arms. In moving terms he said our nation requires a group of professionals, such as the four brave men who had died, who will remain aloof from politics, fight its country's battles, and in the end be willing to give their lives as the ultimate payment for the cost of freedom. Consequently, the highest calling of a free nation, above any other profession, is to be a soldier.

The eulogy was unquestionably the most moving thing I have ever heard. Warriors fought back tears, and some even cried openly. The Texas Warrior King concluded his last magnificent speech before his soldiers at TRAC, we stood at attention, taps played in mournful reverence, and those beautiful colors to which we had all sworn allegiance were cased and removed from the building in gallant ceremony.

It was then that I as an enlisted E-5 in the U.S. Army found myself. From that point on, I knew where I wanted to be, whom I wanted to be with, and what I wanted to do with my life. First of all, I wanted to be in Vietnam participating in the war; second I wanted to be in the company of warriors; and third, I wanted to be a soldier.

Years later I was stationed at Ft. Campbell, Kentucky, the home of the 101st Airborne Division, of which I happened to be a proud member. I belonged to 311th MI Battalion and one afternoon I had to do some coordination in one the infantry brigade headquarters for upcoming training. As I was walking up the stairs I noticed a number of Vietnam War photographs of the 101st in action, so I paused to take in a little of the division's history.

Lo and behold! The pictures all were of General Tallman, or then Colonel Tallman, back when he was a combat brigade commander in the 101st. I expressed to the military intelligence captain who was with me that I knew who Colonel Tallman was, and that I believed I had the last photograph of Brigadier General Tallman, taken before he was killed (An NCO at TRAC headquarters snapped a picture when General Tallman awarded me the Bronze Star Medal). The captain told me the building we were in was the "Tallman" building, hence the reason for all of the pictures of Colonel Tallman. The building housed the headquarters of the brigade that Colonel Tallman had commanded during the Vietnam War, a tour before he was assigned to TRAC as Chief of Staff, and then as the Texas Warrior King's replacement.

With the death of General Tallman, a new general took over TRAC. He was Brigadier General Fairfield. His aide was Second Lieutenant Dennis Treece, with whom I worked closely in Saudi Arabia years later in Desert Shield and Desert Storm.

One day after some incredible good luck in targeting in Bien Hoa province—some of our targets had set off hundreds of secondary explosions—Brigadier General Fairfield flew to CTAP and awarded Robertson and me Bronze Stars—our second in less than a month.

The next day, Brigadier General Fairfield flew into a contested area to visit an ARVN unit and its American advisors. While there, the enemy attacked and both General Fairfield and Lieutenant Treece were wounded, fortunately not fatally. Treece recalls that as he and the general were medically evacuated out of the fire-fight by Huey helicopter for emergency medical treatment, he could see the intensity of the battle going on below. Tracers, both enemy and ARVN were going off everywhere. At the same time, Treece saw a Vietnamese woman at a nearby village casually walking along with a stick over her shoulders to which two buckets were attached at each end. The woman seemed to be totally unconcerned with the carnage that was occurring around her.

As a result of the deaths of Brigadier General Tallman and the three other officers, and now the wounding of Brigadier General Fairfield and Lieutenant Treece, black humor was very much in evidence at TRAC: don't decorate Smith and Robertson with any more Bronze Stars or you may be next.

But I did get one more Bronze Star (my third)—and the Vietnamese Cross of Gallantry. The last week in Vietnam, the senior TRAC intelligence officer (G2), Colonel Stein, stood me up in front of my peers and superiors and awarded me my third Bronze Star. And the Vietnamese awarded me their equivalent of the American Bronze Star, the Cross of Gallantry. The awards were for successful B-52 strikes.

When I came back to the States as a one-tour soldier, several times senior NCOs questioned me about my three Bronze Stars and Cross of Gallantry that I wore on my khaki and dress green uniforms. None of them challenged me as to whether or not I was entitled to the decorations, but they did have a puzzled look as to how a young "MI puke" could be so decorated.

Robertson told me once that he believed I had a psychic gift and could "sense" where the enemy was by looking at a map. But I had my share of misses which proved his theory didn't hold water. From time to time Army reconnaissance teams would land in the middle of Arclight craters, just seconds after a strike, and more times than not they would locate dead, dazed, or dying enemy, but every now and then they would report back that nothing was in the Arclight box.

On my last day at work our six ARVNs had a party for me. I guess saying goodbye to those wonderful little guys was the hardest day of my life. They served a Vietnamese delicacy that I haven't had since: brazed duck heads. They really weren't too bad. Just don't invite me over to relive the culinary experience.

Years later as I was going around Vietnamese refugee camps throughout Southeast Asia interviewing refugees about Vietnam, I always thought maybe I'd run into at least one of those guys. But I never did. When I walked out of the office I never saw them again. I hope they didn't end up in re-education camps, but if they stayed in Vietnam after the fall, they definitely would have been in for a rough time.

I got one of my buddies to drive me from Plantation to Camp Alpha, which was a departure point in Saigon for military servicemen. I was there for a couple of days and caught a flight to the states. As we neared the California coast, excitement reigned supreme, and as soon as we landed cheers from 200 throats filled the air.

For some on the aircraft, Vietnam had been a boring place to kill a year while waiting for life to start back in the world. For others Vietnam had been a world of erotic and hedonistic pleasures. For a few the year of Vietnam passed in a stupor of illegal drugs and alcohol. For some Vietnam had been pure hell. For me it had been an adventure beyond belief. Regardless of the different mental or emotional baggage we were bringing back, at that moment we were all of one mind: it was great to be home!

The author, on the left, and Bill Gadoury, with his back to the camera, inspect a crash site near the Mekong River in northeastern Thailand.

Cutting through jungle in the Ashau Valley.

CHAPTER SIX

INVESTIGATION IN THE PHOU PHAN MOUNTAINS

Bill Gadoury and I got along great at the JCRC Liaison Office in Bangkok. He was a personable guy and made friends easily inside and outside of the embassy. LTC Harvey thought the world of him and on excavations of crash sites in Laos, he was Harvey's right-hand man. When I was at the Liaison Office, Bill was an Air Force NCO, but he later retired after I left and was immediately hired on as a civilian employee. He became responsible for directing the investigations in Laos.

Bill was also popular with the private MIA hunters who operated out of Bangkok. These are true believers who are certain American POWs were held in Southeast Asia after the withdrawal in 1973. Some of them bum around Bangkok living from hand to mouth, but a few do quite well as employees of various MIA groups or wealthy, eccentric individuals. They are hired to obtain MIA information outside the scope of the U.S. government. These individuals frequently express that the government's resolution efforts, particularly JCRC's operation, are fraudulent. They vehemently make accusations that elements of the U.S. government are in an active conspiracy to hide the fact that Americans were knowingly left behind as prisoners in Vietnam and Laos. Some of them believe the CIA undertook an active plot to kill American prisoners of war to keep them from surfacing and embarrassing the conspirators that are in the U.S. government.

All of this is pure, unadulterated nonsense, but incredibly, some very important and influential people in the United States have fallen for it hook, line, and sinker. To me it is scary that there are educated Americans in high positions who actually accept such silliness and put private MIA hunters on their payroll.

Ironically, the private MIA hunters didn't get along with each other, and they checked in with Bill from time to time to find out what the others were up to.

One of the MIA hunters was Vinnie Arnone, a short, stocky guy with glasses. I saw him several times when he came up to the second floor in the embassy, where we were located, to speak with Mather or Gadoury. Mather had known him for years. Mather told me Vinnie had participated in Bo Gritz's foray into Laos a few years before.

Vinnie conveyed to me he had been a Green Beret during the war, but I never was clear on the details of when and where. Vinnie is one of those guys who assumes everyone else knows fully what he is talking about; consequently, the listener is bombarded with years of incidents and personalities that may or may not be in the least familiar. Vinnie once showed me a photograph of himself and Bo Gritz together in uniform. I suppose the picture was taken in Vietnam, since Gritz had extensive special forces combat experience there. (General Westmoreland wrote an entire chapter about Gritz's combat exploits in his book, A SOLDIER REMEMBERS.)

Vinnie eventually went broke and had to go home. The American Embassy loaned him money to get back to the states, but stamped his passport invalid so he couldn't use it again until he paid the money back. Just before Vinnie left, he came by and tried to get some help from JCRC so he could stay in Thailand longer. He said he believed what he was doing was important, and his contributions were valuable to finding living Americans he believed were being held in Laos. Bill Gadoury told him bluntly to give it up and go home.

A young private MIA hunter who contacted Gadoury frequently was Barry Flynn. Barry was in Thailand working as "Chief of Staff" to Bo Gritz. Barry was also a wheeler dealer on the side and was trying to sell equipment to the Thai police. He also had contacts with the Burmese drug lord, Khun Sa, which made U.S. Drug Enforcement Agency (DEA) personnel at the American Embassy in Bangkok raise their eyebrows. Barry and Bo had both been to Burma to talk with Khun Sa about MIAs. According to Barry, Khun Sa was really a great guy who was trying to get the people who live in his feudal Burmese kingdom to develop crops other than opium.

Bill Gadoury was JCRC's official Thai and Laotian linguist. He had learned Thai in Thailand back during an Air Force tour in the war years. His formal Thai training consisted of attending night language classes as part of his off-duty education, but his main education in the Thai language came about when he met a lovely Thai lady and married her. Bill said she was his "long-haired dictionary." She must have done a good job. People who speak Thai tell me that Bill's Thai is excellent.

In preparation for the JCRC Liaison Office assignment in Thailand, Bill was sent to Laotian language school in Washington D.C. Thai and Laotian are different languages, but they are similar in many ways, much like Spanish and Portuguese. At least that's what Bill says. I never learned enough of either one to tell the difference.

I've always had a hard time describing the way people look, but if you are interested in seeing a picture of Bill Gadoury, get the November 1986 issue of NATIONAL GEOGRAPHIC MAGAZINE and find the article entitled "Missing in Action." (The article is about a JCRC and CILHI MIA recovery operation in Laos.) Look at the bottom photograph on page 695. Bill Gadoury is the guy on the extreme right with the light brown hair and medium build. He's wearing a white shirt and blue jeans.

Bill is a handsome guy with a lot of charm, and pretty Thai girls always perked up when he would talk to them. One afternoon, Bill Gadoury and I, and Sataporn, the Liaison Office driver, were visiting a camp for Laotian refugees on the northeastern Thai-Laotian border. Several attractive Thai girls work in the camp as humanitarian service workers, and Bill was kidding them for a few seconds as he usually did in his lighthearted way. As we walked on by, I heard one of the girls say something excitedly in Thai to the other one. I asked Sataporn what she said, and he told me: "She say, she not be able to sleep tonight after talking with Mr. Bill today."

One day Bill told me of his efforts to locate an F-111 that supposedly had crashed in the Phou Phan (pronounced "POO-PAN") Mountains in Northeastern Thailand. The mountains, which are located along the Mekong River on the Thai-Laotian border, were heavily contested during the war by Thai communist insurgents and the Royal Thai Army. The F-111, which had completed a night bombing mission over North Vietnam, was returning to its base in Thailand when it was reported missing. An Air Force radar supposedly briefly picked up the aircraft as it was entering Thailand, but then it disappeared from the screen.

One theory of the crash was the aircraft hit a cloud bank which disrupted its terrain-following guidance system, causing it to make a steep drive and crash.

Although the Phou Phan Mountains were under communist insurgent control for a period of time during the war years, they are no longer. The insurgency movement was not defeated by force of arms, but died as a result of a budding friendship between Thailand and China. After the war, Thailand became eager to mend fences and made overtures to China. As a return gesture of friendship on its part, China ended its support of the insurgents. The insurgents surrendered to the Royal Thai Army, pledged their eternal loyalty to the king of Thailand, and were promptly resettled elsewhere.

Since there were now no insurgents running around the Phou Phan Mountains shooting government officials and blowing up things, Bill Gadoury reasoned that it was time for an investigative team to go into the mountains and spend some time systematically questioning villagers who might know what happened to the aircraft.

Bill asked me if I wanted to go to the Phou Phan Mountains with him to conduct an investigation. I didn't even have to think about it; I told him I'd love to go. We hit Mather with the idea, and he thought it was great. Mather called up Harvey and he gave the trip his blessing. Gadoury said that Mather and Harvey were always under the gun about the F-111 case. After all, the JCRC Liaison Office was located in Thailand, and it was embarrassing not to be able to find an aircraft that had supposedly crashed in our own backyard. Hence, their immediate readiness to send a team to the Phou Phan Mountains was understandable.

As soon as we got the green light from Harvey, Bill and I began making preparations to go. We requested a four-wheel-drive Toyota from the embassy, which was available in the embassy motor pool. Mather said we could take Mr. Sataporn, the Liaison Office driver. In addition, Bill printed several hundred leaflets, written in Thai, that gave the details of the crash and requested information from anyone who might know what happened to the aircraft.

And off we went. It took a couple of days to get up to the Phou Phan Mountains by vehicle. Our first stop was at the province police headquarters to get the police commander's permission to operate on his turf. Bill presented the police commander with a letter of introduction from the American Embassy as well as from the Thai national police headquarters in Bangkok.

The province police commander was cooperative, but said there was no way he was going to let two Americans roam around by themselves in the Phou Phan Mountains, regardless of how humanitarian their intentions were. He expressed that he would not agree to let Bill and me enter the area unless we were accompanied by an armed Thai escort. He voiced that even though there was now no threat from an armed communist insurgency, some of the villages were hostile to outsiders and to official government personnel. But he wasn't worried so much about that as he was about drug traffickers who were growing marijuana and other illegal drug crops. He was afraid what would happen to us if we accidentally ran into a drug operation in some isolated area while out looking for a crash site.

The police commander explained that the Phou Phan Mountains fell within two police districts, and he told us he would contact the commanders of those districts and give them instructions to give us assistance. We made plans to go meet the district commanders the next day.

That night, and for the rest of the time we were conducting investigations in the Phou Phan Mountains, we stayed in a little Thai town called Muhkdahan, which was located on the Mekong River. While in the little town, we could hear what local people said were "war drums" beating across the Mekong River in Laos. Thailand and Laos were having territorial disputes at the time and both sides were hyping up their population for war. A couple of days before there had been an extensive battle between the two sides in northern Thailand. U.S. military officials at the American Embassy said casualties had been high on both sides, and in Thailand a military hospital had been filled with the large numbers of wounded.

The next morning, Gadoury, Sataporn, and I drove to the two district headquarters to meet the district police commanders. Neither of the headquarters was located within the Phou Phan Mountains, but on the western and eastern edges of them. Gadoury, just as he had done at the province commander's office, spoke only Thai to the district police commanders. I generally sat like a bump on the log and every now and then, in a break in the conversation, Gadoury would tell me what had transpired.

At one of the district headquarters, a commander had not gotten the word from the province headquarters giving us permission to work in the province, but that eventually got all worked out. Bill and I expected that. After years in the military, both of us had firsthand experience with going somewhere and the folks we were going to work for or with had no idea we were coming.

The district police had official liaison contacts in all of the villages, and they put the word out to the contacts to canvass the locals about any crash sites they knew about. Word came back quickly that indeed the locals in one village knew about a crash site in a field near one of the Phou Phan Mountain villages.

We entered the area the next day with a squad of Thai policemen who were to accompany us into the village and provide protection. They looked like they were going to war, not escort Americans to interview Thai villagers about a missing aircraft. The advanced automatic weaponry they carried was sufficient evidence they believed the Phou Phan Mountains to be a dangerous place for outsiders.

Also we learned from the police that there was another criminal element they constantly dealt with in addition to drug traffickers: wood poachers. Cutting trees illegally for timber was big business all over Thailand, not just in the Phou Phan Mountains. Thailand's forests are rapidly disappearing and the government has enacted strict legislation in an attempt to curtail the wholesale stripping of the trees. The only trees that can be legally harvested are those that are selected by a government forestry agency.

During the war when the F-111 supposedly crashed in the Phou Phan Mountains, the terrain was covered with thick forests. Now much of that was gone. As we drove through the mountains, it was hard for me to visualize that the largely open areas had once been one of the most beautiful forests on earth, or so Americans who had seen it told me.

LtCol Mather said that JCRC, when it was a much larger organization, was located in Nakhon Phanom, which is in northeastern Thailand near the Phou Phan Mountains. Mather said bulldozers cleared out a large area in the thick forest for the construction of a base on which JCRC was eventually located. As Bill and I travelled around the Nakhon Phanom area, I found it almost impossible to believe a forest had ever been there at all. Only a few scattered trees remained here and there to give circumstantial evidence of the mighty forest that once existed. The ancient, majestic forest described to me by others won't be seen again for many lifetimes to come.

One of the district policemen had served in Vietnam, and I got Bill Gadoury to interpret for me so I could find out where he had been located during the war. We swapped war stories as Bill interpreted. Thailand sent a large number of combat troops to Vietnam and even had some MIAs.

Bill Gadoury and I agreed to furnish fuel for the police truck that followed us and food for the policemen while we were out in the boonies. We would keep track of how much we spent and JCRC would reimburse us when we got back. Early in the morning of each day before going out to conduct investigations, Bill and I went to the local Thai market to buy the food for the day, which consisted of sticky rice (a main staple of the population of northeastern Thailand and Laos), a fiery hot sauce, beef on a stick, roasted chicken, and several other things that I'm not sure what they were. Bill is an expert on Thai and Laotian food, so he had no problem in getting all kinds of things the locals liked. He also bought something called "Nam," which he said was made from raw pork. He recommended that we not eat any of it because of the danger of trichinosis, but he said the Thais in that part of Thailand love it.

Many of the people who live in northeastern Thailand speak Laotian as their first language, although they also speak Thai. But many of the rural people also speak dialects. Bill could always communicate with them in either Thai or Laotian, but he said that when they spoke dialect, he couldn't understand them. Several of the policemen with us spoke "Yao" to each other, but would speak Thai or Laotian whenever they wanted to communicate with Bill.

We drove out to the village and picked up a local farmer who took us to the crash site, which consisted of a large hole in the ground in the middle of a field. Nothing remained of the aircraft except fragments of metal, plastic, and pieces of glass. The major pieces of the wreckage had been dug out long ago and sold as scrap.

When Bill questioned the farmer closely about the incident, he said that when the plane crashed, the pilot bailed out and was picked up by a large American helicopter. The farmer's description of the aircraft sounded like a "Jolly Green," a U.S. aircraft used for search and rescue operations. The farmer said immediately after the aircraft impacted, U.S. military officials flew out to the crash site by helicopter. In addition to investigating the crash, they compensated the farmer for the damage to his field. The farmer told Bill he wasn't unhappy about what had happened to his field since he was able to dig metal out of the crash site to sell. Bill and I used a compass and a map to determine the exact location of the crash site for future reference.

The farmer's story did not fit the case of the F-111 we were looking for. The witness said the pilot bailed out and had been rescued by a helicopter, and U.S. officials had come out to the site and made compensation for damages. In contrast, the crew in the F-111 likely perished in the crash, and no Americans ever came to the crash site.

The district police informed us that another of their liaison contacts had located a second crash site. We picked up the new witness and he took us out to the site. The story this time was that an American propeller-driven aircraft had crashed and the pilot was killed. American personnel flew in by helicopter and extracted the body of the American pilot. The witness found the crash site for us, which had fewer aircraft pieces than the first site had. And there was no hole, likely because the aircraft had not buried itself as at the first crash site we visited. At the second site, I found the heel of a boot, which indicated to me a crew member or pilot had not exited the aircraft before the crash.

Again the circumstances of the crash did not match what we knew to be the circumstances of the loss of the F-111, so we moved on.

Bill and I spent the next several days travelling through the Phou Phan Mountains. We stopped in the little villages and Bill would start talking to the locals and passing out his leaflets. Sometimes Bill would have in excess of one hundred villagers gathered around him.

At one little village there must have been twenty pregnant women, and it seemed like all of them showed up to surround Bill Gadoury as he was giving his talk. Bill and I joked that there must be something in the water that caused that particular condition. I took a picture of Bill surrounded by a bevy of pregnant gals and later gave it to him. On the back I made a note kidding him about his "harem."

In one village, the local people all told us that "Uncle Nut" (pronounced NOOT) would know where the crash site was. In unison everyone started nodding their heads and saying, yes, Uncle Nut would definitely know. Immediately Bill asked to speak to Uncle Nut, and someone ran to get him.

A sagely looking gray-haired man confidently strode up to the group with all the intention of solving whatever problem the village and the ignorant Americans had. With all the eyes of the village on Uncle Nut, Bill asked him if he knew anything about an aircraft that might have crashed somewhere in the vicinity. Uncle Nut's mouth dropped open and the disappointment was reflected in the eyes of one hundred villagers. The illusion had suddenly vanished. Uncle Nut was a mere mortal like themselves.

At other villages, witnesses told Bill about crash sites, but as he got more and more of the details, he realized they were the same stories about the crash incidents we had already investigated.

It was an incredibly interesting experience to wander around Thai villages, some of which did not even have electricity. As I walked around I particularly enjoyed watching the women weave cloth on their hand-made looms. Weaving is a primary income producer for women in northeastern Thai villages. I bought some lovely pieces of material from the local people that I gave to my wife when I got back to Bangkok.

At one of the villages we visited, one of the policemen found metal that he thought must be part of an aircraft. Bill and I went to look at it and saw that it was a large fragment of an exploded bomb that likely had been dropped on communist insurgents years before, definitely not a piece of aircraft. The policeman was not convinced. Bill told him that an aircraft could never get off the ground if it were made of material as heavy as the piece that he had found.

After a week travelling around the Phou Phan Mountains, Bill and I gave up and headed back to Bangkok. We had a great time and told a lot of stories to each other, but no F-111.

On the way back, we drove by Bill's in-laws, who lived in a tiny rice farming village. Bill showed me around their house, which sat on stilts. At night the family pulled the entrance ladder up into the house to keeps out the farm animals and potential intruders. The family meals were cooked on a charcoal fire in a little balcony room at the edge of the house. Bill and his wife bought a western-style bed for her parents, but they ended up putting it in a closet in the house. Bill said they set it up for him and his wife when they visit. Bill's in-laws and extended family members all sleep on straw mats on the wooden floors.

Bill took me to see the local Buddhist wat (temple). On the temple is a sign that says "The Bill Gadoury Memorial." I laughed and asked Bill what on earth it was for. Bill said he purchased a sound system for the temple, and the temple monk put up the sign in honor of the gift.

When I got back to Bangkok, I fell deathly ill. I was sicker than I had ever been in my life. I had diarrhea and was nauseous at the same time. At the height of the illness, I would lie on my bed for hours at a time, wishing I could die. In a week's time I lost fifteen pounds. The doctor at the embassy said that I was suffering from a water-borne parasite, and he gave me some medication to get me back on track. We had drunk only bottled water the entire trip, but somewhere along the line I had picked up the parasite and it took a full week to get rid of it.

Remarkably, in all of my trips in the three years I was at JCRC, that was the only time I got sick. This was a miracle in itself, in that I consumed some really questionable stuff, particularly in Vietnam. But one thing that undoubtedly helped was the Doxycycline that we took for malaria prevention. "Doxy," as we called it, also killed stomach bacteria and kept us from coming down with stomach ailments. And we always carried bottled water with us wherever we went.

Because I was sick, I had been away from work at the embassy for a while and recuperating at home. One evening Bill Gadoury called me up at my home and asked if I was well enough to travel. I asked him what he had in mind. He said one of the district policemen in the Phou Phan Mountains had called him and said he had found another crash site. As weak as I still felt, the old excitement suddenly came back and I was ready to go. "Let's do it!" I said.

This time Bill and I flew up to northeast Thailand on a Thai commercial aircraft, and Mr. Sataporn drove up and met us. We landed at a military airport and Sataporn was waiting with the four-wheel-drive embassy Toyota. We drove to Muhkdahan and stayed in the same hotel where we had previously been during the first trip to the Phou Phan Mountains.

The first evening in Muhkdahan, Bill and I went to a restaurant that prepared special northeastern dishes. Bill wanted me to try a dish of Red Ant Egg Salad. I had been about to die for the last week, and now Bill was trying to get me to eat a concoction called Red Ant Egg Salad. Never in my life would I have dreamed that anyone would think of eating ant eggs, but sure enough it was on the menu. I was just getting better and didn't know if I should try it, but, fool that I am, I did. The main ingredients were white eggs from a red ant bed, mixed with lettuce and tomatoes and doused with red pepper. Surprisingly it was really good, but the last thing someone recovering from dysentery should be eating. Somehow I got it down and even enjoyed it, though the next day as we bounced around in the four-wheel-drive vehicle, I regretted my decision to try it.

The next morning Bill and I linked up with the district police commander and a squad of armed policemen and drove to the newly located crash site. All of the wreckage on the surface was gone, but there seemed to be large pieces buried under the surface. Bill bargained with the village leader to obtain laborers to dig them out for us. For a set price, Bill hired fifteen rice farmers to dig into the crash site to retrieve aircraft pieces, which we intended to take back to Bangkok.

Bill also bargained with villagers to supply food to us and the Thai policemen. Also, for a set price we bought a chicken dinner, and we watched a Thai farmer set up a net and chase chickens into it. They became entangled and were retrieved by our cooks. Bill also bargained for some things to go along with the meal, such as sticky rice and vegetables. I paid for the meal in Thai Baht, and when I got back to the embassy and filed for reimbursement, I wrote on the voucher: "One chicken dinner for eleven Thai policemen." The embassy finance officer never batted an eye. I got paid for the full price of the meal.

I also bought a knife as a souvenir from one of the locals for two dollars. He told me he had made the blade from metal taken from the crash site.

After a day of digging we had quite a few good-size pieces, some of which had serial numbers still clearly visible. Also, one of the workers recovered a wristwatch without the band.

After getting what we believed to be enough parts to identify the aircraft, we loaded up the pieces of wreckage, gave our thanks to the villagers, said goodbye to the policemen who had been with us for a good portion of our adventure the last few weeks, and started the long journey back to Bangkok.

In Bangkok, we mailed the aircraft parts to Honolulu, and the JCRC analysts sent them to the corporation that made the F-111 aircraft. The engineers at the company determined the pieces of wreckage did not belong to an F-111.

The analysts theorized that since the wreckage didn't pertain to an F-111, perhaps they might be of an F-4. An F-4 involved in an MIA incident had taken off from a base in Thailand, made one radio check, and dropped off into the Twilight Zone never to be heard from again. Analysts had always believed the F-4 had crashed in Laos, but the analysts thought just maybe the wreckage we had recovered were pieces of an F-4. It was a long shot, but after further examination of the items, that idea fizzled.

The analysts eventually determined that because of the location of the crash site and the fact that the recovered parts did not correlate to the F-111 and F-4 cases, the crash site likely was a resolved incident.

Just before I left JCRC in 1990, two Thais from a village near the Phou Phan Mountains came to the American Embassy gate and requested to see Wi-yam-R-Ga-do-ry (William R. Gadoury). They had Bill's business card with the embassy address. Bill brought them up to his office to talk to them. They said they found the wreckage of an aircraft. They even showed us photographs of the alleged crash site.

To make a long story short, their story turned out to be a typical scam that JCRC typically dealt with. But what was interesting was the location where they had supposedly found the items. It was on the projected flight path of the ill-fated F-111 that JCRC analysts had determined the aircraft would likely have been flying before it crashed in the Phou Phans. It was a mystery to Bill and me how they could have possibly known that, or even guessed so precisely. The chances of a good guess would have been hundreds to one.

As we were scratching our heads in wonder, Bill Gadoury figured out the answer. The leaflets he had made up to pass around villages in the Phou Phan Mountains had a decorative black silhouette of an F-111 on a map of the Phou Phan around villages in the Phou Phan Mountains. At the top and bottom of the leaflet was a synopsis in Thai of what happened to the aircraft and an appeal for information. Immediately behind the silhouette, Bill had drawn a long arrow showing the likely flight path of the aircraft. The aircraft silhouette was on the map directly over where the two Thais claimed to have found the wreckage. They made the whole thing up and based the location on Bill Gadoury's leaflet.

So where is the F-111 crash site? Well, it's not in Thailand; I'm sure of that. I don't have a clue where the aircraft went down, but I know it didn't crash in the Phou Phan Mountains. Had it crashed there, Bill Gadoury would have eventually, either through police contacts or his own pressing the flesh out in the villages, found a witness to the crash. He didn't and I'm convinced no one else will either.

David Atherton on a climb to a mountain crash site. Notice the tough terrain.

CHAPTER SEVEN

PICKING UP THE PIECES

After I returned home from the Vietnam War, I met my wife in Dallas, Texas. She was five months pregnant, as a result of our two week honeymoon in Hawaii. We spent a day in Dallas getting re-acquainted and then drove to Abilene to visit my folks. From there we travelled to Ft. Bragg, North Carolina, where I was assigned to the 1st PSYOPS (Psychological Operations) Battalion, 1st PSYOPS Group. I was there for only six months and then re-enlisted for Arabic language school in Washington, D.C.

Mistakenly, I thought I would never use Vietnamese again. I was interested in learning a language which would enhance my chances to become involved in real-world intelligence missions, not just state-side training. Therefore, I made the decision to forget Vietnamese.

We packed up all of our possessions, which weren't many, and moved to Washington, D.C. We also had with us our baby son Ross, who unbeknownst to us at the time, had within his young body the makings of an incredibly talented classical pianist. Where he got that kind of skill is a mystery to Betty and me. He certainly didn't get it from the two of us. Our musical talents are slightly above the Chopsticks level.

I loved Arabic language school, which was taught at the Anacostia Naval Station, in clear view of the Capitol of the United States of America. In addition to my studying Arabic, Betty and I took Ross frequently to museums and places of culture throughout Washington. Of course, he doesn't remember any of that. Also, he doesn't remember the trips that affected me the most: the Petersburg battlefields, Antietam, Manassas, Fredericksburg, and the Shenandoah Valley.

On one particular memorial Sunday, we read in the Washington Post that the First Lady, Patricia Nixon, was opening up the White House to the public for a special tour. The tour was to be limited to the first 1,000 visitor, first come first served. Betty and I, with Ross in tow, jumped in our car and headed to the White House, and as a result had a tour of the White House that most Americans only hear about. It was grand. The news about Watergate was particularly virulent at that time; consequently, we suspected the tour might have been to take the old town's mind off the steady succession of bad news that was gripping the nation.

After a year in Washington, we moved back to Ft. Bragg, North Carolina. Betty and I bought our first house in a little section called Springlake, North Carolina. Our house was small, and to others with higher incomes, very inexpensive, but to us it was a palace. We spent some of the happiest days of our lives there. From experiences like these one learns that poverty is a relative term.

I was assigned to the 519th MI Battalion, which was an MI unit that previously had been in Vietnam during the war. The majority of NCOs and warrant officers in the unit were Eastern Europeans who came to the United States after World War II. They entered the Army under a special program in which they became American citizens in exchange for their linguistic talents and their usefulness to military intelligence. It was probably the smartest move U.S. military intelligence ever made.

Dave Atherton and Tom McKay were also at the 519th, though Dave was in a different company than Tom and I. I saw Dave quite a bit, but I got to know Tom better because we were in the same duty section. Tom and I were in "A" Company, which was a unit of language-qualified interrogators. The members of the company spoke a hodgepodge of languages. Tom and I both spoke Vietnamese, and in addition, I spoke Spanish and Arabic.

Later, Tom saw an opportunity to leave the 519th and get into a special forces unit at Ft. Bragg. The 519th was a "leg" outfit, and Tom, an airborne-qualified and adventuresome kind of guy, was just not happy working with a bunch of MI soldiers who were marking time until they could get back to civilian life. Although the soldiers at the 519th were highly qualified, linguistically and technically, they were in reality civilians at heart, and not interested in being the type of hard-core military professional that Tom wanted to be.

During my time at Ft. Bragg, Vietnam fell. I was depressed for weeks. I would have been even more depressed had I known the awful truth that since the American withdrawal, the Congress of the United States had cut off almost all aid to South Vietnam, while the Soviet Union had rebuilt North Vietnam from top to bottom. When I left Vietnam in late 1972, the North Vietnamese army was in shambles. Now an impressive juggernaut was advancing on a weakened South Vietnam, and there was nothing to stop it.

Other Vietnam veterans and myself watched on television as the provinces of Vietnam fell one by one to the communist onslaught.

The American public, by the time of the final North Vietnamese invasion, was so sick of Vietnam, no politician in his right mind would have advocated re-entering the conflict to stop the offensive. Although the North Vietnamese units, massed in the open, could have been easily decimated by air power, it was politically impossible. And by that time, because of congressional legislation, it would have been illegal.

If the administration in power during the early part of the Vietnam War years had shown the same type of national resolve President Bush showed in hitting Iraq with full force, we would have never had to go through the national convulsions that our country was subject to in the late 1960s and the early 1970s. The demons released in American society at that time might very well have stayed in the bottle. As an example, the horrendous drug problem our nation suffers from today can be traced directly to the counter-culture movement that began when the Vietnam War turned sour. Concerned American youth, alienated at the grass-roots level, attempted to find meaning to life through a wide range of mind-altering drugs and retreatist behavior.

And perhaps more importantly, had the Vietnam problem been resolved early, the voice of the Left in American politics would likely not have gained respectability in American life. The political power the Left attained in the war years was translated into political action, which has been unleashed against the primary institutions of American society: religion, the family, public schools, and colleges and universities.

I believe the Left's destruction of traditional values has been at the heart of the reason our nation has been decaying around us since Vietnam. Not only did we let the lives of thousands of Americans and South Vietnamese soldiers go down the drain for nothing, we planted the seeds of our own national decline.

During the war, the political wisdom of the Left was that if the U.S. pulled out of an immoral war, and the so-called corrupt puppet government was abandoned, our problems and the problems of the Vietnamese people would be solved. Well, they weren't solved. In addition to all of the problems caused in our own country, Vietnam still bleeds in the form of being one of the poorest nations on earth. In addition, thousands of South Vietnamese officers and government officials unjustly rotted for years in re- education camps, the Vietnamese population in the south was terrorized for more than a decade, and the plight of the Vietnamese refugees is pathetic.

As a result of the timidity of our national leadership, primarily in the early days of the war, Cambodia, Laos, and Vietnam have gone through hell. And it all could have been avoided early on. Never in history has the price of political ineptness been so high. We could have and should have won in Vietnam.

I think anyone who has ever read THUD RIDGE, a definitive history of the air campaign in the early years of the Vietnam War, would be appalled at the restrictions under which American pilots operated. In addition to silly rules of engagement, it took three years to bomb a list of targets recommended to be struck in the first thirty days of air operations by the senior Air Force command.

But perhaps the worst crime of all in Vietnam was to have allowed the Ho Chi Minh trail to continue to function throughout the course of the war. Year after year, lethal war material flowed down the trail to be used to kill American and South Vietnamese soldiers. The criminality of allowing that to go on when it could have been stopped defies imagination.

The trail, according to senior ground commanders, who have spoken out in memoirs after the war, could have easily been cut by sending allied combat troops into Laos in the early days of the American involvement, hence bringing the war under American control.

Toward the end of the war, the United States provided logistical support for South Vietnamese units that entered Laos to cut the trail, but military experts have stated the operation was poorly conceptualized and was doomed from the start. By then, the American public was so turned off by the war, and accordingly, American forces were unable to put their full weight to any offensive measures that would look like they were seeking a military solution to the conflict.

The United States did in fact establish bases at the bottom of the Demilitarized Zone (DMZ) in Vietnam, but the last base in the chain, Khe Sanh, stopped near the edge of the Vietnamese-Laotian border, almost in view of the Ho Chi Minh Trail. The American bases on the DMZ, such as Con Tien, the "Rockpile," and Khe Sanh, were quite effective in slowing down wholesale infiltration coming across the DMZ from North Vietnam into South Vietnam, but had idiotic restrictions on them: they were prohibited from engaging target in or directly across the DMZ. Once enemy units crossed the DMZ into South Vietnam, or fired on American soldiers, they were fair game, but not before.

In 1989 I was in charge of an MIA investigative team that was operating just south of the old DMZ, and my counterpart on the team was a senior Vietnamese official. One day the Vietnamese and American team members took a break and visited the old Marine Corps base at Con Tien. As we were wandering around, I pointed in the direction of Laos and suggested to my counterpart that U.S. and South Vietnamese forces should have stationed combat units across Laos, all the way to Thailand. I argued that had we done so, the Ho Chi Minh Trail would have been cut and North Vietnam could not have continued the war. He merely shrugged and said the United States never had the political will to do such a thing. In other words, it was a non-issue and not worth debating. He was right.

Shortly after the fall of Vietnam, a number of us Vietnam veterans who could speak Vietnamese were sent to the various military posts where Vietnamese refugees were being inprocessed into the United States. The posts were Indian Town Gap, Pennsylvania; Camp Pendelton, California; and Ft. Chaffee, Arkansas. Tom McKay got orders for Indian Town Gap. Paul Rester, with whom I had served in Vietnam and who was now at another military intelligence unit at Ft. Bragg, got orders for Ft. Chaffee where there were 50,000 Vietnamese refugees. Shortly afterward, I also got orders to report to Ft. Chaffee.

Looking back now, it's incredible to me that we were able to process 50,000 refugees at Ft. Chaffee with almost no problems whatsoever. There were a few minor incidents, but the refugees behaved themselves and pretty much were model citizens. The area where the refugees lived at Ft. Chaffee was cordoned off by wooden saw horses. At each intersection that led into the Vietnamese area, Army military policeman were stationed. Most of the time they dozed while sitting in folding chairs at their posts, and Vietnamese kids played around them.

I didn't do intelligence work at Ft. Chaffee. When I first got there, I was assigned to a job moving Vietnamese refugees from point "A" to point "B" while they picked up clothing, etc. The job was easy since it was just a matter of pointing groups of a hundred or so refugees at a time in the right direction and telling them what they needed to do.

After my job as a language-qualified traffic cop, pointing Vietnamese in the right direction for inprocessing, I worked in a legal aid office preparing marriage and birth certificates. Many of the refugees had departed Vietnam without any type of documentation, and I worked as a translator and interpreter in assisting refugees in filling out affidavits that would substitute for the legal documents they had left in Vietnam.

Being a Vietnam vet and a hot-shot E-6 (I had gotten promoted back at Bragg), there wasn't too much I didn't know about Vietnam, the Vietnamese, or what ought to be done when faced with complex legal problems. Or so I thought. When in doubt I tended to make my own rules.

As an example, one day an attractive young Vietnamese woman came to the legal aid office with a very cute little Vietnamese girl. She said the little girl didn't have anyone in the whole world and she was concerned she and the child would be separated when they left Ft. Chaffee.

I said in Vietnamese to the woman, "Do you want the child?" She replied, "Oh, yes!"

I said in Vietnamese to the child, "Do you want this lady to be your mommy?" She nodded in the affirmative. In a matter of a few minutes, I typed out a legal birth affidavit showing the unmarried woman to be the lawful mother of the child. She signed happily.

I called over other Vietnamese in the room, total strangers to the woman and the child, who signed as witnesses saying that they knew the woman was in fact the legal parent of the child (generally Vietnamese will sign anything). Then I got a notary who worked in the office to notarize everyone's signature. And presto! a document that was valid in any court in the land.

I hope for my sake they all lived happily ever after. And if not, I hope the statute of limitations has run out on that particular case.

While at Ft. Chaffee I met Bill Bell. At that time Bill was still a lanky, raw-boned soldier. When I worked with him years later in Bangkok, he was a hefty, middle-aged bureaucrat. Life does that to us all. Once at his home in Bangkok, Bill showed me pictures of himself going through airborne training when he was 18 years old. He was a dashing young airborne warrior with black wavy hair and looked solid as a rock. But even warriors get old and fat.

I had never met Bill, a fellow Texan, before Ft. Chaffee, but friends of mine had talked about him for years. He was widely known in military intelligence circles.

Whenever I think of Bill, I think of the joke about the guy named "Charlie" whom everybody knew. One day two of Charlie's friends were in Vatican Square and they looked up and saw Charlie and the Pope on the balcony waving to the crowd. One of them said to the other, "Say, who is that guy standing there by Charlie?"

That's the way it was with Bill. It seems anywhere I've been in the Army, I've run into someone who starts telling a story about Bill Bell.

Bill had recently suffered a tragedy. His wife and a child had been killed in a plane crash in Vietnam. Bill had been assigned to the American Embassy in Vietnam when the North Vietnamese were advancing on Saigon, and he was one of the last Americans out of Vietnam. Before he left, he put his family on a C-5A Galaxy aircraft that had flown in to evacuate Vietnamese refugees, many of whom were small children. The aircraft crashed shortly after takeoff, likely shot down by a Strella missile fired by North Vietnamese troops.

I've known Bill Bell a long time now, and I've learned over the years he has a special feeling for people who are going through emotional trauma. I'm sure he's able to empathize with others because of the personal hurt he has had to face in his own life.

Once, Bill and I were in Hanoi as part of an MIA investigation, when he learned that the mother of one of our Vietnamese drivers had died. Bill asked me if I would go with him to the Buddhist wake that was being held for her. I said I would, and he and I went along with our Vietnamese team members who were going to visit the family of the deceased.

During the ceremony held in the home, Bill explained to me the significance of the events that were transpiring in the ceremony. When the family and friends started lighting the candles on the family altar, Bill and I were asked to participate. I'm a Christian and normally I would have excluded myself from a Buddhist ceremony. On this occasion I wanted to participate, and I did so with a clear conscience. I know the Lord would have wanted me to be as respectful as possible at that moment to the family, even though we shared different faiths. Bill told me what to do and I joined with him and the others in paying last respects to the memory of the Vietnamese woman.

Bill's genuine outpouring of sympathy for the bereaved family crossed political, international, and cultural boundaries more effectively than any professional diplomat could ever do. Bill proved to me that he had a quality to his character that was as precious as gold.

The Bill Bell I know is tough and is all business when it comes to the job or relations outside of his family and friends. I would not ever want to take on Bill as an adversary as others have foolishly tried to do. He could be ruthless in a confrontation.

However, I've watched Bill at close quarters for years and I know about the soft spot he has in his heart for those who are less fortunate than himself. He's done charitable things that no one else knows about but me. Once he gave 300 dollars to a refugee whom he had known years before back during the war when the refugee was an ARVN officer. I don't think anybody in the section would have done that except Bill. The refugee was a friend who needed help. Bill is by no means an easy touch; it's just that he can be a generous person when he sees someone whom he truly believes to be in need.

There was one thing I noticed happening to Bill at Ft. Chaffee. He was falling in love. He followed a beautiful Vietnamese teenage girl around like he was a lost puppy, and I learned later after I left Ft. Chaffee, he finally married her. Her name is Xuan (Spring), and my family and I got to know her well in Bangkok. Bill and Xuan have some beautiful, well-mannered, smart kids, one of whom, a son, was in one of my wife's classes at the International School of Bangkok.

The last week I was at Chaffee, I got a call from someone who introduced himself as special agent so-and-so. He wanted me to bring him my personnel records I had brought with me from Ft. Bragg. He said he was doing a security check and needed them. I was busy and didn't feel like hunting him down, so I suggested if he wanted my personnel records, he could come see me. Then he said something to the effect that he could care less if I made warrant officer or not.

"Warrant officer?"

He said, "Didn't you apply to become a warrant officer?"

I said, "I'll be right down!"

I had applied to be a warrant officer some months before back at Ft. Bragg, but had forgotten all about it. One day my good friend Sergeant First Class Al Coy, a Mexican American from Texas, told me he was en route to personnel to apply to become a warrant officer. Al had been a captain aviator during the war, but along with thousands of other officers after Vietnam had been "RIFed" (Reduction In Force). Since Al had prior enlisted time, he was eligible to become an enlisted man again, and he chose to do so. Al asked me if I wanted to put in my application too. I said, sure, and off I went with him. In a couple of days I put all of the paperwork together, submitted it, and hadn't thought about it again until I was called at Ft. Chaffee.

To make a short story long, I was accepted and Al was told he had been rejected. I don't think Al ever forgave me. We were always friendly when we ran into each other after that, but I suspect that deep down inside he felt I had stolen his warrant officer slot. Maybe I had.

A few hours before I left Ft. Chaffee before Christmas of 1975, those of us who worked at Ft. Chaffee with the Vietnamese dedicated a monument at the entrance of the post to show that we had processed 50,000 refugees through "Task Force New Arrivals." Sixteen years later, I spent a lot of time at Ft. Chaffee as an intelligence evaluator assigned to the Joint Readiness Training Center, and every now and then, I'd stop to read the plaque on the monument. I'd look around and reflect on the empty World War II barracks of Ft. Chaffee, which I could see in my mind's eye as teeming with thousands of Vietnamese refugees. But no sounds now came from the buildings, save an occasional gust of the Arkansas wind, and the ghosts engraved on memory.

There is now an identical monument next to the Vietnamese one: it's dedicated to the thousands of Cuban refugees who came to Ft. Chaffee in 1980 during the Mariel Boat Lift. The two monuments stand as a witness to the hideous cruelty of the great socialist experiment, inspired by Marx and brought to life by Lenin like Frankenstein's monster.

After I returned to Ft. Bragg, I was promoted to Warrant Officer One (WO1), or "Wobbly One" as the troops sometimes called us. After I had been pinned, I walked outside and received my first salute, which cost me one silver dollar—a tradition that goes far back into the dark recesses of the American military past.

The battalion command sergeant major was looking on and told me that once at an OCS graduation, he managed to get stationed at the exit of an auditorium when several hundred brand-new second lieutenants were leaving. In the space of a few minutes and multiple salutes later, he earned several hundred dollars.

From Ft. Bragg, I was reassigned to the 5th MI Detachment of the 5th Infantry Division (Mechanized) at Ft. Polk, Louisiana. The detachment, along with the division, had just been re-activated. The division had been structured to fight in Europe. In the event of an impending Soviet attack in Europe, the division would have have deployed by rail to a port, and shipped to Europe. On one occasion while I was at Ft. Polk, the division practiced its combat role by sending a brigade to Germany to participate in the yearly REFORGER (Return of Forces to Germany) exercise. I went along and spent two months in Southern Germany in charge of twenty interrogators that were tasked to provide interrogation support to the division. One of the armored divisions stationed in Germany played the part of the invading Soviet army. With the collapse of the Soviet Union, it all seems so quaint now.

The 5th MI Detachment had thirty two intelligence specialists commanded by an Army major. That had to be the best unit I was ever in. It was small and we all got to know each other extremely well, and it was there that I met my best friend, Buzz Wilhelm.

Chief Warrant Four Melborne (Buzz) Wilhelm was the funniest and the smartest human being I've ever known. He could crack you up or impart wisdom all in the same breath. He was a huge man—about 6'3" and weighed 250 or so pounds. He had a blond flat top and looked ever bit a Louisiana redneck, although he was from Wisconsin.

I had an NCO in my section who was overweight and Buzz was all the time kidding him about being fat. Buzz was overweight himself so he could get away with it where someone else couldn't. Buzz asked him one day about the new diet he was on. The NCO listed off all of the things on his new low-calorie diet: cottage cheese, grapefruit, unbuttered toast, etc. Buzz said, "Well, the reason I wanted to know what you've been eating was because when I retire I want to start a hog farm. I want to be sure and feed those hogs something that I know will fatten them up." The NCO, who usually had a quick comeback for Buzz, was for once totally speechless.

Buzz made so many redneck statements that you'd think he was prejudiced. But I recall vividly what Buzz did when a black soldier was not promoted when Buzz thought he should have been. Buzz complained to the commander and the soldier eventually got his deserved promotion. No one except the commander and myself ever knew what Buzz had done. I don't think the soldier ever knew what had happened. Buzz was definitely no liberal, but he had a sense of justice that transcended race.

Once a couple of the troops in the detachment found a gas mask in the woods that was totally shot. It was full of holes and was falling apart. Some basic trainee must have lost it years ago during some long forgotten training exercise. One day when we were conducting an exercise at the gas chamber, Buzz exchanged the tattered gas mask with the commander's new mask. We all were watching and waiting for the commander to test the mask before going in the chamber, but he made no attempt to do so. Finally, someone suggested that he check his mask, since we were all getting a little nervous that he might actually go into the chamber with the defective mask. The commander said he thought it would be okay. But just before going in, he pulled out his mask to take a quick look—and he almost fell over from shock. We all had a good laugh and gave him back his mask.

Once several of Buzz's troops were arrested for having bought stolen U.S. government tools. It was a stupid mistake on the part of a couple of outstanding soldiers, and they ended up getting court martialed. In spite of the verdict, Buzz gave them maximum scores on their efficiency reports. The commander was livid and called Buzz into his office several times to try to get Buzz to change the scores. The commander said that troops who had been court martialed were not outstanding and should not be given outstanding ratings. But Buzz wouldn't budge. Buzz contended they did everything he told them to do in a most outstanding manner and that's how he was rating them. Buzz's rating stayed, although the commander wrote a disclaimer on the efficiency reports, as was his lawful prerogative.

One time Buzz and I were out on a field exercise and a jeep drove by that must have had ten military policemen hanging precariously from the vehicle. Buzz yelled, "Stop that jeep!" They stopped and in the midst of chewing them out, Buzz told them, "Now write yourselves tickets!" Their commander happened to see Buzz lecturing his troops and came over and said, "What's going on here, Chief?"

Buzz said, "I caught these troops in a unsafe act in a military vehicle and told them to write themselves tickets." The troops looked at their commander for guidance.

The commander said, "You heard him, write yourself tickets!" The ten MPs pulled out their ticket books and meekly wrote themselves tickets.

I heard and saw a lot of funny things in the 5th MI Detachment. Buzz and a couple of the other folks were an absolute riot and kept me laughing for the three years I was there. But I'll have to say the funniest thing I saw at Ft. Polk was the night Hookfinn was "tortured."

The 5th MI Detachment built a mock prisoner of war camp at Ft. Polk, at which I frequently had the honor of being the camp commander. Every few months we trained units from the 5th Mechanized Infantry Division in resistance to interrogation, indoctrination, and imprisonment. We went all out in our training. We had black uniforms, a communist flag, and loud speaker equipment. The camp looked vicious: it was surrounded by watch towers and razor-sharp concertina wire. The training consisted of sleep deprivation, hunger, and physical and mental harassment. The regimen was brutal.

One night my interrogators, all dressed up in their enemy uniforms, "tortured" a black infantry soldier named Hookfinn. They didn't really torture him, of course, but he believed they did. My interrogators put a six-inch piece of wire to his head and told him it was electrified, and then started a countdown: "Ten, nine, eight...three, two, one...ZZZZZZ!" Hookfinn was sure bolts of electricity were going through his body. He screamed in pain that could only be felt in his mind. "I'll talk! I'll talk!" he yelled. My interrogators yelled back: "Shut up! We don't want you to talk. We just want to torture you!"

Hookfinn was a member of an almost all-black infantry squad, and as his fellow soldiers were sitting in the camp watching my interrogators in action, they decided to help them torture Hookfinn. Hookfinn's own comrades held him down, took the short piece of wire from my interrogators, which was hooked up to absolutely nothing, and proceeded to "electrocute" him too. I'm sure to this day Hookfinn believes with all his heart he was tortured one night at Ft. Polk by his own fellow soldiers. Hookfinn, wherever you are. I'm sorry I let them do it.

In mock POW camps you could never tell what was going to happen. Sometimes a little dirtball who you think would spill his guts right off the bat, would play hard core to the end. But other times, a little pressure would push someone right off the edge. And then we had collaborators who would actually sell their comrades for food or cigarettes.

At the end of three years at Ft. Polk, Louisiana, I called my assignment manager and he told me that I would shortly be reassigned overseas. He gave me a choice: Alaska or the Republic of Panama. I thought for a minute and chose Panama. It's ironic to think that had I said Alaska, my family and I would have had a completely different set of experiences and friends.

I travelled to Panama alone to get housing at Ft. Amador, and then Betty and the kids flew down. Ft. Amador, which looks like a Florida tropical park, is built on a causeway that runs out into the Bay of Panama. It's one of the most beautiful places we've ever lived. From one window in our quarters we could see Panama City across the bay; from the other we could see ships going through the canal.

I was a real jock in those days and often ran out to the tropical islands at the end of the causeway, a round-trip run of over five miles. I used to set some blistering times, which surprises me now as a military retiree whose main exercise these days seems to be pushing myself away from the table.

My family and I got to Panama just a month before the old U.S. Canal Zone became one of the Provinces of the Republic of Panama. It was interesting seeing for a very short period the last vestige of America's colonial empire. One minute after midnight on a day in October 1979, the Canal Zone officially passed into history as it came under the authority of the Republic of Panama. My family and I watched from our window as a huge Panamanian flag, brilliantly outlined by spotlights, was raised on nearby Ancon Hill. Out in the canal ships sounded their horns in salute to the newly unified county. The next day in Panama City, the jubilation of the populace reigned supreme.

Even though the Republic of Panama had taken over all of the territory that encompassed the old Canal Zone, the United States still had the mission of the defense of the Panama Canal, hence my unit, the 193rd Military Intelligence Company of the 193rd Infantry Brigade, spent hundreds of hours in the jungle training to expel any potential invader.

As Chief of the IPW Section (Interrogation of Prisoners of War), I had nine Spanish-speaking interrogators assigned to me. We had an absolute blast. During exercises we had the mission of obtaining information from American and Panamanian soldiers, playing the part of guerrillas who had be captured. We would interrogate them, obtain information, and send a completed report to the brigade intelligence officer (G-2). Sometimes I would surprise myself as to how well we did on these exercises.

The exercises, which were very realistic, were "live play." If the soldiers didn't capture guerrillas, then we didn't get prisoners to interrogate. If we did get prisoners, but were unable to interrogate them successfully, then we had no information to pass through intelligence channels. If the brigade received no intelligence, then it operated blind.

The infantry companies designated as guerrilla units were free to attack American troops and bases when and where they wished, to include the commanding general's headquarters. The fact that the guerrillas could actually "win" enhanced the training considerably. The training my interrogators and I received in Panama was the best I ever had in the Army. After a couple of exercises, my section could have gone into combat and done it for "real," which was the object of the training.

In 1980, the Mariel Boat Lift began in Cuba and thousands of refugees began pouring out of that country. My section was tasked to support governmental agencies involved in monitoring the exodus, and we deployed first to Miami and then to other makeshift refugee camps in the United States, to include Ft. McCoy, Wisconsin. We interviewed hundreds of refugees to obtain intelligence information about Cuba.

I discovered in a hurry that working with Cubans wasn't anything like working with Vietnamese refugees years before. The Cubans proved to be an emotional, violent people, while the Vietnamese refugees were very passive. At Ft. Chaffee, Arkansas, we herded thousands of Vietnamese from place to place using only one or two military policemen and a couple of Vietnamese linguists to give instructions. With the Cubans, it was necessary to have a full contingent of military policemen, and sometimes even federal marshals, to move a small group anywhere. And someone usually got stabbed in the process.

I saw more blood at Ft. McCoy than the entire time I was in Vietnam. Cubans frequently would get into fights with each other, and inevitably someone would end up lying on the ground in a pool of blood.

There were unquestionably genuine refugees that came out of the Cuban boat lift, but Castro opened the doors of his prisons at the same time and flooded us with the dregs of Cuban society. Castro said in a speech that the United States had always gotten the best and the brightest of Cuban society; now it was time to get the dregs. And we got them in spades: the United States ended up with drug addicts, pimps, prostitutes, mentally deranged, and hardened criminals of every ilk. Toward the end of the boat lift the first question that we immediately asked newly arrived Cubans was, "In which prison were you held?"

In contrast to the Cubans who arrived during the last part of the boat lift, when Castro emptied the jails, the Vietnamese refugees were the cream of the crop of their nation. They were the same quality of refugee that the United States used to get from Cuba in the early 1960s when Fidel Castro first came to power.

At the end of my three year tour in Panama, I returned to the U.S. and took the Intermediate Arabic Course (Egyptian Dialect) at the Defense Language Institute at Monterey, California. After graduating, I was sent to the Military Intelligence Warrant Officer Advanced Course at Ft. Huachuca, Arizona, where Tom McKay and I were students together. On graduation day, as my family and I were driving off to my new assignment, I stopped to talk to Tom for a few minutes to say goodbye. Tom said he had just been informed he would be going to Bangkok, Thailand, to the Joint Casualty Resolution Center as a Vietnamese linguist. "What do those folks do?" I asked, never dreaming that within three years I would be his replacement and become fully aware of the mission of the unit.

From Ft. Huachuca, my family and I drove to Ft. Campbell, Kentucky, where I was assigned to the 311th MI Battalion of the 101st Airborne Division. I loved every minute at Ft. Campbell. I was the chief of an interrogation section that had all Arabic speakers and on one occasion I had as many as twenty-six soldiers and one civilian working for me.

The civilian, who was the battalion's Arabic instructor, was Mr. John Ashy. I had first met John when I was TDY for a few days at Ft. Gordon, Georgia. At that time he was an enlisted Spec Four (Specialist Fourth Class) who had two days left on his tour in the Army. John, a college graduate, was Lebanese and spoke fluent Arabic. John told me he was going to Florida to open up a diner and sell Arab dishes. I told him, "Why don't you come to Ft. Campbell and work for me as an Arabic instructor?" I had already been given permission to hire an instructor if I could locate someone who would be willing to relocate to Ft. Campbell. He agreed and I picked up the telephone, made a few calls to make the arrangements, and hired him on the spot. John and I have been great friends for years and as of this writing he is still at Ft. Campbell, but is now teaching Special Forces soldiers. Some of his students were with me in Saudi Arabia and Kuwait during Desert Shield/Storm.

In the event the division deployed to the Middle East, my section would have had the mission of interrogating Arab prisoners of war in support of combat operations. Also, frequently elements of the division went on alert for possible deployment due to international incidents that were usually reported in the press. Invariably elements of my section would go on alert also to potentially provide linguistic support to the operation. But sometimes the incidents were not reported in the press and we would get orders to pack our gear, and a few hours later told to unpack, with no explanation as to where we might have been going or what we would potentially have been doing.

One Sunday morning just a few days before Christmas of 1984 I got a call and told to report to the intelligence officer of an airborne infantry battalion at Ft. Campbell. The battalion had been alerted for an EDRE (Emergency Deployment Readiness Exercise). The entire battalion and I were loaded into three C-130 Air Force transport aircraft, and flown to Ft. Stewart, Georgia. There, in bitter December cold, the battalion assaulted a mock prisoner of war camp and rescued frozen soldiers playing hostages. Then we all loaded into the aircraft and returned to Ft. Campbell in time for Christmas.

Christmas of 1985 was a sad time at Ft. Campbell. An aircraft carrying several hundred soldiers returning from a six-month tour of duty in the Sinai, crashed near Gander, Newfoundland. Everyone aboard perished. The MI battalion had six soldiers on the aircraft, who had been providing Arabic language support to the unit. Two of the linguists had been fellow Arabic students with me at the Defense Language Institute. The fort and the town of Clarksville were crushed by the tragedy. At the grade school where my wife taught, it seemed that almost every class had at least one student whose father had died.

President Reagan and his wife flew to Ft. Campbell and met with family members of the deceased. Showing the utmost love and concern, they shook hands and hugged each of those present. One of the mothers of a fallen warrior broke down in tears in the arms of the First Lady. As the President looked on, his face evidenced the sense of hurt and loss that the entire nation felt toward its sons and daughters who had died in the tragic accident.

During a memorial service for the soldiers at Ft. Campbell, I was assigned as an escort officer to families who attended the ceremony that took place on a frigid Kentucky parade field. At the end of mournful taps, a formation of Air Force jets screamed over the field where the 101st Airborne Division was standing at attention. As the aircraft formation reached the center of the field, one jet broke from the pack and flew away alone. According to Air Force tradition, this symbolized the loss of a comrade in arms. The symbolism was not lost on me or any of the others. Twenty thousand soldiers were fighting back tears as they watched the aircraft render its final tribute to fallen comrades.

In 1986 an Army board made a selection of warrant officers to attend the Senior Warrant Officer Course at Ft. Rucker, Alabama. Being selected, in addition to being an real honor, was nice in that it practically guaranteed that I would be promoted during my next assignment to CW4 (Chief Warrant Four), the highest warrant officer rank. The course was considered to be the best "ticket punch" for advancement. My assignment manager, CW4 Walt Johnson, gave me a class date and told me he would be reassigning me back to Panama after I graduated.

But I wouldn't be going back to Panama. It didn't even enter my mind as I signed out of my unit and drove out of the front gate of Ft. Campbell en route to Ft. Rucker that my next job would be picking up the pieces of the Vietnam War.

The author with Nguyen Manh at an excavation.

SFC Jim Williams with former Viet Cong crossing a river in the Ashau Valley.

After over two decades, still a formidable-warrior. This old Viet Cong was the guide for a search team in the Ashau Valley.

CHAPTER 8

INVESTIGATING THE "70-NAME LIST"

There is only one MIA left from the Vietnam War. Now that statement is sure to raise a few eyebrows, but it's accurate. After the war all but one of the MIAs were declared to be "unaccounted-for, presumed to be dead." On the very last case that was submitted to the Secretary of the Air Force for approval as unaccounted-for, the secretary declined to sign the document and stated that one American would remain "MIA" as a symbolic gesture in the effort to resolve the fate of those who did not come back home from Vietnam.

In spite of the legal definition, the term "MIA" is used unofficially by almost everyone in the federal government, although in official government documents the term is "unaccounted-for." The Defense Intelligence Agency hasn't quite gone over yet. Its office for MIA matters is called The Office of POW/MIA Affairs.

In attempting to obtain information about MIAs from the Vietnamese, JCRC had been going back and forth to Vietnam for years to joint U.S.-Vietnamese technical meetings; however, the Americans couldn't get the Vietnamese to cooperate to let American investigators and recovery specialists go to specific sites to investigate cases on the ground. Sometimes during technical meetings, the Vietnamese would take American delegations on a side trip to where a plane had crashed and where the Vietnamese were digging up wreckage. But the activities were in most instances totally unilateral, and the U.S. government was eventually billed for recovery expenses the Vietnamese had incurred.

The first time I ever went to Hanoi as a member of one of Harvey's delegations, the Vietnamese loaded us into a Toyota van and took us to a crash site south of Hai Phong City. Bill Bell took advantage of the situation and interviewed several witnesses to the crash.

Only once before, in August of 1985, had the Vietnamese permitted Americans to come to Vietnam to dig into what allegedly was a downed B-52, but after several days of digging in miserable weather, nothing was found. Bill Bell theorized that a B-52 had not crashed there at all, but an errant Soviet-made SAM missile had landed there. That dig, which netted absolutely nothing, cost the U.S. taxpayer $100,000 dollars. Tom McKay showed me a photocopy he made of the check before it was given to the Vietnamese.

In February 1987, President Reagan appointed General John J. Vessey, Jr. (Retired), a former chairman of the Joint Chiefs of Staff, as his personal emissary to Vietnam for POW/MIA affairs. General Vessey led a mission to Vietnam in July 1987. Accompanying General Vessey were Colonel Richard Childress, from the National Security Council, and

Ms. Ann Mills-Griffiths, head of the National League of Families.

Colonel Richard Childress had presidential-level staff supervision of the POW/MIA issue. Dick Childress, who once shared an office with Ollie North at the NSC, was one of the more influential Americans in the U.S. government in the search for MIAs. He had tremendous influence in setting U.S. policy regarding MIA investigations and ultimate relations with the Vietnamese government.

Ms. Ann Mills Griffith was the head of the National League of Families, the powerful MIA family organization. In her position, she commanded instant respect from elected and appointed officials alike. Career officer and politicians knew fully that she had the ear of MIA family members who could bring tremendous pressure to bear should they become unhappy about something.

Childress and Griffiths frequently travelled together to Bangkok, Laos, and Vietnam. Consequently, when they flew in things were in an uproar at JCRC headquarters in Honolulu and the American Embassies in Laos and Thailand for a couple of days. The pair definitely had the bureaucrats' attention during those brief visits.

Colonel Childress' and Ms. Griffiths' impact on the MIA issue was significant; unquestionably, they were the ones largely responsible for getting the resolution of the fate of MIAs elevated to the "highest national priority" by two American presidents. Childress has since retired from active duty and at least for a while was involved in business dealings in Laos. Ms. Griffiths remained very much active in the MIA issue. In addition she continued to be interviewed frequently on national television about MIAs.

General Vessey met with Nguyen Co Thach, the Vietnamese Foreign Minister, and reached an agreement that the two sides would begin resolving cases of unaccounted-for Americans in Vietnam.

After years of stonewalling American requests to get serious about resolving MIA cases, the Vietnamese decided to allow Americans to conduct searches inside of Vietnam. Why did they do it? Part of the answer has to do with the fact that Vietnam's major ally and benefactor, the Soviet Union, was starting to have severe social and economic problems. The Vietnamese were legitimately getting nervous that the "brotherhood of socialist countries" (anh em xa hoi chu nghia) might not be as reliable in the future as it had been in the past. Therefore, the Vietnamese hoped that progress in the search for MIAs would eventually secure diplomatic relations with the United States, which would open economic doors for investment opportunities.

In the past the American government had repeatedly told the Vietnamese that withdrawal from Cambodia would be the first step toward diplomatic relations, and the level of relations would depend on the progress the Vietnamese showed in resolving MIA cases.

Vessey and Thach agreed that the two sides would start investigating what the Americans called "discrepancy" cases. These were incidents where very strong evidence indicated that the individuals involved came under the control of North Vietnamese or National Liberation Front (Viet Cong) forces, yet the Vietnamese government claimed to have no knowledge of what happened to them. These cases have been of concern to the American public, particularly with all of the rumors about U.S. prisoners still being held captive in Indochina.

And the evidence of some of the cases was extremely compelling. For example, several cases that I later investigated in Vietnam dealt with pilots seen exiting their aircraft with good chutes in populated areas—but never heard from again. Of the 2,400 some odd cases, roughly 220 fell into the category of being discrepancy cases.

It always amazed me that the Vietnamese themselves picked up the word "discrepancy" and used it in describing MIA cases in which there was evidence the Americans had exited the aircraft or were known to be under the control of Vietnamese forces. To me, discrepancy has a negative connotation to it. I thought it strange that Vietnamese diplomats, some of whom were totally fluent in English, would have no problem in using the term.

Harvey thought it would have been more prudent to use the term "compelling evidence" cases, but the U.S. government continued to use the word "discrepancy" as an official category. And the Vietnamese government continued to accept the category, seemingly without any problem with linguistic semantics.

The plan General Vessey and Foreign Minister Nguyen Co Thach came up with was that joint American and Vietnamese investigative teams would initially investigate seventy of the several hundred discrepancy cases, and when these were concluded, discussions would be conducted to determine future investigative activities. The list of the first seventy cases that were to be investigated was thereafter referred to as "The 70-Name List" by both the U.S. and Vietnamese sides.

The investigations of the 70 cases were conducted over seven periods, called "iterations." The First Iteration was in September of 1988, a little more than a year from the date of the meeting between General Vessey and Foreign Minister Nguyen Co Thach. The Seventh Iteration was in August of 1989. On each iteration, two, and sometimes three teams, investigated three, four, or more cases. Each team had as a minimum a Vietnamese-speaking team leader from the JCRC Liaison Office at the American Embassy in Bangkok, a case analyst from the JCRC headquarters in Honolulu, and a graves registration specialist from Central Identification Laboratory Hawaii (CILHI: pronounced "Sil-High"), also located in Honolulu.

During the investigations which were conducted throughout the entire country, the Vietnamese had counterpart teams that accompanied the U.S. teams. Their organization, called the "Vietnamese Office for Seeking Missing Persons" (Co Quan Viet Nam Tim Kim Nguoi Mat Tich), was staffed with officials from the Vietnamese Foreign Ministry, the Ministry of Defense, and the Ministry of the Interior. Each joint team had a Vietnamese official from the Foreign Ministry, a military officer from the Ministry of Defense, and a representative of the Ministry of the Interior. The official from the Ministry of the Interior was responsible for the security of each team and also paid the team's bills that accrued as the team travelled around the country. All expenses incurred by the joint teams were reimbursed by the U.S. government.

The joint U.S.- Vietnamese teams travelled throughout Vietnam in eight 1988 four-wheel-drive Jeep Cherokees which were flown to Hanoi by U.S. transport aircraft. In a country where there are virtually no private automobiles, and the government vehicles are basic and drab, the Jeep Cherokees with their bright sporty colors attracted attention everywhere they went. Whenever the teams would stop, large crowds would gather to take stock of the cars and their strange American passengers.

I missed the First Iteration in September 1988. Bill Bell and Jim Coyle were the team leaders on that one. I was absolutely crushed that I was not selected to participate, but Bill and Jim, even though civilians, were both senior in rank to me, and there were only two positions for team leaders. I would gladly have gone as a team member, but on the first iteration the teams were going light and no additional personnel were going along except those who were going to fill designated jobs as case analyst and graves registration specialist.

The international news media gave close coverage to the investigation, and Bill and Jim were both interviewed by international news organizations.

Bill Bell was to be the overall ground commander during the investigations. In addition to being responsible for the operation, Bill would also be a team leader responsible for investigating cases out in the boonies. There is no question Bill had the leadership ability and qualifications to be in charge, just as he was fully qualified to eventually be the Director of the POW/MIA office in Hanoi, a job that he took after I left JCRC. Bill is a very impressive person and able to sit down with the highest-ranking officials as an equal and discuss most issues.

Right now is a good time to stop briefly and explain some ground rules that I'm going to use for the remainder of this book. I intend to describe the iterations in which I participated in Vietnam, but will only be giving limited information about individual MIA cases we investigated and what we found at specific crash sites. American investigators at JCRC are still not allowed to give out that kind of information; therefore, I will continue to abide by that policy. Besides, I feel information such as that goes beyond the public's right to know and infringes on the privacy of MIA families. Witnesses frequently gave us graphic information about how MIAs died, and I think that is much too personal to repeat here. I don't intend for this book to be a sensational thriller.

On the Second Iteration, I went to Vietnam as a member of Bill Bell's Team. Harvey was going to give me my own team during the upcoming Third Iteration, and my mission as a member of Bill's team was to be his understudy and learn all I could about being a team leader. It was a great idea. Bill Bell and Jim Coyle had been thrown into the First Iteration cold, and I had the luxury of going into the water a little at a time and learning from their mistakes.

The Second Iteration was eleven days long and lasted from October 24th to November 3, 1988. The first few iterations were relatively short, and then they eventually got longer and longer. By the time I left JCRC, they were averaging twenty days in length.

The two teams, seven Americans in all, departed Bangkok on the 24th of October in a small, twin-engine, C-12 military aircraft. We crossed Laos, entered Vietnam, and landed at the Noi Bai airport just outside of Hanoi. Four Jeep Cherokee vehicles, purchased by the U.S. government for our work in Vietnam, were waiting for us. After clearing Vietnamese customs, our drivers took us to the Foreign Ministry Guest House in downtown Hanoi. We spent the evening in Hanoi and then the next day had a series of meetings with our Vietnamese counterparts and prepared equipment.

The next day, the two teams headed to their respective zones of operation. Jim Coyle's team worked west of Hanoi, as Bill Bell and I were going to do also, but generally Jim's team was going to stay close to the city.

Bill Bell's team travelled to the northwestern provinces of Vietnam, through some of the most rugged terrain in all of Southeast Asia. Our team travelled as far as 300 kilometers (180 miles) from Hanoi. One hundred and eighty miles may not sound like much, but in Vietnam with the horrible roads, it's quite a distance.

We drove to Son La Town, Son La Province, which took a full eleven hours across treacherous mountain roads with thousand foot drop offs. But the scenery was absolutely spectacular and made the trip worthwhile.

As we were driving along, white-knuckled from the close calls of oncoming traffic, it did not come to my mind that I would be making the exact same trip on two more occasions before I left JCRC.

I was really surprised along the way to see so many villages of ethnic minorities. The Vietnamese told me the ethnic minorities we saw were the Hmong (pronounced MOHNG), Mung, Black Tai, White Tai, Red Tai, and Meo (cat people). When I was in the south during the war I saw Montagnard people from time to time, but I didn't realize there were other distinct groups besides them. Vietnam has many ethnic minorities, each with its own language and culture. The style and color of clothing are all unique to the different areas.

We got into Son La Town after dark and checked into the province guest house, which had electricity but no running water. The place was a two-story building that I believed, because of its dilapidated condition, must have been at least a century old and built by the French. I was surprised to learn the building was erected in 1966 by the Son La Province People's Committee.

Early the next day, Thursday, communist party and military cadre from the Son La Province headquarters came over to the guest house. We briefed them on what we hoped to accomplish and requested they give us support in finding witnesses to MIA cases that the joint team would be investigating.

The head of the Son La group was a grandfatherly and pleasant retired army officer, Colonel Tho, who had served many years in Laos during the war years. I would get to know him well during the iteration, and two additional iterations in the future. Colonel Tho was accompanied by several army officers and a beautiful woman wearing stylish western clothing. She was introduced as the province photographer.

Bill, suspicious as always, believed she was likely a seductress spy for the Ministry of the Interior, the state security apparatus. When Bill first told me that, I thought he might be right. But, having gone through three iterations in Lang Son Province, I believe she was who Colonel Tho said she was: the province photographer. Bill Bell's theory is admittedly much more intriguing, but typical of most of his conspiracy theories, it didn't pan out. She remained totally circumspect and never attempted to entrap any of the Americans.

As for sexual conduct: we had been briefed, threatened, warned, admonished in no uncertain terms that we would not have sexual relations with Vietnamese women—period. In addition, we all had to sign a statement saying that not only would we not have such relations, but if we did, we would report it the next duty day. I was the security officer in the Liaison Office in Bangkok and every iteration I had the duty of briefing the sexual prohibitions, plus getting any new people coming on board to sign the document.

Some of our team members on iterations got what I considered a little too cozy with Vietnamese girls, but I personally don't know of any instance where any of them violated the prohibition. There were undoubtedly opportunities to do so. At hotels throughout Hanoi we were asked occasionally if we wanted girls to spend the night with us. And on one occasion when I was in Hue, a hoodlum-looking pimp came up to several of us and attempted to interest us in some attractive young ladies who were discreetly watching from the distance.

After the meeting with the Son La Province officials, the American and Vietnamese team members, and the Son La province officials, all piled into our two Jeep Cherokees and Soviet-made jeeps belonging to the province headquarters. We drove into the center of Son La Town looking for evidence of an aircraft that had crashed there years before, according to American records.

We talked to several local people who said they had lived in the city during the war and that no aircraft had ever crashed there. They did say that a nearby antiaircraft battery had shot down a jet but they didn't know where it had impacted. At the site, the Vietnamese province officials showed us a bomb crater and a bombed-out building that they said had been a hospital during the war.

Several years before, Bill Bell had interviewed a former resident of Son La at a refugee camp in Thailand. The refugee drew a sketch of Son La for Bill and identified the bombed-out building as having been a military barracks, as opposed to a hospital. Bill Bell had brought the drawing with him and he was quite happy to show his American team members that he had caught the Vietnamese trying to pull the wool over our eyes by showing us a bombed-out military barracks and claiming it had been a hospital. But we were all still nice back then and kept such things to ourselves. In future iterations when we would get propagandized, we'd bluntly say what they were telling us was garbage.

From the center of Son La we headed toward a village a few kilometers out from Son La, where locals officials told us a crash had allegedly occurred. We met with village officials in a community long-house, a huge rectangular structure on stilts. The elders of the village showed us metal parts and what they said was a pilot's helmet, which looked to me like a motorcycle helmet. They said the items had come from an aircraft that had crashed in a ball of flames on a nearby mountain years before.

We took pictures of the items, made a few notes, and then got some villagers to lead us on an exhausting but incredibly beautiful climb up the mountain to the supposed crash site. We found absolutely nothing that remotely looked like a crash site and felt we had been the victim of a wild-goose chase. The purpose of the search was never really clear to us.

Our Vietnamese team members apologized and said the local people in the village had approached them and said they had information, and they had no way of knowing what they were going to show or tell us. They said they had been taken for a ride as much as we were.

The American members of the team theorized that the locals thought they could make some bucks by selling an MIA story to us. Who knows.

I was really worried about Bill Bell on the climb. He's a heavy smoker, overweight, and out of shape, and he had no business making a climb like that. His heart started racing when we were going up the mountain and I thought surely we'd be carrying him down.

Bill hated mountain climbing with a passion, and on future iterations, he was insistent the Vietnamese get us helicopters to preclude making dangerous mountain climbs. I chuckled at the idea of using helicopters at the time, but when I eventually saw how well they worked, I had a change of heart. Generally the helicopters worked beautifully when the weather was good, and were useless when the weather turned bad. But some of the trips we eventually took were in such remote areas, I don't know how we could have gotten into the investigation sites without them.

On one particular iteration I went on, had we not had a helicopter, we would have had to cut our way through dense jungle and make horrendous climbs across dangerous mountains. But with the helicopter we were able to conclude an investigation in the course of a day.

On Friday morning, October 28, 1988, local cadre took us to a crash site near a village several miles away from Son La, and we did indeed find aircraft wreckage. But we had to dig up a garden to do it, and the owner was furious. Our Vietnamese calmed him down by telling him they would reimburse him for the garden.

We talked to locals who claimed to have witnessed the crash. According to them, a pilot ejected from the aircraft with a good chute, but was shot by local militia as he was coming down. The witnesses said that later on that day regular army troops buried him in the vicinity of where he landed.

Several days later we attempted to do a field recovery of the MIA and hired thirty local people to excavate the possible grave site for us, but we found nothing.

During the dig, Bill expressed to me his concern that he would end up paying for the excavation out of his own pocket. He said he hadn't gotten any authorization from Harvey or anyone else to excavate suspected grave sites. I told him not to worry about it. I told Bill he was the ground commander and if he saw the mission necessity of doing something like that, no one was going to second guess him. I said if he got charged for the dig, I'd pay for half. But there was never any problem; the finance office in Honolulu picked up the tab for thirty laborers without batting an eye.

Excavations are supposed to be done in a scientific manner under the direction of an anthropologist. All we had on our team was a graves registration specialist. He was a nice guy, but not very scientific, and certainly not qualified to direct an excavation. When it became obvious the dig was going nowhere, he went "divining" for remains with a bent copper rod. He said a forensic anthropologist with a Ph.D told him that a divining rod made of copper would "dip" when passed over remains. As he walked back and forth with his copper divining rod, a crowd of Vietnamese watched him with all of the awe and respect they would give a true mandarin sage

I later told Harvey about the copper divining rod. Harvey rolled his eyes and said, thank goodness no one from the international news media saw him doing that. Harvey said it would have been disastrous if a story got out that JCRC investigated cases with divining rods.

After our unsuccessful dig, we visited an old French prison in Son La Town that had been turned into a museum. The purpose of the visit was to check the files and exhibits to see if there was information about pilots captured or killed in the vicinity of Son La. The director of the museum was in Hanoi, but a young woman who worked there eventually let us in after a little coaxing from the silver-tongued Bill Bell.

The woman took us on a guided tour of the prison. The walls were still standing, but most of the interior had been gutted by what she said were American bombs. She took us down into some of the underground dungeons where she said contemporaries of Ho Chi Minh, Le

Duan and To Hieu were held during the war against the French. Le Duan became party chairman after Ho Chi Minh died in 1969. A sign on the prison wall said To Hieu had been martyred in the prison.

She told us no Americans had ever been held in the prison, but she was only partially correct. Ernie Brace, an Air America pilot captured in Laos, had been held there for at least a day and a night while awaiting transportation that would take him to the Hanoi Hilton, approximately 300 kilometers away.

She let us into musty storage rooms in the museum that contained documents and a lot of ethnic minority artifacts. We started going through the documents that were piled around on shelves and tables and began to make notes and take photographs of things that interested us. However, as we dug more and more into the museum's records, she became increasingly fearful that she had done something that would get her in trouble with the director when he came back from Hanoi. She told us we would have to leave. No amount of persuasion by us or our high-ranking Vietnamese escorts could change her mind. We kept stalling, but she finally put her foot down and told us we had to leave, and we did.

I can't really blame her. Vietnamese workers live on near-starvation wages as it is, and jobs are at a premium. If she were to be fired from her job, the results would be catastrophic for her and her family.

The next day, local officials led us to another mountain crash site and we photographed wreckage and wrote down numbers from some of the larger pieces. We also interviewed witnesses to the crash. On this particular case, a pilot in a propeller-driven aircraft was looking for another pilot who had been lost a day or so before. The aircraft was hit by antiaircraft fire and crashed. Witnesses said the aircraft must have gone in fully loaded because there were repeated explosions from the crash site all one afternoon.

Throughout our trips around Son La Town, we were mobbed by the local people—just like celebrities. Usually we were asked if we were "Lien Xo (Soviets)," and they usually were surprised when we told them we were Americans. But some of them had lived such isolated lives, they didn't know anything about America. One guy asked me if I was Chinese. Also, our vehicles attracted considerable attention. And, of course, the brand new, air conditioned Jeep Cherokees with AM/FM radios caused a commotion.

During our time in Son La, we took our meals in the Son La guest house dining room. The food was quite good, though one morning Bill Bell got upset with a bowl of Vietnamese soup he was served. Pho (pronounced "fuh") is a delicious soup with noodles and meat and usually served at breakfast. Bill put his ladle-like spoon into his bowl of pho and up came what looked like a tiny rib cage with red meat. Bill turned to me with a look of disgust and said, "What is this?"

I said, "Bill, I think it might be rabbit."

Bill looked down at the rib cage in disgust and then looked up at me and said, "I've been coming to Vietnam for over twenty years and I've never seen a rabbit in this country yet!"

The next day, we loaded up the vehicles and headed back in the direction of Hanoi. This time the trip was not going to be as tough, since the plan was to stop a little way past the halfway point and investigate a crash site.

However, on the return our driver seemed to be a little more reckless than usual and we thought we had bought the farm a time or two when we met trucks, buses, people, livestock, or carts around deadly curves and over hills. The driver usually used his horn long before he touched the brake. We had a few close calls, but nothing serious occurred other than grazing a cow and killing a few chickens. The chickens would not have been a total loss since the locals undoubtedly would have made use of the fresh "road kill."

We reached the village of Mai Chau, Mai Chau District, Ha Son Binh Province in the late afternoon. One of our escorts from the Foreign Ministry in Hanoi made arrangements for us to stay in the district Communist Party headquarters. The building had three rooms, a conference room, and two large rooms with a half dozen or so bunk beds in each. The conference room was in the center and had a larger-than-life statue of Ho Chi Minh. Behind Uncle Ho was a red flag that hung on the wall. The two rooms with the bunk beds were separated by the conference room, and we four Americans stayed in one end room, while the Vietnamese were in the other. We had outhouses and a well to draw water from for bathing. We had a beautiful view of a rice field that was being harvested by villagers. We also had complete freedom to walk around, though any time we started to wander off, one of our friendly escorts on our team from the Ministry of the Interior would make some pretext to join us.

The next day, the team climbed a nearby mountain to take a look at a crash site. I talked Bill Bell into staying down below to interview witnesses about another case, while I took the team up the mountain. He agreed. It made all the sense in the world. He was the best linguist and most suited to interview, and I was in the best shape and most suited to climb mountains.

We climbed the mountain and found the crash site up near the summit. The wreckage from the crash was scattered down the side in a large swath for several hundred feet. Engines and the larger pieces that the villagers had been unable to salvage were still clearly visible. We recorded information from aircraft data plates, shot several rolls of film, and then climbed back down the mountain.

In consideration of the feelings of the MIA family, I won't divulge what we discovered about the fate of the pilot, except to say that we obtained evidence that later proved conclusively the pilot died in the crash.

Down below, Bill was successful in his interview and was able to get significant information about a case that had occurred nearby. The information would likely be enough to resolve the fate of the airmen involved.

That evening we were mobbed by local people who had come from miles around to see the Americans. There were also a large number of ragged-looking children among the crowd. The graves registration specialist handed out pieces of candy from a large bag he had brought to Vietnam just for such an occasion. Bill Bell laughed and said, "Those kids aren't going to eat that."

Surprised, I looked at Bill for an explanation. Bill said, "All their lives their parents have told them foreigners poison kids. A Vietnamese kid from the North would never eat candy an American gave him."

Sure enough, none of them would eat the candy. The graves registration specialist was perturbed and tried to get several of the kids to try a piece. One of them said in Vietnamese, "You eat a piece first, Uncle." (Uncle is a term of respect.)

Bill Bell told the graves registration specialist what the problem was, and he made a big production of unwrapping one and eating it in full view of the unruly mob of urchins. But they still wouldn't eat the candy. They kept their eyes on the American, fully convinced he was going to drop dead any moment.

The next day, we headed back to Hanoi. On the way we stopped and had a meal in a city called Hoa Binh, where the Soviets were constructing a huge dam on the Da river. The Vietnamese told us they hope the power will eventually transform the northwestern provinces of Vietnam, just as the huge Tennessee Valley Authority projects in the United States improved the lives of thousands of Americans during the Great Depression.

One thing about being on a team with Bill Bell, you can always count on eating well. He always had American-style food stashed away somewhere. On this stop he pulled out two large cans of chili and asked the restaurant owner to heat them up and pour them over rice. Fixing the rice was no problem, but the cook couldn't figure out how to get the chili out of the cans with the fancy crank-style can opener Bill gave him. Bill showed him how to use it, and the look of surprise and pleasure on the cook's face was all-inspiring. After an absolutely delicious meal, Bill presented the cook with the can opener—which couldn't have been a more appreciated gift, even if it had a fifty dollar bill attached to it.

It was at the restaurant that I learned not to enjoy pork in Vietnam. The public latrine in the restaurant was in a pig pen. The pig kept the latrine clean, thereby serving the multiple function of being the sewer and future dinner at the same time.

We reached Hanoi in the late afternoon. The next day, Wednesday, November 2, 1988, both teams assembled with their Vietnamese counterparts and wrote joint reports of investigative findings which were signed by Bill Bell and Jim Coyle and their Vietnamese counterparts who participated in the investigations.

On Thursday morning, November 3, the Vietnamese took us to Noi Bai Airport where we were to meet our small military plane that was to carry us back to Bangkok.

While at the airport we watched from a distance a solemn ceremony conducted by military personnel from our headquarters in Honolulu who had flown in by a C-141 jet transport to pick up twenty-one sets of remains that were being repatriated by the Vietnamese government. We had to stay in the distance because U.S. policy is that the appropriate attire for such an affair is a uniform or coat and tie. At the conclusion of the ceremony, the caskets were loaded aboard the aircraft. The back door of the aircraft was closed, and the big plane rumbled aloft en route to Guam and then Honolulu. Americans, who had their departure delayed for twenty years or more, were finally going home.

Fifteen minutes later, we also were in the air for the two and a half hour flight back to Bangkok. Our adventure, but not our excitement, was over.

The author and a graves registration specialist aboard a rented Sampan checking out a water crash site.

The author standing in front of the "Hanoi Hilton." A lot of horrible things happened to American POWs behind those walls.

Ngo Hoang at the crash site of an F-4 fighter aircraft. The pilot was shot by village militia while trying to reach rescue helicopters.

CHAPTER 9

IN THE PRESENCE OF MINE ENEMIES

When I was travelling around Southeast Asia interviewing refugees about MIAs and making trips into Vietnam as a leader of MIA investigative teams, in reality I was involved in two missions. In addition to my primary job of resolving cases of MIAs, I was looking for a way to rid myself of the ghost of Vietnam that haunted me.

Over the years I've tried to pin down why Vietnam was such a troubling experience for me and others who participated in the war. I've come to the conclusion that there is something in the collective national psyche that was damaged by the war and in turn affected those who served, regardless of the intensity of involvement.

Although many veterans had horrible combat experiences or were mistreated as prisoners of war, the majority were rear echelon soldiers who could only hear and see the war in the distance. At worst, the war was hideous beyond belief; at best it was an interruption of plans for the future. For most, the memory of the war is a stain, something that can't be cleansed with the mere passage of time. The ghost of Vietnam still festers in the dark recesses in the minds of so many who served.

I was partly able to come to grips with the war by sitting down with my old enemies, one-on-one, and talking through a lot of things that bothered me about them and their country. I slowly came to see them as fellow human being with the same hopes and aspirations for their country and children as I had for mine. I came to understand that my enemy was like myself in more ways than I wanted to admit.

During a trip to Honolulu in June of 1988, I got to know several of the Vietnamese with whom I would eventually be making trips throughout Vietnam during MIA investigations. Now it may sound funny that I got to know them in Honolulu, but it's true. LtCol Mather and I were designated as official escorts for a delegation of Vietnamese who were visiting the Central Identification Laboratory, Honolulu, and the Headquarters of the Joint Casualty Resolution Center. The purpose of the visit was to acquaint officials in the Vietnamese Office for Seeking Missing Persons (VNOSMP) with U.S. investigative and identification techniques.

The delegation had flown from Hanoi to Ho Chi Minh City and then on to Bangkok, all on Air Vietnam, the national Vietnamese carrier. At Don Muong International Airport, Mather and I were waiting for their arrival with American Embassy vans. We assisted them through customs and took them to the Vietnamese Embassy where they spent the evening.

Mather had purchased tickets for them to fly directly from Hanoi to Bangkok on Thai International, but their own government would not allow them to fly on a foreign carrier when Air Vietnam was available. So Mather had to make arrangements for the U.S. government to reimburse the Vietnamese government for the additional tickets.

The delegation had a day to spend in Bangkok, and Mather put me in charge of taking them around to see the sights in Bangkok. They had to get permission from their embassy to go, but only three of the six members of the delegation ended up going. The other three had been in the Vietnamese Foreign Service for years and had been to a number of foreign countries, including Thailand. They were not particularly interested in seeing Bangkok. Two of the three who went with me were seeing a foreign country for the first time and were totally wide-eyed as we walked around Bangkok to see the sights. They even got excited when they saw a traffic jam for the first time.

Vietnam is still in the bicycle age, but Bangkok is a modern metropolis, a fact which became readily obvious to all three. The difference between the two countries is like night and day. To make sure they appreciated the difference, I took them to see Central Department Store, which was down the street from where I lived. It is as modern as any department store anywhere in the world. The main department store in Hanoi is like an old-fashioned American dry goods store. They were definitely impressed. Of course, I subtly pointed out how successful capitalism had been in creating tremendous wealth for the people of Thailand.

Mather gave each of the Vietnamese nine hundred U.S. dollars for TDY expenses and their eyes bulged when they saw the money. The average Vietnamese makes an equivalent of one hundred and twenty U.S. dollars a year. Mather was handing them about eight years earnings for the average Vietnamese worker. The security officer on the team, who was a real young guy, took charge of all of the money. It would be his responsibility to safeguard the money and pay all of the bills.

I've often wondered what happened to the money the Vietnamese didn't spend during the trip. In the U.S. government, if an employee spends less than the daily per diem allowance for meals and incidentals on a TDY (Temporary Duty) trip, he or she gets to keep what is left over. I wondered if the security officer let them have any of it at the end of the trip.

Bill Bell told me later that the older delegates didn't care for the young security officer and said he was "spoiled." His parents were supposedly bigwigs in the Communist Party in Vietnam, and he had been able to obtain schooling and a prestigious job with their influence. The older delegates had worked their way up in the Communist Party and had been required to prove themselves every step of the way, starting during the war against the French.

Mr. Nguyen Can, who was a senior diplomat in the North American Division of the Vietnamese Foreign Ministry, headed the delegation. Can is very suave and speaks perfect idiomatic English. He has a slight accent that is barely noticeable to native English speakers, but other than that his language level is on a par with educated Americans.

Bill Bell was always suspicious of how Can and some other Vietnamese diplomats could speak English so well when they didn't grow up with it. Bill's reaction to this mystery, as it was to anything else involving the Vietnamese, was to develop a conspiracy theory as an explanation. Bill theorized that Can and others who could speak English well might have been taught by American POWs who remained behind after the war. Bill got the idea from a story in the international press about a Japanese girl who had been kidnapped years ago by North Korean special operations types and forced to teach Japanese to agents in North Korea.

This conspiracy on the part of the Koreans was something Bill had no problem in transferring immediately to the Vietnamese. Bill never stopped to consider other plausible explanations, such as the fact that the Vietnamese we dealt with in the Foreign Ministry were the cream of the crop of the nation intellectually; hence, learning a foreign language well would have been a minor challenge for them.

Bill Bell had flown to Honolulu a week before Mather and I left Bangkok with the Vietnamese. He was to be the primary interpreter and was getting a preview of all of the briefings at CILHI and JCRC that would be given to the delegation.

Harvey, as the commander of JCRC, had been scheduled to host the delegations, but he came down with malaria from a recent excavation in Laos and spent the entire time in the hospital. LTC Jordan, the Deputy Commander of JCRC, took over Harvey's functions and oversaw all of the details of the visit.

Mather and I checked the six Vietnamese into a fancy hotel in downtown Honolulu and they stayed in two rooms. They wanted to all stay in one room, but the hotel only allowed four adults in each room, so they had to get two. When I started travelling around Vietnam during the MIA investigations, the Vietnamese always stayed in one room in the Vietnamese guest houses.

It was in Honolulu that I started to get to know Ngo Hoang well. Hoang, an older man with gray hair and a hilarious sense of humor, always broke out in loud laughter when he heard something funny. Hoang was born in the South and had willingly gone north at the time of the partition of the country in 1953. He had fought against the French as a combat soldier. His overseas assignments as a diplomat accredited by the Vietnamese Foreign Ministry had been in India and the Philippines.

Our time together in Honolulu started a friendship that would continue over the next two years during the MIA investigations all over Vietnam. Hoang and I travelled together frequently and would talk about just about every issue under the sun. I believe him to be a fine, moral man even though he's a communist to the core.

Bill Bell used to call him "Bac," which is a highly revered term for "most senior uncle." "Bac" means that the person you are talking to is older than your father, which, given the respect due to the aged in Vietnam, signifies an elevated position. Ho Chi Minh, for example, was called "Bac Ho." Hoang was not older than Bill's father, and should have been called "Chu," which would be the title of address for someone younger than your father. But Bill always called him "Bac" and David Atherton and I picked it up and called him that too. Hoang wanted to know what I did in the Army, so I told him in general terms that I had been in military intelligence for my entire career. I even told him about my job of targeting B-52 strikes during the Vietnam War. Hoang conveyed that he too had been in intelligence during the French War as a member of a Viet Minh reconnaissance unit. Hoang expressed that it was important for countries, regardless of political ideology, to have strong and competent intelligence services.

In Honolulu Bill took the Vietnamese to a place where they could get Japanese stereo radios really cheap. All six bought identical stereos. I took several of the Vietnamese over to the Good Will Store and they thought they had died and gone to Heaven. They bought all sorts of used kitchen ware and clothing.

At the end of the conference, Mather, Bill Bell, and I escorted the six Vietnamese back to Bangkok. They spent one day there before flying back to Vietnam. Bill Bell got special permission from the American Embassy to have them over to his house for a party. Permission was necessary because we were not allowed to have anything to do with Vietnamese outside of official functions. The U.S. did not have diplomatic relations with Vietnam and any personal contacts outside of official business was prohibited. The Vietnamese had a great time at Bill's house and years later they would mention how much fun they had. They particularly enjoyed meeting and talking to Bill's Vietnamese wife, Xuan.

The trip to Honolulu had been my first prolonged contact with Vietnamese from the part of Vietnam that my country had been at war with just a few years before. During the next two years as I travelled through Vietnam, I got to know many other Vietnamese as well. I really enjoyed meeting them and finding out their philosophies on life; what they did during the war, if they were about my age; how they felt about Americans; and their hopes for the future.

When I would first meet Vietnamese in Vietnam, it amazed them to no end that I could speak Vietnamese. When I'd walk through the streets of Hanoi, or wherever, and stop and chat with the locals, they would almost fall over when I spoke to them in Vietnamese. Then when I would tell them I was from the United States, they'd almost fall over again. A double surprise. Not only a foreigner speaking Vietnamese, but a tool of capitalist America to boot! Vietnamese frequently hang out in night clubs, which are social places to sit around and visit friends. Although alcoholic beverages are sold in the clubs, the usual fare is Vietnamese green tea. Vietnamese of both sexes go to night clubs to talk, listen to music, and generally kill time. Spending hours in a night club in the evenings doesn't have the same connotation as hanging out in a bar would have in the United States.

After a day of conducting MIA investigations, American team members would usually wander over to the main drag of whatever community in which they were staying and visit the local night clubs. We attracted a lot of attention because Vietnamese aren't used to seeing Americans, particularly in their night clubs. One by one they would come over to our table to find out where we were from and what we were doing in their community.

Often in such places I would run into combat veterans who had gone down the Ho Chi Minh Trail in the old days and fought against Americans in the South. When I first started travelling to Vietnam, I was hesitant about saying I had been a soldier in South Vietnam during the war, but I found most held no prejudice against me for having served. Toward the end of my tour of duty in JCRC, I openly told the Vietnamese all about where I had been in South Vietnam during the war, though I remained reluctant to tell them I targeted B-52 strikes. I just assumed that someone who survived a B-52 strike might harbor a resentment against a soldier who was involved in those operations.

I don't think American soldiers would be as willing to let bygones be bygones as the former North Vietnamese and Viet Cong soldiers were to me and other veterans like Bill Bell, Jim Coyle, and Dave Atherton. I've run into many American veterans over the years who hated Vietnamese. I never saw the same kind of hatred on the part of Vietnamese veterans.

In fact, I was only aware of two minor instances when American members of the team ran into local people who expressed any negative feelings against them. I can't say the same for other countries I've visited such as Panama and Mexico. In Vietnam the local people were almost always courteous and would generally say something positive when they would meet us, such as, "America, Number One!" And when they would say it, they would usually give a big smile and a thumbs up.

When I would meet local people, invariably one thing they would talk about, assuming public security officers were not around, was how bad the economic conditions were in Vietnam. They could barely make ends meet. In fact, some parts of the country existed year after year under such depressing conditions I have no idea how the people even survived. Each month they made only a tiny pittance, yet food prices were high. And when the government ended the complicated system of subsidies in 1989 that kept the prices of certain food staples artificially low, many Vietnamese families suffered tragically.

The elimination of the subsidy system had to be done for Vietnam to make any kind of economic progress, though it was incredibly painful. Scarce food items, with low subsidized prices, were actually being used as fodder for farm animals. In a time of extreme economic hardship, waste was rampant.

When I was travelling through Vietnam, most Vietnamese made an equivalent of fifty cents a day. As long as they could keep their living expenses at that level, they could somehow make it. When they reached the point where they couldn't survive any longer on that amount—when their living expenses reached a dollar a day—it was then they loaded up their families into boats and headed to what they believed would eventually be the promised land of the United States, Canada, or Australia. In 1989 and 1990, as a result of the drastic revisions in the subsidy programs, Vietnamese refugees poured out of Vietnam in record numbers, only to find the resettlement countries would no longer would take them.

Most of the Vietnamese who fled the country have come from places where it was relatively easy to leave. Areas along the coast that had a fishing industry were particularly susceptible to an escaping population. But areas that were landlocked and far from the traditional refugee escape route were submerged in misery. The population could not leave and had to endure the grinding poverty and despair.

I remember talking to a businessman in Hanoi once, and he was telling me how bad things were economically and how hard it was to operate a business in such an economy. I asked him why things were so bad, and he started giving me all of the official reasons, such as the war, the American embargo, and a series of natural disasters. Then he looked around to make sure no one was listening and asked me what I thought was the reason. I told him it was the fault of the government (nha nuoc). He laughed and nodded his head in the affirmative.

The Vietnamese economy has gone through so many ups and downs and played havoc with Vietnamese life, but in recent years there have been some bright spots. When I visited Vietnam for the last time in 1990, the economy in Hanoi seemingly was coming to life because of all of the capitalist measures Vietnam was adopting. In contrast, in the past, life in Hanoi had been pure hell, even for senior government officials. And with the horrible economic conditions, the state security apparatus was even more vigilant in watching for those who might express dissent.

Bill Bell told me a story about the economic plight of some local people he saw in Hanoi in the early 80s, when so many Boat People were fleeing Vietnam. One afternoon, he and other members of an American delegation stopped at a sidewalk refreshment stand in Hanoi and bought soft drinks and peanuts. Bill said the peanuts were rancid and he and the other with him didn't eat them. Bill recalls that after they paid the bill and were walking off, several local people, who had been watching from a distance, ran over and quickly scooped up the foul-tasting peanuts.

Doing any kind of business transaction in Vietnam with a government-run business is a mess. Checking out of hotels takes forever, getting a clerk to wait on you is like pulling teeth, and generally doing anything requiring a government employee to perform some sort of service on your behalf is a major undertaking. On a number of occasions I've tried to buy something in a store, only to be told, "I can't help you, the person who operates that counter isn't here."

The American team members used to joke that Vietnamese workers had the "RCA dog look." If you remember, on RCA records the corporation logo was a dog with its head tilted to one side and an ear up against the horn of an old-time radio. Often as we would drive around Vietnam, we'd see Vietnamese standing around with their hands in their pockets, their heads tilted to one side, and their mouths open hence the apt American description of the Vietnamese look.

I'm convinced that a government controlled economy creates indolence and leads to all kinds of negative social phenomenon. In Vietnam so many people are idle or underemployed, and as a result the typical stance is one of able-bodied people standing around with their hands in their pockets doing nothing. Years of inactivity tends to do that to people.

One thing that surprised me about Vietnam was the number of beggars and homeless people. I had always thought of a socialist country as eradicating things like that, but they definitely exist there. And it's not just Vietnam, I also saw pitiful beggars in China. Socialism does very little about the social problems that it's usually given undue credit for solving.

When I first travelled to Hanoi in 1987 as a member of one of Harvey's delegations, Hanoi was a dump. The economy was terrible, public services were a mess, and the city generally looked dilapidated. But that was the old Hanoi. When I last visited Hanoi in March of 1990, the city was clean and little shops and stores had sprung up everywhere—seemingly overnight. I haven't seen Hanoi for a while, but my guess is that it has progressed even more by now. I believe the reason for the dramatic improvements was the capitalist measures implemented by the government to give a shot in the arm to the economy. One of the economic decrees was that it was now possible to have up to twenty employees without taking the state in as a partner. Just a touch of capitalism worked wonders.

On one iteration, JCRC sent a U.S. Air Force C-130 transport aircraft to Ho Chi Minh City to pick up a joint U.S.- Vietnamese team that had been doing forensic work in a public security office. Vietnamese public security officers had confiscated skeletons from dealers, who were trying to pawn them off to unsuspecting opportunists as MIA remains. The team was examining the remains to see if any of them could possibly be Caucasian or Negroid (none were; all were Mongoloid). The plane picked the Vietnamese and American team members up in Ho Chi Minh City and transported them to Hanoi. I was watching as the plane was being unloaded in Hanoi, and to my surprise off came a pallet of tables and chairs. I investigated the phenomenon further and found out that one of the senior Vietnamese members of the team was starting a restaurant in Hanoi, and he had taken advantage of the trip to purchase furniture for his business. He had nice tastes, too.

Here was a Communist Party member engaging openly in the evil of all evils: capitalism. And ironically the U.S. taxpayer was footing the bill for the delivery of his restaurant furniture. I couldn't pass up the opportunity to kid him about it and call him a capitalist.

Vietnam has also made basic changes in its socialist agricultural policies and initiated capitalist incentives at the farm family level. Huge government-run farms still exist in Vietnam, but grass-root changes have been initiated in regard to letting families own cattle and negotiate profit arrangements on farm plots. Within an amazingly short period of time, Vietnam has become the third largest exporter of rice in the world, after the United States and Thailand.

Vietnam is definitely doing much better, and hopefully the communist party hacks who made such a mess of the Vietnamese economy in the first place aren't waiting in the wings to take it all back.

People ask me if American team members were followed when we were travelling around Vietnam. The answer is, no. The state security apparatus, which is invisible but very real, does not follow people around. State security has informants in every hamlet of every village and every block of every town and city and doesn't need to follow you anywhere. Any time a stranger, not necessarily a foreigner, enters an area where he normally does not work or visit, the antenna of the local informants go up, and the stranger's movements and contacts are reported.

There generally is no problem now with Vietnamese talking with Americans. But according to the Vietnamese, at one time during the hyper period of vigilance after the war, conversation with a foreigner, particularly an American, would mean the knock at the door in the middle of the night and a sentence without trial in a re-education camp.

The state security system operates like zone defense in basketball. Defensive players don't follow offensive players around on the basketball court. Defensive players are responsible for a zone, and when an opposing player enters, the person responsible for the zone watches the offensive player until he or she leaves the zone.

In Vietnam, just as in Cuba, the state security system is overwhelming. These countries follow the principle of the "tenth man," in which every tenth person is an informant. The same was true in Eastern Europe before the sweeping political changes. At a gathering of ten people, one will be reporting on the activities of the other nine. Since the majority of employees work for the government, the state security system exists also in the work place. Each duty section has an informant reporting on the political loyalties of the other employees.

At times state security lets up, just as it did in China, but it is always watching and taking notes. Should the cat start trying to get out of the bag, state security agents appear from seemingly nowhere to tie up the bag.

Once I asked a government official, whom I had gotten to know fairly well, if Vietnamese could listen to Voice of America without getting into trouble.

He said, "Of course! If you have an ear plug stuck in your ear, how is anyone going to know what you are listening to? How could anyone possibly control such a thing?"

Then he said, "That's the problem with you Americans. You always believe the worst about Vietnam."

I said, "I've heard some other things about Vietnam and I wonder if they are true. I've heard there are prisons all over the country filled with people who have criticized the government. Is that true?"

He thought for a minute and said, "I think that's probably true."

Bill Bell and I were in Hanoi once at a night club when local people came over to talk to us. This was when I first started going to Vietnam and wasn't sure about how things worked in Hanoi in regard to security matters. I told our guests we didn't want them to get in trouble with security people in the neighborhood and it might be better if they not join us. They said it wouldn't be any problem. They knew who the "antennas" were and if any of them came in, they would leave.

As I became more aware of how the country functioned, I realized the local people knew their limits and what they could get away with. As long as they portrayed the correct public attitude and were careful in their conversation with certain people, their minds were free. Those who were unable to play the game correctly ended up in re-education camps.

I spent hours talking with my Vietnamese counterparts on the MIA investigative teams. Sometimes we would drive for days to get to an investigative site, and I really got to know them well after having been in a vehicle with them hour after hour, day after day.

Our Vietnamese counterparts were all loyal Communist Party members. They never, even in their unguarded moments, gave any hint of being dissatisfied with the regime or its policies. They were definitely the "New Socialist Man" and had all of the benefits of Vietnamese society. They did not live well by Western standards by any stretch of the imagination, but they were the ones who could be considered successful in Vietnam.

A few of our counterparts were revolutionaries from the old days. I already mentioned a little of Ngo Hoang's background. Ho Xuan Dich, who would eventually be my counterpart when I led an MIA investigative team in the Ashau Valley, was, like Hoang, a diplomat accredited by the Vietnamese Foreign Ministry. In the old days, Dich had been imprisoned in French jails, and had fought in the Battle of Dien Bien Phu. Once on a trip to Hue, Dich pointed out to the Americans in his vehicle a place where he had been imprisoned for a period of time by the French. He also showed me his war wounds. He had scars all over his legs that he said were caused by a French grenade.

I had gotten to know Ngo Hoang fairly well in Honolulu, and as we travelled around Vietnam I got to know him even better. He is an old revolutionary and definitely believes in the communist system, yet he's a genuinely nice guy. He used to like to debate with me constantly, in a friendly way. He would hit me with Marxist theories that I recalled studying in Political Science 101 as a college freshman, but I hadn't heard of or thought about since.

As an example, he talked to me once about the Marxist Theory of Surplus Value. He explained to me that if a capitalist hires a worker for five dollars and sells the fruit of the worker's labor for ten dollars, then he has effectively stolen five dollars from him. I laughed and said that was ridiculous. I argued in return that the capitalist was an investor who was risking his money in a business enterprise. The worker was able to participate in the fruit of the capitalist's investment without having to put up one dime of his own money.

Hoang related to me the Marxist Theory of History. He said in the beginning of human history, individuals formed tribes for protection. As society progressed, the tribes evolved into feudal societies, which evolved into capitalism, and which will ultimately evolve into socialism. Socialism, in the natural progression of time, will become communism where everyone works according to his ability and takes out according to his need. Also, the state will wither away in this magical kingdom. I told Hoang the idea that socialism would turn into communism was a fairy tale and I couldn't believe he could actually believe such a thing.

I said, "You don't really believe that, do you Uncle?"

He answered, "Yes, I believe it with all my heart."

I told him that socialism was an aberration of human history that is doomed to failure, and capitalism democracies will be the wave of the future.

Little did I know it, but in Eastern Europe and the Soviet Union it would be happen much sooner than I thought.

As we drove around Vietnam, I'd point out to Hoang what I would see as glaring deficiencies of socialism, and Hoang would tell me, "Don't look at Vietnam as an example of socialism. Vietnam is not a good example of a socialist system."

Then I said, "Well, where is a good example of socialism?"

This was before the overnight radical changes in Eastern Europe and socialism still reigned supreme in those countries. I figured Hoang would try to argue those countries were good examples of socialism, but he didn't. He just said, "Well, there are some good examples."

I pressed him and said, "Well, where?"

He laughed and waved his hand and said, "Somewhere."

Hoang and I never argued. We just bantered back and forth in a good natured way. Hoang is incredibly bright and interesting in talking and debating about everything: religion, politics, customs, the war in which Vietnam had been involved, or whatever. His interests and opinions are boundless.

Ngo Hoang had the ability to give and take, and he would break into a loud guffaw if you scored a point. But Ho Xuan Dich was serious and doctrinaire. Dich was definitely the hardest of the hard-core, but he also had a sense of humor that we would work on until we got him laughing.

Dave Atherton used to tell him, "Under capitalism, man exploits man; but under communism, it's the other way around."

Dich wouldn't get it, and would say in his high-pitched voice, "Yes, yes, that's correct, capitalism exploits man and communism doesn't. Yes, that's definitely true."

Dave and I worked on the witty saying with Dich for days, but he still couldn't figure out what we meant. Dave and I got out a dictionary and looked up all of the possible Vietnamese meanings for "the other way around" and "just the opposite."

Finally after days of trying, Dave somehow finally hit the right meaning, and Dich's face brightened. "I get it!" he squealed in his high-pitched voice. "They're the same!"

I talked for hours with Dich. Americans often see him as a comic figure because of his eccentric mannerisms, but he's very astute and well aware of what is going on in Vietnam and the rest of the world.

Dich told me that Vietnam had no intentions of ever giving up socialism. He said socialism in Vietnam followed Ho Chi Minh's philosophy of two steps forward, one step back. Dich said it's very true that socialist development in Vietnam had run into severe economic problems, but the Vietnamese Communist Party's strategy is not to give up everything it had fought and sacrificed for over the years. Dich said it may seem Vietnam is adopting capitalist principles, and indeed in some ways it is, but the Communist Party is merely taking one step back to regroup before continuing the country on the socialist path to communism.

Dich said Vietnam went from feudalism to socialism without going through capitalism. He said that what the Communist Party was doing was allowing the development of a capitalist base, but maintaining sufficient controls to avoid the injustices inherent in capitalism. At an undetermined period of time in the future, the Communist Party of Vietnam would assume state ownership of the private businesses that had developed and take two steps forward into socialism.

When we Americans travelled around Vietnam, occasionally officials would extol the virtues of the Vietnamese revolution, but generally they knew Vietnam was a basket case and didn't insult our intelligence with such drivel. But every now and then a local official would say something that had a superior overtone of a teacher correcting an errant student. Once a province official asked me what changes I had observed in South Vietnam since the "puppet" (nguy) government had been deposed in 1975. I'm sure he was expecting that I would say that I had seen wonderful, miraculous changes in the South under the new regime. I told him that, yes, indeed, I had seen changes; South Vietnam under the "puppet" government was so much richer and more modern.

I could tell from his expression that wasn't what he wanted to hear.

Not often, but occasionally, the Americans would get hit with little digs from local officials about American aggression. When we first started visiting Vietnam, we'd ignore them, but after a while we'd say we didn't appreciate things like that. Our team members sometimes intervened on our behalf when a district or province leader made an inflammatory comment. Once Jim Coyle was attending a briefing presented by a district official who said, "The American imperialist aggressor aircraft crashed in the vicinity of...." This was just hype the local people were used to saying and I don't even think the official realized he was being offensive to the visiting Americans. Jim's Vietnamese counterpart stopped the briefing and told the speaker that Vietnam's relations with the United States had changed and that kind talk was no longer used.

Bill Bell could answer digs in a flash. Bill is like a verbal "Zorro" in his responses; suddenly his opponent would have a big "Z," or perhaps better said, a double "B," emblazoned on his chest after a Bill Bell comeback.

Once a particularly aggressive public security officer cornered Bill in a night club and was berating the American support of the South Vietnamese government during the war. Bill told him, "The reason we did that was because we were afraid you guys would lock the southerners up in re-education camps, and we just wanted to protect them. Of course, now that we know you better, we realize you guys would never had done anything like that."

One thing that amazed me in Vietnam was the openness of the population in expressing religious sentiment. In spite of the professed atheistic policy of the government, churches and shrines throughout Vietnam are openly attended. I once visited a crowded service at a Catholic Church in Hue. Also, Buddhists make yearly pilgrimages to various shrines throughout Vietnam.

Bill Bell professes to be a Buddhist, and once his team members took him to a very special place that has a dozen or so stops for the faithful to burn incense and meditate. I watched at one shrine as Bill lit candles and offered prayers. I think Bill was completely serious about his adopted faith. How a boy from rural Texas could ever have become such a proficient Vietnamese and Thai linguist and have such exotic spiritual interests, I'll never know.

A Vietnamese official told me once that you couldn't be a party member and be actively involved in religious services. The Vietnamese members of our teams all professed to be atheists, but when we would pass Buddhist shrines, several would bow their heads and put their hands in a praying position. I'd usually comment that I didn't think new socialist men should be doing something like that, which would usually cause a sheepish grin.

Our team members were very superstitious. For example, anytime we were taking photographs there must not be three people in the picture. If there were, that meant something bad was going to happen to one of them.

I'd laugh and say, "Look, you don't believe in the supernatural, right?"

And they would answer, "Of course not."

Then I'd say, "Then what difference does it make if three people are in a photograph? Are you telling me the bogey-man, which you don't believe in, is going to get you because you were the third guy in a picture?"

Then without even paying any attention to the logic of my argument, they would say, "Oh, but it's bad luck to do that."

Dave was all the time pulling practical jokes on the Vietnamese team members. Once when we were in the Ashau Valley, our team members asked us for Doxycycline to protect themselves from malaria. But they were concerned that the medication might cause impotence. Dave assured them that malarial medication wouldn't make them impotent.

So assured, they took the medication, but decided they would double the dosage for a couple of days to make up for the days they hadn't been taking any. One morning at breakfast, Tran Trien, our state security team member, took his two tablets while Dave and I watched.

Dave nonchalantly asked him, "Mr. Trien, did you take your malaria medicine this morning?" Trien told Dave that he had.

Dave asked, "How many did you take?"

"I took two."

In mock horror, Dave yelled, "Two! Oh, no! You were only supposed to take one! You're going to be impotent for the rest of your life!"

All of the Vietnamese at the table looked at Dave with their mouths open and fear showing in their eyes. They also had taken two tablets. But I couldn't keep a straight face and they quickly realized Dave was pulling their leg. We all burst out laughing.

Once several years ago, Bill Bell, a Vietnamese diplomat, and myself were travelling in the same vehicle back to Hanoi from an investigation. As we were driving along we started talking about the bases in the Philippines. I commented to the diplomat that what Vietnam should do would be to lease Cam Ranh Bay to the Americans, so the United States could pull out of the Philippines. The diplomat laughed and took it as a joke, which it was.

But then I said, "Think of what Vietnam could do with the money that the United States pays the Philippines every year."

After thinking of the money angle of the deal, it didn't seem to be such a bad idea anymore. Bill and I could see that the wheels in the diplomat's head were really turning.

A few days after we returned to Bangkok, the Vietnamese government announced over its international radio service that the United States would be welcome to begin resumption of its use of the facilities at Cam Ranh Bay.

Bill and I couldn't believe it. The coincidence was unreal. We had always suspected the Vietnamese were reporting everything we said, and we wondered if the Vietnamese diplomat had given the higher ups in the government the idea about Cam Ranh Bay.

We knew that whenever a Vietnamese official told us something, it wasn't just an offhand remark. Anything they said had been approved for release. Bill and I wondered if perhaps they saw us the way they saw themselves and assumed anything we told them had to be officially approved. Who knows.

One thing is for certain, Vietnam is fully in control of its own destiny. Whatever path it chooses to follow, it will be its own choice and not someone else's. Vietnam may be a poor country, but it's completely in charge of whether it will continue on in socialism or develop a capitalist democracy. This is in contrast to other poor countries, like the Philippines, whose future is unknown. Without question, Vietnam is master of its fate and captain of its soul.

The author and Air Force Master Sergeant Gary Flanagan en route to a mountain crash site in Northwestern Vietnam.

The author interviewing a crash witness.

David Atherton and the author with Vietnamese province officials.

The author interviewing a witness to a crash.

CHAPTER 10

MIA TEAM LEADER

In late November of 1988, JCRC was making plans for the Third Iteration that was to occur the first couple of weeks of December of that year. LTC Harvey had designated me as a team leader of a third investigative team, in addition to the two teams that had been investigating in Vietnam during the last two iterations.

One morning during that time period, LTC Harvey called the Liaison Office from Honolulu wanting to talk to Bill Bell. Bill was not in the office and neither was Jim Coyle, so Harvey asked to speak with me.

Harvey didn't beat around the bush. He asked, "Do you know anything about some heavy drinking that's been going on by some of the guys on the teams during the iterations?"

I paused before I answered, and then mumbled a barely audible, "Yes, sir."

I don't know how Harvey found out about it, but a couple of the guys had been putting away quite a bit of booze. It was done in Hanoi and off-duty, but several of the team members were getting blitzed immediately before and after investigations. One of the guys was fortunate that he wasn't hurt one night when he fell down the stairs in a restaurant in Hanoi.

Harvey asked who the individuals were, and I haltingly told him the names of two of the team members I had seen polluted at times. I didn't want to answer, but when a commander of a military organization asks a specific lawful question, then his subordinate is obligated by law to tell him the truth.

Harvey was furious. He asked, "Well, did Bell say anything to them about it?"

"No, sir."

"Did you say anything to them about it?"

"No, sir."

"Did Jim Coyle say anything to them about it?"

"No, sir."

Harvey was livid. I thought he was going to have a stroke on the telephone. He said, "I expect you guys to be in charge. You and your folks are representing the United States government and JCRC. If you, Jim, or Bill see something that you know to be wrong, you will correct it! Do you understand?"

"Yes, sir."

"Are you aware of anything else that the guys have done I should know about?"

I was afraid Harvey was going to ask that. I muttered a reply: "Yes, sir."

I told him that Bell was concerned that two of the guys had slipped out of the guest house in Son La in the middle of the night and went wandering around on their own in the town. Bell told me that most of the towns in Vietnam have a curfew, and he was concerned that they could easily have been picked up or even shot by the Son La Public Security Service.

Harvey started in again on whether or not Bell or I had said anything to them about it, and all I could answer was a weak, "No, sir."

When Bill came in to work, I told him what had happened and he was not at all pleased. He liked being the guy in charge and he could visualize some senior officer going to Vietnam with us to baby sit because of all this. Harvey called back later and took Bill through the ringer just as he had taken me. Bill never said so, but I knew he was irritated with me. I don't know what he expected me to do in the situation, but I wasn't going to lie to the boss. But I also knew that Bill was concerned that a couple of the guys were getting a little rambunctious and needed to be brought under control—which Harvey did back at Honolulu before they left on their flight to Bangkok.

On the 5th of December, 1988, our JCRC investigative teams boarded a U.S. Air Force C-130 transport aircraft at the military side of the Don Muong International Airport in Bangkok. The C-130 had been flown in from the Philippines to support our operations. We departed Bangkok, crossed Laos, and landed at the Noi Bai International Airport in Hanoi. Our U.S.-taxpayer-bought Jeep Cherokees were waiting for us to take us to the old Foreign Ministry building in Hanoi where we had our gear stored. We loaded up the vehicles with our equipment, had a meal, and headed south down Highway 1, the major north-to-south highway that runs all the way down to Ho Chi Minh City (formerly Saigon).

The three teams were composed of nine Americans and an equivalent number of Vietnamese, not including drivers. We were on the highway, truly an exaggeration to call it that, from early afternoon until late at night. We finally arrived at the town of Vinh in Nghe Tinh Province at about 11:30 p.m., where we stayed at the state-run guest house.

From the outside, the guest house looked like a modern building. But on the inside it was a dump, as places like that usually are in Vietnam. In Hanoi and Ho Chi Minh City, several of the hotels meet what could be considered minimal Western standards, but I haven't seen any other places that come close to what an average American would expect in the way of accommodations and services.

As a major staging point at the beginning of the Ho Chi Minh Trail, Vinh was a city that had been attacked often by American aircraft during the war. North Vietnamese troops and truck traffic would assemble in the vicinity of Vinh and head west to Laos, and from there would enter Vietnam or continue on to Cambodia and then into Vietnam.

After I left JCRC, my good friend Army Chief Warrant Officer (retired) Melborne (Buzz) Wilhelm told me that during the war, one of his missions as an imagery interpretation specialist was to locate targets from aerial photography in and around Vinh. Buzz told me that Vinh had been totally decimated. He said one of things he remembered from the photographs of Vinh was the ruins of a huge Catholic church. I told Buzz the city had been totally rebuilt since the war and about the only destruction still present was the ruins of the church, which I had visited. Little else can be seen as evidence of years of American bombing.

The next morning while still at the guest house, we broke into three teams with three Vietnamese and three Americans on each team. Ngo Hoang, from the Vietnamese Foreign Ministry, and I were the team leaders for our joint team. My good friend Dave Atherton was to be the team NCOIC. Bill assigned a CILHI graves registration specialist to us to make up the third team member.

Bill Bell and Jim Coyle's teams travelled further south down Highway 1 to Dong Hoi town, which they were to use as a base to investigate sites in rugged terrain in Binh Tri Tien Province and on the Laotian border. Soviet helicopters with Vietnamese pilots were to be flown to a nearby PAVN (People's Army of Vietnam) base to support them, but during the entire time of the investigation the weather was miserable and the aircraft were not able to get off the ground. As a result, Bill and Jim's team ended up investigating cases by vehicle and were unable to finish all of the cases that had been assigned to them.

My team stayed in Vinh and met with representatives of the Nghe Tinh Province People's Committee, who would be escorting our team to various crash sites in Nghe Tinh province. Hoang, Dave, and I had a meeting with several representatives of the province people's committee and put together a plan of actions of what we wanted to do during the iteration.

After the morning meeting, our joint team and province representatives travelled further south on Highway 1 to Ha Tinh town, where we got rooms at the local guest house. The guest house, a province government business, was very neat and tidy, unlike most places where we stayed in Vietnam. The husband and wife management team, even though they were government employees, were conscientious and had really gone out of their way to fix up the place. They even employed a gardener who cut bushes around the guest house into the shapes of animals. This was the first of several pleasant trips that Dave and I would make to Ha Tinh, and we got to know the guest house employees well. We particularly liked the food they prepared; once they even put on the dog for us, literally. More about that in a minute.

In the late afternoon, our team and province representatives all drove over to the headquarters of the Thach Ha District People's Committee, which was located just outside of Ha Tinh. There we met district cadre and talked to them about a crash incident that had occurred in their district during the war. We were particularly interested in a case where the pilot was seen to have ejected with a good chute. A Vietnamese army captain, who was a member of the district people's committee, briefed about a crash incident that appeared to match the MIA case we wanted to investigate. But the members of the people's committee all played dumb when it came to the fate of the pilot. In fact, they looked almost embarrassed when we asked them if there were any witnesses that we could interview about what may have happened to the pilot.

After the meeting, representatives of the Thach Ha District People's Committee called Ngo Hoang over for a meeting to which Dave Atherton and I had obviously been excluded. Dave and I wondered what was going on.

A few minutes later, Hoang came out of the meeting and said he had something to tell us. He said the people's committee had told him that the local militia had gunned down the pilot of the case we were investigating. Hoang said the pilot had landed safely, tried to make it to a search and rescue helicopter, but was gunned down before he reached the helicopter. Hoang added that during the escape attempt, the pilot shot and killed a Vietnamese female militia member.

The next morning, the joint team, the province representatives, and the district representatives (quite a large entourage by now) travelled to Viet Xuyen village, Thach Ha district, Nghe Tinh province to investigate the case in which the pilot had been killed. Hoang told me that the village lost forty four people back during the war, and he didn't know what our reception would be like.

But our greeting was pleasant. The village turned out for us and we were met by the chairman (a woman) of the village people's committee, the village party secretary, and a number of other local village officials. At the village we interviewed witnesses to the incident, one of whom was the brother of the female militia member who had been killed by the pilot. After interviewing several villagers, we took a walk through the rice fields where the incident occurred. We paused briefly several times on the way while the witnesses told us what had happened at the various places. As Dave and I stood at the very spot where the pilot died, we felt like we were involved in something almost sacred.

There are a number of details about this case that I don't want to get into in consideration of the feelings of the surviving family members of the MIA. I will just synopsize the investigation by saying that the remains of the pilot were recovered and repatriated at a moving ceremony in Hanoi. Back at CILHI in Honolulu, the remains were proven by dental examination to pertain to the pilot of the incident.

After we left Viet Xuyen village, I told Hoang that I was relieved that our reception had been good. He said it was obvious to him that the villagers did not hold us responsible for what had happened during the war to their village. He told me the crime (his words) was Johnson's and Nixon's, not the American people's.

The next day, the team drove to the headquarters of Cam Xuyen district, also in Nghe Tinh Province, where we met representatives of the Cam Xuyen District People's Committee. Our joint team was briefed by the district's military representative regarding information they had discovered about an MIA case we had asked the district to look into. The case involved an American aircraft that was reported missing after it had attacked a target in the vicinity of Cam Nhuong Village, which was located within the district in which we were now in.

After the briefing by the district's military officer representative, our joint team, plus province representatives, plus district representatives, plus Cam Nhuong village personnel, travelled to Cam Nhuong Village. Our large entourage of vehicles and officials looked more like a circus parade than an MIA investigative team. We all went in convoy to a fishing cooperative in Cam Nhuong village, Cam Xuyen District. There the Americans were shown around the cooperative like touring celebrities. We were given the grand tour of the boats, the processing equipment, and the catch of the day, which included huge lobsters.

At the fishing cooperative, Dave and I interviewed the wartime commander of an antiaircraft battery who said that the aircraft had crashed in the ocean just off the coast, and sank. The pilot had not exited the aircraft. The former antiaircraft battery commander took us to the spot where his antiaircraft gun was located when the aircraft was shot down. He pointed in the distance to an area of ocean where the plane had crashed.

Hoang rented a thirty foot motorized fishing boat and a crew, and we sailed out to the water crash site. We anchored directly over the crash and took azimuth readings to determine our exact location. Dave used a fishing line to estimate the depth of the water (about 30 feet).

Another fishing boat pulled up along side of us and gave us several kilograms of shrimp they had caught. The boat crew boiled the shrimp which we ate for lunch. What an ironic turn of events! American and Vietnamese officials and soldiers were eating shrimp together on a boat with a former soldier who commanded the air defense batteries that shot down the aircraft that was directly below us. Strange is too weak of a word to describe what I felt at the time.

After taking measurements and notes, and after ministering to our fellow Vietnamese team members, who survived the Ho Chi Minh trail and years of combat in the South, but fell easy victim to a gently rocking boat, we returned to land. We were met by perhaps a thousand people who lined the shore to get a look at the Americans.

We were literally mobbed, and even the Public Security Service personnel had difficulty keeping the press of the crowds away from us. Some of them even used switches to literally beat the kids off of us when they got too close. We found that in the larger towns we got only curious stares, but here in the rural areas we were a major attraction that might have just as well come from Mars.

One difficulty that we had when surrounded by hundreds of people was finding a place to use the rest room.

Everywhere we went in rural areas we were followed by crowds of curious people who were watching our every move. One of the more humorous moments occurred once when Dave Atherton found an outhouse, which he decided to take advantage of. A mob of several hundred Vietnamese surrounded the outhouse while he was inside.

Another funny incident happened about this time when an adult local villager asked me what country I was from. I answered, "I'm from the United States."

He said "Oh yes, Bei-jing."

I replied, "No, the United States."

He then said, "Cu-ba?"

I said, "No, no, America. The United States (Hoa Ky. My)."

Then he nodded very sagely, "Oh, yes, of course.

Mos-co-ba."

The brief conversation left questions in my mind regarding the quality of the Vietnamese educational system of Cam Nhuong Village.

Several years later I was in Hong Kong at a refugee camp when a teenage Vietnamese refugee told me about the day Americans came to his village and rented a boat from his uncle to go out to a water crash site. I customarily carried photographs with me to show the refugees in the camps, and I happened to have several pictures with me of when I was in Cam Nhuong Village. He was thrilled to see pictures of the home folks, most of whom he instantly recognized.

We left Cam Nhuong Village and returned to the guest house at Ha Tinh town in Thach Ha district. It was here that my team was first introduced to a Vietnamese delicacy that is worthy of mention: Seven-Course Dog (con cay bay mon). Now believe it or not, Dave and I had requested the meal. We had seen signs all over northern Vietnam advertising "Fresh and Tender Young Dog," and we wanted to give it a try. I got through most of it okay, except for the sliced dog liver. I just couldn't quite get that down.

Dave told the CILHI graves registration specialist with us that it was goat. During the meal Dave started making doggie sounds, and our fellow team member finally caught on. He was not at all amused. He expressed in no uncertain terms that we had unfairly taken advantage of him in getting him to eat a food that was loathsome to him. He undoubtedly was right.

When we got back to Bangkok and I related our latest adventures, the embassy doctor told me, "If you guys are eating dog meat, you're fools." He said dogs are extremely susceptible to rabies, and cooking will not kill the rabies virus. He said if we got the symptoms we were going to die.

Needless to say I didn't knowingly eat any more dog meat. Jim Coyle took further precautions and had the rabies vaccination just to be sure. I planned to do it, but it is a three-shot affair, once a week for three weeks, and I never was in Bangkok long enough to get all three shots scheduled.

The next morning, the team went to Thach Ngoc Plantation, a state-run farm that employs thousands of people. We went there to investigate a crash incident that occurred on the farm during the war. The case was not on the "70-Name List," but was one of several secondary cases that we carried around in the event we found we had extra investigative time.

The investigation of the case on the state farm turned out to be a bonus for us. We were going to the farm anyway to look at the crash site of the aircraft of the case we had just investigated, the one in which the pilot had been shot by the militia. On the way over to the farm, Dave suddenly had an idea that we might could make a quick stop at a nearby hamlet just to look around and ask a few questions about another case. On Dave's maps was a symbol that another crash had occurred near the hamlet, and he wanted to see if anyone there knew anything about it. He figured it would only take a few minutes to make the detour, ask a few general questions, and then move on to our primary destination.

We drove into the small hamlet that was part of the farm system, and we saw a jet aircraft engine lying on the ground out in the open. We got out and examined it and saw that it was perforated with holes, likely from 14.7mm antiaircraft rounds. The rounds had pierced the extremely hard metal in the engine like a hot knife going through butter. We asked Hoang to find witnesses for us to question later about the aircraft engine, and he said he would.

We drove over to the state farm, and in the midst of a mob of people trying to get a glimpse of us, we were cordially greeted by the director of the plantation. In addition to being in charge of the plantation, he also held the position as the state farm's Communist Party secretary. Usually the position of director of a state enterprise and party secretary are separate, but for some reason he held both.

The director was a young guy in his late twenties. He's part of the new breed of educated bureaucrat the government is trying to develop to rescue socialism. All over Vietnam, state enterprises have been entrusted to young executives with the intention that their vigor, youth, and new ideas will pull the socialist economy out of the doldrums. The young executives have been educated in universities in the socialist countries, to include Cuba. (I occasionally spoke Spanish with several of them.) The old warriors from the past, who in previous years served in the leadership roles in state enterprises, hadn't been done away with; they merely had been moved over and were serving as advisers to the new leadership.

We walked to the crash site of the aircraft of the pilot who had been killed by the militia. It was a gigantic water-filled crater that villagers had dug into many times over the years to extract metal. We went to a nearby hamlet (a number of hamlets usually make up a village) and looked at pieces of aircraft metal that local people had carried off. It was at the hamlet that we ran into the largest mob of people to date. They trampled gardens and tore down banana plants in their zeal to get a close look at the Americans.

We were invited to lunch hosted by the director of the state farm. The dining room was in a large room decorated with pictures of Ho Chi Minh, Lenin, Engels, and Marx. During the meal I attempted to make small talk with a uniformed state security officer who was sitting at the end of the table away from the others. He was the state farm political watchdog, and it was obvious he took his duties seriously. He ignored my attempts to chat with him.

After lunch, the director introduced us to witnesses that we had asked Hoang to round up for us, those who knew about the aircraft engine we found. The witnesses told us the pilot had evidently ejected from his aircraft, but landed dead in his parachute. He was buried by workers at the foot of the hill on which he had landed.

Dave and I asked Hoang to hire some workers for us, and under the guidance of our graves registration specialist, we attempted to carry out an impromptu excavation to locate the grave. A storm had come up and we stood out in the rain watching the dig, which continued for the rest of the afternoon. But too many years had gone by and the workers could not recall the exact spot of the grave site, and we eventually called it off.

Several days later, the joint team departed Nghe Tinh province and moved further south down Highway One into Binh Tri Thien province. Since we were now in another province, we would have to coordinate with the officials of that province in order to investigate cases there.

Vietnam has a very strict chain-of-command—just like a military organization. In order to coordinate anything, our three Vietnamese team members from the central government— each respectively representing the Foreign Ministry, the Ministry of Defense, and the Ministry of the Interior—had to coordinate with their counterparts at the province level, which were the representative of the province foreign office, the representative of the province military command, and the representative of the state security office. Then these province officials had to coordinate with the district people's committee, the district military command, and the district security officer. The district officials then coordinated with the village or state farm people's committee. By the time we finally got down to the local level to investigate a case, we had a large group of people travelling in a caravan of U.S. Jeep Cherokees and Soviet vehicles.

Our link up with the Binh Tri Thien Province officials was to be at the town of Dong Hoi. To get to Dong Hoi, we had to cross a swift, wide river by ferry. Now when you think of a ferry in a Western country, you imagine a large boat that is self-propelled and takes a large number of passengers and vehicles efficiently from point A to point B. Not so in Vietnam. At this particular river crossing point on Highway 1, vehicles load onto a rusted barge that can hold a half-dozen trucks and cars at the most. A beat-up, rusted hulk of a boat belching black smoke pushes the barge across. The ferry has to strain upstream against the current in order to eventually drift down into the landing place on the opposite shore. Once on the other side, an awkward and hazardous unloading operation begins. Meanwhile, long lines of vehicles wait their turn to use the ferry on the return trip. Fortunately we had an official document that said we had "uu tien"—priority—which let us go to the head of the line.

In Dong Hoi we stayed at the guest house, which was typical socialist style: modern and attractive on the outside, but filthy and deteriorating on the inside. State workers shuffled around performing their duties. Also at the guest house, we met up with the two other teams that unfortunately had been grounded because of bad weather and had been unable to get out to their mountain search sites.

On 11 December, 1988, which was a Sunday, we took the day off to get a jump on the joint U.S.-Vietnamese reports that would be required of the teams before we could depart Vietnam.

Early the next morning, we departed Dong Hoi with our Binh Tri Thien Province escorts. We travelled north up Highway 1, took the ferry back across the river, and proceeded to the headquarters of the Quang Trach District People's Committee, Binh Tri Thien Province. After a briefing and coordination meeting, we piled into our Jeep Cherokees and Soviet vehicles, and with our large escort drove across country over Strategic Route 22, one of the war-time branches of the Ho Chi Minh trail. Had we continued to follow the old route, we would have ended up in Laos.

We drove to Huong Ban village that was at the foot of a very high mountain. There in the village we interviewed villagers about an aircraft that had crashed on the mountain. The villagers also told us that there were CBUs (cluster bomb units: small mines, really) all over the mountain. They said that just a few days before several children were severely injured when they stepped on a "bom-bi" while out in a field tending water buffalo. However, we fortunately didn't see any CBUs during our stay in the area.

We took an exhausting two-hour climb up an incredibly steep slope to the crash site, which was located just below the peak of the mountain top. That's where crash sites seem to always be: always at the top never at the bottom. The valley below was sprawled out before us in a majestic setting. The wreckage of the aircraft had mostly been hauled off for salvage, but there still remained some large pieces that we examined. We recorded numbers from the larger parts lying around on the surface, made drawings of the crash site, and took photographs.

Almost exactly one year later, a CILHI team retraced our steps to the crash site and conducted an excavation in and around the crash site. To protect the privacy of the MIA family, I won't go into detail about what they found, except to say they obtained evidence that the pilot died in the crash.

On the way back down the mountain, we stopped for a break on the banks of a lovely mountain stream. By this time we were out of water so we filled up our canteens. We used iodine tablets to purify the water. The water was probably safe to drink, but after my experiences with dysentery in the Phou Phan Mountains in Thailand, I wasn't about to take any chances.

During our rest stop, Dave told me about the time he and Bill Bell had climbed Tam Dao Mountain. The mountain was part of the range that American pilots had dubbed as "Thud Ridge." Dave said part of the trek took them around the side of the mountain on a tiny foot trail. At one point the trail got so narrow they had to brace up against side of a cliff to maintain balance as they inched on around. A slip would have meant sudden death in the abyss below. Dave said the experience was horrifying.

Dave said when they got on around the ledge to safety, they both collapsed and rested a while before moving on. Dave said Bill told him, "My whole life passed in front of my eyes."

After a few seconds of thinking about what Bill had said, Dave asked, "Well, did you like what you saw?"

Dave said Bill answered, "No," in a quiet, expressionless tone of voice.

When we returned to the village, Hoang, my Vietnamese counterpart, whom I had asked not to accompany us on the climb because he wouldn't have made it, met us. He told me that we really should leave the area as soon as possible. He said a group of villagers desired a confrontation with us because of previous war casualties in the village, in which five families had been totally wiped out in American air attacks. He said the village and district security personnel had been alerted, but he thought it best if we depart immediately, which we did.

We then took a long night-time drive north up Highway 1 back to the guest house at Ha Tinh town. The guest house was full when we got there, but within a few minutes Vietnamese guests were hustled out of the rooms upstairs to be doubled up with other guests downstairs. Since Americans pay $15.00 a night for a room, and Vietnamese pay fifty cents, the guest house was quite willing to accommodate the foreign visitors. Also, we weren't going to be egalitarian at that particular moment; we were absolutely exhausted and dirty from our climb and long drive.

The next morning, one of the Nghe Tinh Province district representatives told us at a coordination meeting that the province had officially invited us to tour the birth place of Chairman Ho Chi Minh that afternoon. In addition, after our tour we were also invited to attend a reception hosted by one of the senior members of the Nghe Tinh Province People's Committee in Vinh. We accepted the invitation.

That afternoon we travelled to Lang Sen village, Nghe Tinh province, the birth place of Ho Chi Minh. There, surrounded by incredible poverty with people literally dressed in rags, was the most sacred spot in all of Vietnam. We three Americans watched in wonder as our Vietnamese counterparts and province escorts stood in awed reverence. With tear-stained eyes, they listened as tour guides told about the early life and hardships of Ho Chi Minh. However, one of our elderly escorts, whom I will not name here for fear of ever embarrassing the old gentleman, briefly took away from the dignity of the moment by blowing mucous out of his nose at the edge of the gathering.

From Lang Sen village we travelled to Vinh town and checked into the guest house. The appointed time of 5:00 p.m. for our reception came and went. About 7:00 p.m. our host, who was the deputy of the head of the province people's committee, arrived and greeted us. He apologized for the lateness of the hour and said that he had just returned from several flood-stricken districts in the province. He asked if we had received the necessary cooperation from the province and districts in order to carry out our tasks, to which we replied that we indeed had. He made a few comments in which he said the war was over and it was now time to get on with the task at hand of alleviating the suffering caused by the war. We agreed. We thanked him for his hospitality, chatted for a few minutes, and then he departed. Obviously he was a very busy executive with places to go and people to see.

The next morning and afternoon, we drove back to Hanoi up Highway 1. On the 15th of December, two military aircraft landed at Noi Bai airport, one to pick up thirty-two sets of remains after a very solemn and moving ceremony, and the other to take half of our group back to Bangkok. Since I was a team leader, I had to stay until the 17th to finalize joint reports with my Vietnamese counterpart. Then on the morning of the 17th the rest of us caught a Thai International flight out of Noi Bai to Bangkok.

The next day, a Sunday, all of the employees of JCRC went to work at the embassy to get ready for a technical meeting in Hanoi the next day. Bill Bell, Jim Coyle, and I had to translate technical material into Vietnamese for the talks. I didn't get home until about 11:30 p.m. I couldn't have been more beat, for obvious reasons.

On Monday morning, I flew to Hanoi on a military aircraft with a six-member delegation led by LTC Harvey. We were picked up at Noi Bai Airport and taken to the government guest house where we had lunch, and then in mid- afternoon we began a series of meetings with the Vietnamese regarding the joint strategy of case investigation for the coming year.

That evening the Vietnamese hosted an official dinner for us. The next day, we had more meetings, and that evening we hosted an official dinner for the Vietnamese at which we treated them to turkey and dressing, which had been cooked by Xuan Bell and brought to Hanoi on our military aircraft by Bill. Bill also brought tapes of traditional Christmas music, which the Vietnamese, all self-proclaimed atheists, absolutely loved. A Christmas hymn by Tennessee Ernie Ford was their favorite. Before calling it an evening, we gave the Vietnamese Christmas gifts we had wrapped. They got as excited as our own kids do on Christmas morning. We all had a splendid time.

The next morning, we returned to Bangkok by military aircraft, which brought to conclusion a time of high adventure. Undoubtedly, December 1988 in Vietnam will always be a memorable highlight in my life.

The author on a boat with a joint team.

The author standing next to a parachute and a helmet that belonged to an Air Force pilot, who fortunately survived the war.

CHAPTER 11

FREEZING TO DEATH ON THE CHINESE BORDER

The iteration that took place in January of 1989 was nasty cold. As far as I know, it never freezes anywhere in Vietnam, but the wet drizzly weather of northern Vietnam, particularly up near the Chinese border, can eat into your bones like nowhere else.

The Americans that participated in the January iteration went over in two groups, an advance party and a main body. I was part of the advance party that left Bangkok for Hanoi on January 12, 1989, on a U.S. Air Force C-130 transport aircraft. Our mission was to make preparations for the upcoming joint investigative iteration, which would begin when the main body arrived. Bill Bell was in charge of our small group, but Lieutenant Colonel (Army) Bill Jordan, the JCRC Deputy Commander, would be the mission commander once he landed with the main group.

On the way over, we had a rough flight and bounced around in the turbulence. The cloud ceiling over the Hanoi area was about 1,000 feet, which is lower than some of the surrounding mountains. The radar at the airport starts at seven miles out, but the mountains are nine miles out. Consequently, landing at the Noi Bai International Airport in such conditions is dangerous. We almost went back to Bangkok, but at the last minute the U.S. Air Force pilot decided he could bring the aircraft in safely. Bill Bell, the best linguist, was up in the cockpit getting landing instructions from Hanoi air controllers as to the headings we needed to follow for an approach.

The aircraft crew chief, not knowing anything about our language abilities, asked me to get on the radio and talk to the air controller during the descent. There was absolutely no way I was going to entrust the safety of the aircraft, and myself, to my Vietnamese proficiency. I speak well enough, but when lives are at stake, to include my own, I make sure. I woke Bill up and told him he was needed in the cockpit.

The Vietnamese air controller, thinking Bill was the pilot, asked him where he grew up. Bill said, Texas, in the United States. The controller then said, he meant before Bill left Vietnam. Bill realized the air controller thought he was a Vietnamese who had left Vietnam and had grown up in the states.

On Friday the 13th, my birthday, the advance group met with our Vietnamese counterparts in Hanoi to plan the strategy of how we were going to go about investigating various cases. At one of these meetings, I handed out to the Vietnamese some used paperback books and magazines. I also passed out Vietnamese Bibles. You would think that I had given them each a hundred dollar bill. The junk they have to read is monotonous beyond belief since everything that appears in the public media has to go first through various control organizations to ensure it has the correct political content, etc. Consequently, anything published in the West is really coveted.

That evening, I celebrated my 42nd birthday at a private restaurant in Hanoi. I had a nice steak cooked to my liking by a capitalist entrepreneur, who proved once again the free market is inherently superior to a collective product. The service was good, the price was reasonable, and the meal was splendid.

At the restaurant, our group sat next to two Russian couples from the Soviet Embassy in Hanoi. One of the men in the group was the medical doctor at their embassy. One of the women spoke English really well, and as the meal progressed, she interpreted as the two groups began to converse. I had seen many Russians before, but this was the first time I ever had an opportunity to talk with any. They expressed a dislike for living in Vietnam and said the two years they were required to stay there was a real hardship, and they couldn't wait to get back to Moscow.

The Russian woman who spoke English said it was her birthday and they were celebrating. Since it was my birthday too, the guys in my group sang "happy birthday" to both of us, which the Russians thoroughly enjoyed. One of our guys went to the kitchen and popped American-style popcorn in one of those little pans that has the expandable tin foil top. He brought it to their table and they were thrilled. In return they gave the Americans a bottle of Russian vodka.

Bill Bell always brings American music cassettes to play in restaurants that we visit. Afterward he leaves the tape just to spread a little American culture. This particular evening the tape he got the restaurant to play had songs like "Okie from Muskogee," "I Can't Stop Lovin' You," and several other popular U.S. hits from a few years back. We sang along in unison with the songs, and then the Russians would sing some very beautiful and moving songs to us, though we couldn't understand one word of them. One of them sounded like the "Volga Boat Song" we used to sing in grade school.

When Bill Bell and I were in Hanoi in March 1988, he passed out tapes of a Vietnamese musical group in the U.S. called "New Wave." Those tapes must have been copied hundreds of times because within weeks they were being played all over Vietnam. Once I was at a party hosted by a Vietnamese official in one of the more remote western provinces and I heard "New Wave" playing in the background. Here in the absolute middle of nowhere came the sounds of a Vietnamese American group singing pop Vietnamese music. I even heard "New Wave" playing in state-run department stores in Hanoi.

The next morning, the main group arrived by U.S. Air Force C-141 jet transport from Honolulu. The aircraft also carried our purified water, military-type prepackaged meals that we needed when we were out in the boonies, assorted tools and equipment, and four new four-wheel drive Jeep Cherokees, which now made a total of eight that we had in the country.

Including the advance team and main body that had just arrived, we now had twenty-four Americans in Hanoi. The Americans split up into five teams. One team, under the leadership of Dr. Curley, CILHI senior anthropologist, stayed in Hanoi to examine skeletal remains. The remains had been confiscated from all over Vietnam from illegal remains dealers. The mission of the examination team was to determine whether any of the remains could be Caucasoid or Negroid, and therefore possibly American. If so, they would be sent to CILHI in Honolulu for further study. But even if remains have been identified as non-Mongoloid, this is not total proof the remains were American MIAs. The French had also fought a war in

Vietnam and left behind tremendous numbers of their own soldiers, many of whom were Caucasoid and Negroid.

Bill Bell's and Jim Coyle's teams flew by Soviet transport helicopters to Binh Tri Thien Province. Their Vietnamese drivers had already left two days earlier with the teams' vehicles and equipment. They were to pick up Bill and Jim's teams at an Army air field in Binh Tri Thien Province. Bill and Jim and their team members were fortunate, because going by vehicle, it would have been a twenty-hour drive to their destination over miserable roads, and only a fraction of that by helicopter.

Another team, of which Dave Atherton was the team NCOIC, had the mission of excavating a grave site. Jim Coyle's team in the last iteration had located the grave of a pilot. Jim, always erring on the side of caution, elected not to excavate the remains at that time, but let an excavation team recover the remains during the next iteration. The recovery team was successful, and the remains were eventually repatriated to the United States in a moving ceremony at the Noi Bai International Airport in Hanoi.

Jim, always acting on the side of caution, would not dig for remains. In contrast, if Bill or I heard from witnesses that remains were buried nearby, we'd get out the shovels and start digging, knowing full well LTC Johnnie Webb, the CILHI commander, would have a fit if he knew we were digging without an anthropologist present. Had we ever botched a recovery, we would have found ourselves involved in a legal technical mess, and Harvey and Webb would have been all over us.

Jim was determined to let the anthropologist excavate graves, even though he could have dug the remains right out of the ground at that time. The grave site was even sunken, so he knew exactly where the remains were. In all my digs, the graves had been "area" excavations, because the witnesses could not remember the exact burial site. Bill and I didn't like to wait for the anthropologist on a future iteration because we felt that if word got out to remains traders, they would rob the grave.

And that may have happened at least once. On one particular case that JCRC investigated, some months later a CILHI excavation team went to the site and saw that local people had already done extensive digging in the area themselves. The excavation team found no remains, but they did obtain evidence that the pilot died in the crash.

Just before I left JCRC, LTC Harvey gave the order that no team would excavate graves without a CILHI anthropologist present. But this didn't stop Bill Bell from digging "test" holes. He claimed he wasn't really digging for remains, but was checking out soil conditions for a future excavation (wink, wink). And if he just happened to stumble onto remains while digging test holes, so much the better. Bill's reasoning was totally bogus, and he knew it. But Bill is the type of guy who is not going to sit around when he knows he can recover remains and resolve a case then and there. Bill operated under the assumption that forgiveness is easier to get than permission.

One of Dave Atherton's team members during the excavation was an Army staff sergeant by the name of Mike Janitch. Mike was later hired by JCRC as a civilian, GS-11 interviewer a year or so I left the organization. At the time of the excavation, Mike belonged to a unit in Hawaii and had been loaned to us for TDY (temporary duty).

Mike was a great Vietnamese linguist. When I was taking the refresher course at the Defense Language Institute in Monterey, California, I kept hearing from the Vietnamese instructors about a young Army sergeant who had been a student there several years before and had "maxed" the course. They said he had scored the highest on his proficiency test at the end of the course that had ever been scored by a basic Vietnamese student.

Though Mike and I had not attended DLI together, we both had several of the same instructors. One of them, Mr. Vi, was an eccentric old guy who had taught in the Vietnamese Department at DLI for years. Mike and I both liked him, though his strange mannerisms would drive students nuts. Mike used to do his "Mr. Vi" imitations that would make anyone who knew the old Vietnamese gentleman roll on the floor with laughter.

Mike had a strange sense of humor himself. During the excavation, he had one of his team members take his picture in front of a sign that read, "Hanoi, 100 kilometers." The sign had an arrow that pointed in the direction of Hanoi. Mike mailed the photograph to Mr. Vi with no letter or explanation to go along with it. Mr. Vi must be wondering to this day what that was all about.

Mike was an excellent linguist and interviewer, but he was hampered by the fact that he was not a college graduate. This makes progression to the higher levels of the federal bureaucracy very difficult. Mike asked me once before I left JCRC if I would mind giving him a personal critique of his capabilities and performance, and I did. The only thing I could think of was that he needed to work on his education, and he was already aware of that. But that did not prevent him from being hired as a GS-11 when he went to work for JCRC.

The American members of my team were a U.S. Air Force analyst, an Army CILHI graves registration specialist, and a civilian Ph.D anthropologist. The Vietnamese side of the team consisted of Ngo Hoang, who had accompanied me as the Vietnamese-side team leader during the last iteration; a Vietnamese Army lieutenant colonel, who had fought in the South against Americans during the war; a state security officer; and four drivers. We had four vehicles: two of the brand-new Jeep Cherokees, a Soviet Volga sedan, and a Soviet jeep that carried our gasoline. The Volga is a sturdy, Soviet-made automobile, much like a mid-50s Chevrolet or Ford.

Sergeant First Class Randy Nash was the CILHI graves registration specialist on my team. He had been in JCRC years ago when JCRC was a much larger organization. After the war, he had been seriously wounded by North Vietnamese forces when they opened fire on a JCRC search team. An Army captain who led his team had been killed.

Randy suffered from recurrent bouts of malaria from years of operating in Vietnam, Laos, and New Guinea. Once during an iteration, he had to stay behind in Bangkok because of an attack of malaria that hospitalized him for several days.

I told you several chapters back that if you wanted to see what Bill Gadoury looked like, then look at the pictures in the article about MIA recovery operations in Laos in the November 1986 issue of NATIONAL GEOGRAPHIC. If you turn to page 693, you will see an excellent shot of Randy. Randy is the guy on the right pulling aircraft wreckage out of the way so his partner, Army Captain Bill Bethke, can see what lies underneath. Randy is also in the photograph with Bill Gadoury on page 695. Bill Gadoury is on the far right. Randy is standing is the middle of Laotians who are carrying a heavy piece of equipment.

My team went first to Lang Son Town, Lang Son province, which is located a half a day's journey by automobile northeast from Hanoi, and sixteen kilometers from the Chinese border. The weather was cold and nasty. Lang Son Town was occupied by the Chinese for twenty days in the brief Chinese-Vietnamese conflict in 1979 and war ruins were still evident, though most buildings and houses that were damaged or destroyed have been rebuilt. I've heard American sinologist, say the Chinese were determined to teach the Vietnamese a lesson, and they wantonly destroyed public buildings and monuments in Lang Son Province.

In Lang Son Town, we interviewed witnesses to a case and unsuccessfully tried to find a grave. The witness was a forensic photographer during the war and had taken a picture of an American pilot who had died as a result of the shooting down of his aircraft. The photograph had been in local police records, but had been destroyed when the building holding the records was destroyed by invading Chinese troops. The witness had also been to the grave site, but too many years had passed and he could only remember a very general location on the side of a hill. We decided to dig into the vaguely identified area anyway, just to see what we could find.

Dr. Miller wanted us Americans to do all of the digging ourselves, but standing out in the drizzling cold throwing dirt with a shovel was no fun at all. After a couple of hours of that, I thought, "Hey, I'm the guy in charge. I've got essentially a blank check to hire laborers, and we're going to hire some." I told Ngo Hoang we needed workers to dig. Hoang got fifteen women for us, and they finished up the job under Dr. Miller's supervision.

As usual we could only get a few Vietnamese males to do the digging, which is typical of all of the other digs I had been part of before or since. We'd start with a mostly female crew, but after a few hours, the few males we had would drop out and we would have total female digging crews. I'd rather have Vietnamese females working for me anyway. They would work uncomplainingly for hours in harsh weather conditions and keep their sense of humor. At the end of the day, they would ask if they could work the next day, too.

We dug into the general area described by the witness and recovered two sets of remains, but the CILHI anthropologist, Dr. Miller, determined they were Mongoloid and female. Dr. Miller said that one of the remains had likely been buried over a hundred years before.

The conversation between Dr. Miller and Randy was sort of humorous when we dug up the first remains. Dr. Miller said, "What do you thing the race is, Randy?"

Randy said, "Rice eater, Dr. Miller."

Miller said, "Yeah, I think so too. How about the sex?"

"Female, sir."

Miller said, "Yeah, I think so too."

Randy Nash had been in the remains recovery business so long, the experts usually checked with him first to see if they had overlooked anything in their evaluation. Miller had already come to a conclusion, but he wanted Randy's opinion before making it official.

One thing about working around graves registration specialists and anthropologists, I picked up a lot of interesting facts about remains. By looking at teeth, anthropologists can usually tell if the remains were Mongoloid. A rice diet causes Mongoloid teeth to look different than American Caucasoid or Negroid who has a different diet in the United States.

Anthropologists can generally determine sex of the remains by examining the jaw bone and the back of the skull. Race can be determined by measuring the location of "blood holes" in the long bones where red blood cells are created.

Since Dr. Miller was able to make an immediate determination that the remains were not Caucasoid, which was the racial stock of the person for whom we were searching, Miller ordered the remains to be reburied. They would not have to be exhumed and sent to Honolulu for further examination, although they were photographed for the record of the investigation.

We froze to death in Lang Son. During the day we were outside in the cold, and at night there was absolutely no heat in any of the rooms of the guest house. We were able to keep warm only by putting on extra clothing at night and wrapping up in the one-inch thick down blankets that were in each of the rooms.

The food in the guest house was miserable too. Usually on our trips, the food was quite good, since the Vietnamese cooks put a little extra into the meal because of the novelty of cooking for American guests. But in Lang Son, the staff was cold and indifferent and so was the food.

The next morning after our dig, we did a little sight-seeing. We first toured a nearby cave to see a golden Buddhist shrine located deep in the inner recesses of the cavern. Then we drove to a Vietnamese village located on the Chinese border. Tensions had abated over the years and the border was now open to trade between the two countries. We met Chinese who were operating business stalls on the Vietnamese side of the border and were selling a wide variety of Chinese goods. Our Vietnamese team members did some shopping for Tet, their version of the Chinese lunar new year, and then we began the scenic trip back to Hanoi.

On the way back to Hanoi, I suggested to Ngo Hoang that we have an American style picnic. We stopped on the side of the road at the foot of a lovely karst mountain and had a bite to eat. The American team members broke out a case of American military MREs (Meals, Ready to Eat). The Vietnamese shared a few goodies they had bought on the Chinese border.

That evening in Hanoi, we luxuriated in the warmth of hot showers and warm rooms. After days of freezing in Lang Son, the pleasant warmth was almost hypnotic.

The next morning our team traveled to a crash site and an alleged grave site in Ha Son Binh Province. The trip was just a short drive from Hanoi. We were happy about the short distance, since that meant we could commute from Hanoi and have relatively good and safe food, clean rooms, toilets that worked without having to pour a bucket of water into them (or an outhouse), and hot-water showers—conveniences that just don't exist in government guest houses in most parts of Vietnam.

We hired laborers to dig up a cornfield where witnesses told us they had buried the pilot, and they dug for the better part of the day in nasty drizzly weather. However, there was just too much to dig by hand since the witnesses could not recall the exact spot where they had interred the pilot in the large field.

LTC Bill Jordan, the mission commander, came to the site to observe our digging operation. By that time the job had already bogged down. Our Vietnamese witnesses couldn't remember where exactly in the field they had buried the American pilot. The excavation site had grown from the size of a small room to an olympic swimming pool. We realized the job had turned into a drawn-out affair. Jordan agreed to take charge of the dig to enable my team to move on to conduct investigations elsewhere. It was a waste of time having investigators sitting around watching a dig when we could be gathering information. I left the anthropologist, Dr. Miller, with LTC Jordan, and the rest of the Americans and Vietnamese on our team pulled out. LTC Jordan told me later that the next day he tried to get a mechanical digger, but the machine that finally showed up was a road grader and totally unsuited for a remains excavation. Jordan eventually canceled the dig for that particular trip. The result of the excavation was that the U.S. taxpayer bought itself a cornfield at premium prices.

My team left Hanoi and drove west to Hoa Binh City, where the Soviets were building a huge hydroelectric project. After the town of Hoa Binh, the mountains start. Rapidly we began to climb and weave our way through treacherous peaks until we reached our destination of Son La Town, Son La Province, an excruciating 300 kilometer, 11-hour trip from Hanoi. There we hoped to conclude investigations in which I had participated in October 1988.

Our mission was to try to get more information about the cases in Son La. We were also to visit the Son La museum, where on the last trip a nervous museum employee told us we had to leave because her boss was in Hanoi and she didn't have permission to let us search the museum for material evidence. I was the only member of the team, U.S. or Vietnamese, who had been to Son La previously on the last investigation.

The next morning, Friday, January 20, the joint team had the customary meeting with local officials. Afterward, the joint team visited the Son La museum. We came across some new items that we hadn't seen before, partly because the last trip a number of the storage containers in the museum had been locked, and also because the joint team and high-ranking province officials had been chased out of the museum by the irate female employee. We saw all of the things the team had observed during the last trip, plus some new evidence that eventually proved significant in the eventual resolution of several cases. This consisted of photographs of dead pilots who were later proved to be MIAs. The photographs had been taken by local military intelligence specialists who had been assigned to the regional command.

We also found uniforms, helmets, and personal items that belonged to other pilots who had been captured, but were not MIA. Some of the paraphernalia belonged to Lawrence Guarino, who returned in Operation Homecoming. We also found his "blood chit," which I thought about stealing, but then thought better of it. I've often thought it would have been neat to have mailed it to Guarino. A blood chit is a durable fabric on which is imprinted a pilot's identifying number, an American flag and a request for assistance in five languages.

Strangely, we found a helmet that had belonged to a U.S. Air Force "Captain Kari;" however, no "Kari" had ever been taken prisoner. We found out later that Kari had indeed been shot down, but was rescued by a Jolly Green.

After examining evidence at the museum, I got the museum director to lead the team through the old French prison next door. I had already visited the prison in October when I had been a member of Bill Bell's team and knew my team would find it just as interesting as we did then. As I mentioned previously, it had been destroyed in the fifties during the war against the French, but enough was still standing to get a good idea of how dismal life had been there. The museum employees were quick to point out that many of the martyrs and leaders of the Vietnamese revolution had been imprisoned there at one time or another. We toured the dungeon area—a grim and vicious-looking place. Iron shackles were still visible in the concrete walls.

That afternoon and the next day, January 21, the joint team interviewed witnesses to particular cases. Also we hired thirty ethnic minority laborers, dressed in colorful native garb, to do the digging for us. The Vietnamese on the joint team bargained with the village chief for a sum of money to do the job. The village chief then exhorted his workers with revolutionary fervor for about ten minutes in Black Tai dialect—I could only understand a few words—and then the group went to work looking every bit like a Mao-era "great-leap-forward army."

For the second time, our dig at Son La proved to be unsuccessful, and that afternoon we returned to the Son La guest house to make preparations to leave and have a final meeting with province officials. At the meeting the U.S. team members presented gifts (paid for by the U.S. taxpayer) to various people who had been helpful, and the People's Committee of Son La Province presented us with colorful needlework that had by been made by local Black Tais. The province chief of staff then made a speech, and I said a few words in Vietnamese thanking the province leaders on behalf of the U.S. government and the families of the missing pilots for their cooperation. I told them we had not been successful in finding remains, but the information we did discover would resolve several cases and let American family members know what happened to their loved ones.

Just before the meeting, I had remarked to Colonel (retired) Tho, the Son La Province foreign affairs representative, that I liked the Lenin insignia that he wore. He asked me if I would get in trouble with the United States government if I had one. Hoang answered for me, saying, of course not, that the U.S. was a free country and Americans could wear what they wanted. After the meeting the Vietnamese colonel called me aside and conducted a brief ceremony in front of the military officers from the province staff. He took the Lenin insignia off his uniform and pinned it on my jacket. I was surprised and touched and wore the insignia for the rest of the day. Lenin is definitely not one of my favorite people, but I certainly felt honored that an old soldier would try to reach out across cultures and a war to present something to one of his former enemies that was meaningful to him.

Immediately after the ceremony, we left Son La Town and drove to a town called Moc Chau, which is the district seat of Moc Chau District, Son La Province. The province people's committee had given us a letter of introduction that they said would get us into a trade union guest house for the night, which it did. The next morning, Sunday January 22nd, we retraced our steps to Hoa Binh and then on to Hanoi for a delicious evening meal and a hot shower.

Beautiful Hanoi! The place is a dump by western standards, but when you've been out in the rural areas eating strange things that might include dog and rat, bathing out of a wash basin, using a smelly outhouse or filthy indoor toilet, waking up at night to the sound of little creatures running around in your room, sleeping in beds that showed ample evidence of others having been there before, eating from dishes and bowls that had been poorly washed and were still very greasy, then understandably Hanoi becomes a delectable sight for sore eyes. Hanoi, the jewel of northern Vietnam, where you can buy a steak with all the trimmings and imported Coca Cola. If you're really lucky you might even have a heater in your room that works.

During this particular trip to Vietnam, we noticed some interesting things going on in

Hanoi. Small businesses were springing up everywhere around the city. We heard that in recent months, the government had started to encourage the development of a private sector as one of the means of rescuing the incredibly sick Vietnamese economy. When I first saw Hanoi the year before when I had been a member of an American delegation, I had been struck by how stagnant the economy seemed to be. There had been some amazing changes since then. Hanoi was still miserably poor, but everywhere, shops and outdoor markets were relatively full and people seemed to be dressing better. Vietnamese officials told us businesses could now have up to twenty employees without having to take the state in as a partner. Hopefully these reforms will last without some doctrinaire party hack deciding to strangle the golden goose of what little free enterprise they now have.

The next morning, Monday, January 23, we departed to Noi Bai Airport where we watched from a distance a solemn ceremony in which remains of Americans were being loaded on to a U.S. aircraft for the final journey home. Some of the remains being repatriated were those that our teams had found in previous trips to Vietnam.

After the ceremony, a number of our group boarded the transport aircraft with the remains and returned to Honolulu, with a one day stopover in Guam. The other group, of which I was a part, boarded another military transport aircraft, which flew us back across Laos to Bangkok.

And so ended another incredible adventure. I definitely have some cold memories of a trip on which I thought I was going to freeze to death in northern Vietnam.

Ngo Hoang and author interviewing witness to a crash.

CHAPTER 12

RENDEZVOUS WITH DESTINY

The seventh and last iteration of investigations of the "70-Name List" began on July 31, 1989, when two American teams boarded an Air Force C-130 in Bangkok, flew across Laos, and landed at the Noi Bai International Airport in Hanoi. The two team chiefs from JCRC that would head the investigation were Jim Coyle and myself. Bill Bell, who was usually in charge on the ground whenever JCRC sent investigative teams into Vietnam, was not going to be participating. He was in Washington, D.C., attending a National League of MIA Families meeting.

This is something Bill was very qualified to do. He has a real gift of public speaking and also is able to gain instant rapport with people who have undergone tremendous heartache. Undoubtedly his ability to empathize with people has a lot to do with the pain and tragedy he has dealt with in his own life.

Since Bill was not going to be involved in the iteration, Jim, in addition to being a team chief, was also the overall mission commander. The two members of his team were Master Sergeant Rick John, an Air Force intelligence analyst from Headquarters, JCRC in Honolulu, and Sergeant First Class Randy Nash, from CILHI. Randy had been with me previously on an investigation that had taken us up as far as the Chinese border and then to Son La Province in northwestern Vietnam.

On my team were Dave Atherton, who was to be my team NCOIC; Sergeant First Class Randy Brown, an Army CILHI graves registration specialist; and Sergeant First Class James Williams, also an Army CILHI graves registration specialist.

All of the Americans, except for Randy Brown and Jim Williams, had been on previous iterations. However, both Randy and Jim had been to Vietnam before to participate in the dignified remains repatriation ceremonies that occur periodically at Noi Bai International Airport near Hanoi.

The mission of my team was to operate in old 101st Airborne Division country in Thua Thien and Quang Tri Provinces. Having been in the 101st Airborne Division just before my assignment to JCRC, I was extremely proud to have been selected to lead a team back to battlefields where the division made a lot of its Vietnam history.

One of the places in Thua Thien Province where my team was to be operating was the Ashau Valley, and for several weeks my team members had been studying MIA cases and making preparations to operate there. In addition, I had contacted several senior Army officers who had been in the 101st who had fought in the Ashau. I wanted to get a feel of the terrain and background of the American effort there. In a conversation with a officer who had extensive combat experience with 101st, I learned that the 101st Airborne Division museum at Ft. Campbell, Kentucky, had a map that showed all of the old base camps and helicopter LZs (landing zones) in the Ashau.

Upon hearing that such information was available, I drafted an electronic message to the commander of the 101st Airborne Division, which Spurgeon approved, requesting that the division's intelligence staff photocopy the map in sections and fax them to the JCRC Liaison Office at the American Embassy in Bangkok. The map arrived on the fax machine the next morning. I drafted a message of thanks to the commander of the 101st Airborne Division saying that the American MIA investigative team returning to the Ashau Valley was appreciative of the efforts of the division in assisting in the preparation of our trip. Then I ended the message by writing: "Air Assault!" This is a military courtesy greeting that any member of the division would instantly recognize.

The 101st Airborne Division has a theme song called "Rendezvous with Destiny," and I can honestly say that my team, which was fittingly all-Army, felt we had a rendezvous with destiny. We were the first American soldiers to return to the Ashau Valley since the war.

Upon landing at Noi Bai International Airport, we were met by our drivers and Vietnamese team members. We had gotten to know all of them very well in recent months and our meeting was like a reunion of old friends. From the airport they transported us to the Le Thach Foreign Ministry Guest House in downtown Hanoi.

The guest house is located in a fenced compound that also contains the old Foreign Ministry building, a structure which goes back to the days of the French occupation. The building, in which Ho Chi Minh once had his office, is as much a part of the history of Vietnam as any place in the country. I've seen old photographs of Ho Chi Minh standing in front of the building addressing crowds of Vietnamese after his forces were victorious against the French.

At the guest house, we spent the rest of the afternoon pulling maintenance on our Jeep Cherokees and arranging our gear, which we kept stored in a room at the back of the old Foreign Ministry building. Also, we coordinated with our Vietnamese counterparts who were to be our fellow team members over the next twenty days. Jim Coyle's counterpart was Ngo Hoang from the Foreign Ministry, who had been my counterpart on two previous iterations. Jim also had two other Vietnamese assigned to his team, one from the Ministry of Defense, and another from the Ministry of the Interior. My counterpart was to be Ho Xuan Dich, from the Foreign Ministry. His team members were Major Pham Teo, from the Ministry of Defense, and Tran Trien, from the Ministry of the Interior.

The next two days the two teams travelled to their respective investigative areas down Highway 1, which is the major north-to-south route. Jim and his team's destination was to be Quang Binh Province, and his base of operations was going to be Dong Hoi City. Jim had the mission of investigating three cases in the area of the Ban Karai Pass, a major transit point on the Ho Chi Minh trail. My team, Team 2, had been tasked to investigate two cases in the Ashau Valley in Thua Thien Province, and one case in Quang Tri Province.

Highway 1 is an absolute mess until you get past the old Demilitarized Zone; there the road suddenly improves since it was maintained by American engineers during the war. But before reaching the more modern road, passengers going by vehicle are constantly bounced around due to the terrible road conditions. In addition, heavy truck traffic is constantly on the road, and never yet has there been born a Vietnamese truck driver with the slightest fear of maneuvering a massive vehicle into tight spaces at high speeds.

On the afternoon of August 2, my team, Team 2, reached Hue City, the capital seat of Thua Thien Province. This was to be our base for a few days as we made preparations to operate in the province.

We spent a couple of days in Hue meeting senior members of the Thua Thien Province

People's Committee and being briefed by a province investigative team that had been conducting preliminary investigations of the cases that we were to investigate. Also we were able to get out and see the sights of Hue in the afternoons and evenings. We particularly enjoyed walking around the old Citadel, which had been overrun and held by communist troops during the Tet Offensive some years back. (The movie ""Full Metal Jacket" is a good account of the terrible fighting that occurred in Hue when American Marines retook the Citadel.)

On several occasions as we were sightseeing, former South Vietnamese officers came up and talked to Dave Atherton and me about getting assistance in leaving Vietnam. There's absolutely nothing we could do to help them, except to encourage them to apply to leave through their own government. But they knew all of that; Vietnamese are masters at knowing how bureaucracies work. They just were looking for shortcuts, which is a very Vietnamese way of doing things.

The next day after one such encounter with a former South Vietnamese officer, my counterpart, Ho Xuan Dich, confronted me with information that I was conspiring with former South Vietnamese officers in helping them leave the country. He repeated a conversation I had with one officer who had come to see me, which had been reported by the spy system that exists everywhere in Vietnam. The officer had asked me if there was any truth to a Voice of America news story that said the U.S. and Vietnamese government had agreed that all former South Vietnamese officers would be allowed to leave Vietnam and resettle in the United States. I told him that I had heard the broadcast, and as far as I knew the story was true.

But that's not what a snitch who had obviously been listening to our conversation reported to the Hue state security office. The spy said I had told the officer that the U.S. government would resettle him. I gave Dich my version of what had transpired, and he seemed to believe me, though tensions among the Vietnamese and American team members were close to the surface for a few days afterward.

The next day, the joint team and the province team travelled by automobile from Hue to Phu Bai Airport, which had been a big American base back during the war. There we were to await the arrival of a Soviet-made MI-17 helicopter that the U.S. government was going to rent from the Vietnamese government. The helicopter was to transport us to the Ashau Valley in A-Luoi District, Thua Thien Province.

The amazing thing to me about Phu Bai was that there was little evidence that Americans had ever been there. If you ever visited or worked at a large American base in Vietnam during the war, one of the things you undoubtedly would remember were the guard towers every few hundred feet or so, the incredible amount of concertina wire entwined around the perimeter of the base, the thousands of lights within the concertina, the large numbers of buildings, and the vast amount of equipment scattered throughout the interior of the base. None of that remained at Phu Bai. Only the main airport building would be recognizable to Americans who had served there. The area immediately around the base had reverted to places where water buffalo graze.

At the Phu Bai airport I spent some time talking to a former South Vietnamese officer who had undergone "re-education," but had been rehabilitated and put into a responsible position because of his badly needed technical skills of airport management and maintenance. He was one of the few lucky ones. So many times in travelling throughout Vietnam and refugee camps, I met former South Vietnamese officers and officials who had skills that could have really helped the country after the war, but they were employed in occupations such as bicycle repair. The tragic waste of such expensive talent was criminal. They simply were not trusted by the new regime for ideological reasons and were branded as criminals because of their association with the old "puppet" government.

Upon the arrival of our helicopter to Phu Bai, we boarded and flew to the village of A-Luoi in the Ashau Valley. A-Luoi sits at the foot of Dong Ap Bia Mountain. Most Americans, even those who had fought in the valley, would not recall the Vietnamese name of the mountain, but the American name, "Hamburger Hill," would be immediately recognizable.

One thing that became evident to me as I looked at Dong Ap Bia Mountain was that whoever was in charge of filming the movie "Hamburger Hill" had actually been there. Even though the scenes from the movie were shot in the Philippines, the movie director was able to find terrain that looked almost identical to the Ashau Valley. I saw the movie before and after my trip to the Ashau Valley, and I was struck by the authenticity of the film's portrayal of the features in the valley.

At A-Luoi mobs of local people turned out to see the helicopter and their strange American passengers. Most of the local people were an ethnic minority, which our Vietnamese team members told us were Pa-Coh. They have very distinctive dress and speak a language different from Vietnamese. The Pa-Coh language seemed to be filled with "ng" words that sounded to us like "pring," "krang," and "kring."

In Vietnam most males smoke and most females don't. But with the Pa-Coh people, everyone smokes, even the little kids. In addition to smoking foul-smelling local brands of cigarettes, both men and women smoke cigars and fancily decorated pipes. I'm sure the per capita rate of lung and mouth cancer for Pa-Coh people has to be as high as in place in the world.

At the A-Luoi District headquarters, the joint team and province team met with senior officials of A-Luoi District. These officials had all been Viet Cong during the war. One of these old veterans, who was now the chairman of the A-Luoi District People's Committee, welcomed us in a brief speech. He was a Pa-Coh minority with gaping holes in his earlobes, undoubtedly caused from wearing Pa-Coh ear ornaments in his youth.

I also had a few words to say since I was the senior American present. I gave a few generalities in Vietnamese that consisted of thanking the people's committee for assisting the American government in its humanitarian efforts in allowing a team of American soldiers to return to the Ashau Valley to investigate cases of our missing comrades.

The people's committee informed our joint team that they had two witnesses to an MIA incident that we could interview if we wished. We agreed and right after our meeting, Dave Atherton and I talked to them. They were former National Liberation Front soldiers who served in A-Luoi District during the war. One of them had been a former National Liberation Front lieutenant colonel by the name of Cu Pang. During the war, Cu Pang had commanded five National Liberation Front military districts, one of which was Military District Three, within which the village of A-Luoi was located. The other had been a soldier under Lieutenant Colonel Cu Pang's command and assigned to Military District Three.

During the interview we obtained information about an MIA case that was not on the "70-Name List," which were the cases of primary interest to us. But nevertheless the information turned out to be important in that we were able to obtain solid information about an active MIA case. The case involved a helicopter that had been shot down in Cu Pang's domain, and he and several other Viet Cong soldiers, to include the former soldier who had come with Cu Pang to meet us, had been at the crash site shortly after the crash. Both of these men gave us substantial information that seemed to match perfectly the case that popped up on our portable computer.

After conducting the interviews at the district headquarters in A-Luoi, the joint team reboarded the Soviet helicopter to inspect the investigative sites from the air, but the weather was bad and we had to abort our flight and land. The weather was clear in the center of the valley where we were flying, but there were great sheets of fog that prevented us from flying over the mountains on either side of the valley. We eventually had to fly back to Phu Bai and then return to Hue by car.

The next day, we again returned to A-Luoi by helicopter, but there were still heavy clouds hugging the mountains. We waited a couple of hours and the pilot finally determined that they had cleared enough for us to attempt flying to a landing zone that local people had cut into the jungle for us. We took off from the A-Luoi District Headquarters and flew from the

Ashau Valley over the mountains, but a strong updraft from the area where we wanted to land prevented us from descending into the prepared area. We vainly circled the landing zone and then, when it became obvious to the pilot that he couldn't drop down onto the LZ, we aborted the mission. We flew back to A-Loui and then to Phu Bai. Before landing at Phu Bai, the pilot took us on an aerial tour over the Hue Citadel, which is a magnificent old fortress to see by air or on foot.

The next morning, the joint team drove to Dong Ha Town in Quang Tri Province, a city that was totally destroyed during the war and has since been rebuilt. It is the new capital seat of Quang Tri Province, which is one of three provinces that had just recently been formed from Binh Tri Thien Province. Even though we had not finished our investigations in A-Luoi, we decided that we needed to conduct an investigation in Quang Tri Province, because we had a helicopter we could use that had already been scheduled and waiting for us in Dong Ha. We only had one day to use it, and we definitely needed it because of the difficult terrain in which we would be required to go. When we completed our investigation in Quang Tri, we planned to return to A-Luoi by automobile to finish up our investigations that had been aborted because of the weather.

Immediately after arriving at Dong Ha Town, we met with an investigative team that had been appointed by the Quang Tri Province People's Committee to assist us in our investigations. The province team briefed us concerning what they had done in preparing for our visit. They said that on two occasions in recent weeks they had been to the incident area we wanted to investigate. On the first trip they located helicopter wreckage and interviewed witnesses; on the second, using local labor, they cleared a helicopter landing zone to enable us to enter the area by air to avoid an extremely difficult journey through dense vegetation and rugged terrain.

At the conclusion of the meeting, the joint team, accompanied by the province investigative team, travelled by MI-17 helicopter over spectacular jungle scenery and old battlefields to the incident location. I pulled out my camera to take pictures of the breath-taking view, and Dich told me that it was okay if I took pictures as long as I didn't take any of the interior of the helicopter—national security, you understand. As I looked at the low-tech interior of the beat-up, death-trap, I was thinking that if Vietnamese national security depended on this, the Vietnamese government was in worse shape than I thought.

In fact, after teams had concluded the iteration, we learned that one of the two helicopters the teams had used had crashed and the entire crew perished.

The helicopter landed on a hilltop on which a landing zone had been cut in the forest. From there, the joint team, province team, and witnesses to an MIA incident proceeded through thick mountainous jungle to a helicopter crash site, which was approximately two kilometers away from the helicopter landing zone. Upon reaching the crash site, which was at the bottom of a ravine through which a swift, jungle stream flows, we saw helicopter wreckage.

Also at the incident location, the joint team interviewed a witness to the incident, a former National Liberation Front soldier who was of the Van Kieu ethnic minority. The witness, a resident of a nearby Van Kieu village, gave significant information that may eventually resolve the case the joint team was investigating. A member of the province investigative team interpreted for the former Viet Cong since he did not speak Vietnamese. He said that while he was a local militia soldier of the National Liberation Front, he witnessed the crash of the helicopter and what happened to the crew. The helicopter was shot down by a regular North Vietnamese unit stationed on a hill that was between his village and the Laotian border. (He was unable to identify the location of the hill on a map—throughout the 7th iteration, the joint team consistently had problems in getting specific map locations from the ethnic minorities, even from those who had been officers.)

After we finished up our investigation at the helicopter crash site, the joint team repeated its jungle trek to the waiting helicopter. We boarded and flew over a hundred battlefields in our return to Dong Ha Town.

The next day, we briefed the senior officials of Quang Tri Province on our investigations the day before. At the conclusion of the meeting, they invited us to a special official dinner to be held that evening in our honor, which we accepted.

Also, the Quang Tri Province People's Committee arranged a sightseeing tour for us in the afternoon before the dinner. Province officials accompanied us as we drove up to just below the old demilitarized zone to see Con Tien Hill, which was the location of a U.S. Marine base back during the war. Later, after U.S. forces withdrew, it became a base for South Vietnamese soldiers. It was captured in 1972 by the North Vietnamese after a big battle. We toured the battlefield and saw a lot of war debris still lying around, to include pieces of rocket launchers, artillery shells, remnants of boots and clothing, and a destroyed bunker.

From Con Tien we travelled across the river that marks the center of the old demilitarized zone between what was once North and South Vietnam. The river was where North Vietnamese prisoners were returned to North Vietnamese control in 1973. I recall seeing news footage during that time of North Vietnamese prisoners stripping off their POW uniforms and swimming to the northern shore. On the northern side of the river, we drove a few miles to a white-sand beach on the Gulf of Tonkin and spent a few minutes enjoying the lovely scene before returning to Dong Ha Town to attend our dinner. Even in this little spot of paradise the war was evident: intermittently in the beach sand were artillery shells and bomb fragments.

The next day, we returned to A-Luoi Village by automobile. We went west toward the Laotian border and then followed the Laotian border down to the Ashau Valley road back to A-Luoi, which was about a three-hour trip.

Our journey took us past former American fire bases that formed a chain at the bottom of the old demilitarized zone, the purpose of which was to stop infiltration from North Vietnam into South Vietnam. Some of the bloodiest battles of the war were fought in this area. Khe Sanh and the Rockpile, for example, were nearby. These are just two names of a number of places on the southern edge of the demilitarized zone that undoubtedly would evoke bitter memories from a lot of former American soldiers.

Now back in A-Loui, we began to make preparations to travel into the jungle to investigate cases. Since we no longer had access to a helicopter, our only means of transportation would be by foot. Therefore, the joint team, the Thua Thien province team, and A-Luoi District officials travelled on foot to investigate the area where we were unable to land the helicopter some days previously because of bad weather. The route we travelled was along a former segment of the Ho Chi Minh Trail.

Even though the route had been a road at one time, as evidenced by the rusting remnants of destroyed Chinese trucks and fuel drums all along the way, it was now overgrown with jungle vegetation and difficult to walk through. We passed between two mountain peaks on which were once located U.S. fire bases Tiger and Turnage, according to our information that had been faxed from the 101st Airborne Division. The American members theorized that the U.S. fire bases must have been strategically placed there to cut off supplies being transported on the very trail, or narrow road, on which we were moving.

What we were looking for was a site where Pa-Coh people had allegedly found a parachute, a pilot's helmet, a pair of jungle boots, and a pair of wire-rimmed glasses. The story intrigued us so we decided to check it out. However, several days after we had completed our hike and had returned to A-Luoi, Pa-Coh people brought the alleged pilot's helmet by for us to inspect, and it in fact turned out to be an ordinary GI steel pot, not a pilot's helmet.

But we didn't know that at the time, and we were still full of enthusiasm that we might be able to get some evidence about an MIA case. At our destination, where the so-called pilot's helmet had been found, we began searching the area with metal detectors and by digging. We found remnants of a cargo net with hooks, pieces of burned fabric and cord (possibly parachute material), four pairs of burned jungle boots, a belt buckle, a piece of an entrenching tool, three U.S. Army metal helmets (one was peppered with shrapnel holes), two fiberglass helmet liners, pieces of a flak jacket, scraps of fatigue uniforms, and empty C-ration cans. I theorized that GIs had loaded a cargo net full of trash and damaged equipment, and dropped it over the Ashau Valley, never dreaming that years later Americans would be digging through it looking for MIA evidence.

After a tough morning of digging and sorting through artifacts we had found and having decided that what we had found did not pertain to any MIA cases in the Ashau valley, we stopped work and treated our Vietnamese team members to a meal of Army MREs (Meal, Ready to Eat). After a nice lunch and washing up in a jungle stream, we concluded our investigation and retraced our steps back to A-Luoi Village.

Because we had gotten behind in investigating due to bad weather, we were now facing a time crunch in getting all of our investigations done that we needed to do. Dave Atherton and I decided that it would be a good idea to split up our teams; he'd go with one half and I'd take the other. We briefed Ho Xuan Dich on what we wanted to do. He didn't want to go to any of the more difficult sites because of the terrible terrain we would have to cross. I argued that even though the chance of finding anything was slim to non-existent, we needed to go through the motions to show good faith that we had tried. Besides, I told him, if we didn't go, the critics in the American government would likely say the Vietnamese weren't cooperating. Dich saw the wisdom of making an effort; therefore, he agreed to our plan to split up the Vietnamese and American investigators into two teams.

Jim Williams, a very physically-fit black NCO, and I, went with one group composed of Lieutenant Colonel Cu Pang and other former Viet Cong soldiers. Dave Atherton and Randy Brown went with Ho Xuan Dich and the other members of the Vietnamese VNOSMP (Vietnamese Office for Seeking Missing Persons) team from Hanoi.

Bill Bell, when he found out that none of the VNOSMP team members went with Jim William and me, rode them unmercifully on a later iteration. The truth of the matter was that both of the groups crossed some incredibly difficult terrain, but Bill Bell was not the type to give our Vietnamese counterparts the benefit of the doubt—especially when he could needle them a while.

Early one morning just before sunup, Jim Williams and I set out by foot with our Cu Pang and other former Viet Cong through dense, leech-infested jungle. We were in search of a crash site and a section of jungle where a U.S. pilot had landed by parachute some twenty years before. Jim and I were fascinated that our former Viet Cong guide carried the same AK-47 and CKC assault rifles they carried during the war.

Along our route, Jim and I saw bomb fragments as well as tell-tale signs of the enemy who had once called these jungles home: from time to time we would come across blue Soviet-made commo wire, which North Vietnamese soldiers used in their tactical communications.

Also, we ran into a Pa-Coh family panning for gold. They couldn't have been any more surprised at seeing Jim and me than if an alien spacecraft had landed in the middle of the jungle.

We followed a river into the jungle as far as we could, since there was a semblance of a trail made by Pa-Coh people on the banks of the river. When we reached our planned departure point from the trail, we headed into the dense jungle, cutting our way by machete.

Jim and I marvelled at how well our team members could maneuver through the dense vegetation. They slipped through easily, while we bludgeoned our way through. We saw firsthand examples of the agility and stealth of our former enemies that many American soldiers must have seen only when it was too late. The jungle skills of these tough old soldiers was an amazing thing to behold.

We came to an old enemy base camp where Jim and I looked around the underground bunkers and fighting positions still visible after all of these years. Some of them were covered with thick plastic tarps. One of the former Viet Cong soldiers with us said they had been constructed during the war by a platoon from Military District Three. He said that from time-to-time during the war, he had lived at this very place. Around the bunkers, we saw craters, metal fragments, and scars on trees, which indicated that the area had been attacked by artillery or aircraft.

After vainly searching for aircraft wreckage, we cut our way through the jungle to the spot where American witnesses, hovering above in rescue aircraft, had seen the pilot descend by parachute. We searched the area looking for anything that might have been associated with a pilot—helmet, pieces of uniform, parachute material—but we found nothing.

When it started to get dark, we camped on a river bank in the jungle. The old Viet Cong soldiers made a lean-to from branches and leaves for us to sleep under and then prepared a delicious dinner of local Pa-Coh dishes and fish, which were caught bare-handed by one of our Pa-Coh guides. After a refreshing bath in the river and the native meal, we hit the sack for a well-deserved sleep. Cu Pang insisted Jim and I sleep in the middle of the shelter and he and the others would sleep on either side of us to protect us, which was an ironical turn of events to say the least.

Cu Pang slept next to me and I listened to him talk in his sleep before I finally dozed off. He kept saying in Vietnamese: "Four dollars, five dollars...(bon do-la, nam do-la." I had no idea what he could have been dreaming about, unless it was about the fee the VNOSMP members would eventually pay him.

The next morning, Jim and I ate MREs for breakfast and the Vietnamese had leftovers from the night before. We broke camp and headed back the way we had come. We were en route to Cu Pang's home, which was a Pa-Coh village on the main road that ran through the Ashau Valley. When we reached his house, which was a mud and thatch-roofed dwelling, he invited us in to wait for our drivers to show up and take us back to A-Luoi. While resting and drinking tea and some kind of Vietnamese orange drink, Cu Pang showed Jim and me his wartime decorations. He also introduced us to one of his two wives, who was a lovely young thing many years his junior. In fact, she could easily have been his granddaughter. Jim and I wondered why we didn't get to meet the other wife.

Pa-Coh children came running in and told us that our drivers had arrived and were waiting for us on the Ashau Valley road. We hiked across a stream to the road and loaded into the vehicles. After saying goodbyes and taking pictures, some of which I mailed back to Cu Pang, we headed to A-Luoi.

Dave Atherton's team also had returned to A-Luoi by the time Jim and I got back. Dave said that a local Pa-Coh villager, Cu Le, led them across several mountains to a helicopter crash site. Dave and Randy Brown looked through the wreckage, and after checking the location with locations of known crash sites in the area, decided that the wreckage pertained to a resolved helicopter incident.

From there the Pa-Coh guide led them to an area about 500 meters to the south, where he provided an account of his sighting of remains of a U.S. soldier there in 1972. Cu Le said that two or three days after the sighting, the mountainside was bombed by American aircraft (The American team members saw several large bomb craters in the immediate vicinity). Cu Le said he did not see the remains when he went back to the site sometime after the bombing.

After finishing up their investigation, Dave and his team re-crossed the mountains to get to the main road that runs through the Ashau Valley. Vehicles were waiting for them which took them back to A-Luoi.

Several days later, we all travelled to an area near La Dut Hamlet, Bac Son Village, which is several kilometers from A-Luoi. The village militia commander reported to us that he knew the location of a crash site near there, and we decided to give it a try. The location he described was in the vicinity of one of the crash sites we were looking for, and we decided to check it out.

The militia commander agreed to act as a guide to lead us to the crash site. He led us over a mountain and through thick jungle and then up a muddy mountain trail. When we hit the mud we knew we would run into leeches, and sure enough we constantly pulled off the blood-filled, tiny monsters from hell that had latched onto our boots and crawled up our legs in search of a meal.

When we reached the top of the mountain at the end of our climb, we started down a steep slope on the other side and finally stopped at a jungle stream. There our guide showed us helicopter wreckage. Randy Brown and Jim Williams, our two CILHI guys, began shooting compass azimuths and plotting our location. As the team analyst, Dave carried a map showing all the crash sites in the vicinity, resolved and unresolved. We finally determined that the crash site was likely a resolved CH-47 helicopter incident and was not any of the cases we were investigating.

There was another site we wanted to check out a kilometer or so away, but Ho Xuan Dich and Dave and I seriously considered calling off the search. We were going to have to drop further down into a steep ravine. The route would parallel the course of the stream, which suddenly becomes two raging waterfalls. To get to the coordinate shown on our map, we would have to climb down rocky ledges next to the waterfalls.

Jim Coyle and I had been instructed by our superiors at JCRC not to risk living soldiers for dead ones, which is good advice. Ho Xuan Dich and I both discussed the risks and decided to abort. But when we started discussing how we were going to get back to where we had started, we realized going back was as dangerous as going forward. In considering the odds, Ho Xuan Dich and I made the decision to keep moving downstream, down the sides of the waterfalls, to the bottom of the ravine. There, according to U.S. records, would be aircraft wreckage of an F-4 Phantom.

As we moved ever downward into the forbidding abyss, we crossed the face of a cliff with no vegetation to hold on to. Normally we could find a root or something to grab, but this time there were only slick, protruding rocks that stuck out from the cliff. I went across with Ho Xuan Dich and we were both staring at each other as we inched along. I'm sure that both of us had it in the back of our minds that the other might push the other one off if he had the chance. Old prejudices die hard. We were both visibly relieved when we reached sure footing.

At the bottom of the ravine, we found no evidence that any aircraft had crashed there. After we had looked around a while and satisfied ourselves that nothing was there, we made our way further downstream, and eventually started working up the side of a mountain to get out of the area. We hit the top and started down through a banana grove until we eventually exited onto the main road where our vehicles and drivers were waiting. Those guys with the beautiful Jeep Cherokees were always a sight for sore eyes.

On the morning of August 15, we left A-Luoi and retraced the scenic route to the Laotian border, then north and then east past countless battlefields to Dong Ha Town, Quang Tri Province. We had finished our work in the Ashau Valley and it was time to move on to our last investigation before wrapping up the seventh iteration.

We arrived back in Dong Ha Town, Quang Tri Province. We had one more investigation to do before heading back to Hanoi. The case was not on the "70-Name List," and therefore was a secondary case and had a lower priority. We investigated secondary cases only when we had extra time available. But I definitely wanted to do it because I had a personal stake in it.

My best friend for years was Bill Hanners. Bill and his wife Sherry had lived in an apartment directly below my wife and me in Washington, D.C. Bill and I were young enlisted men who had recently returned from overseas: Bill from Thailand and I from Vietnam. I was studying Arabic at a branch of the Defense Language Institute, and Bill was assigned to an Air Force public affairs detachment. Our two families totally enjoyed the year we spent together, and our friendship has continued up until the present. We still write and call, and Betty and I have dropped in to see them from time to time over the years.

While we were in Washington, D.C. in 1973, Bill told me about a close friend who had been killed the previous year during the 1972 North Vietnamese offensive into South Vietnam. The friend, who was also a distant relative of Bill's, was stationed with Bill at the same base in Thailand. Bill said the friend had flown to Vietnam from Thailand to do some work, and when he finished, he caught a flight back to Thailand. The aircraft was an Air Force search and rescue helicopter.

Anyone who spent time in Vietnam knows that the way American military personnel frequently got around was by hanging around an airfield until they could catch a bird going in the general direction of where they wanted to go. Bill's friend had done that; only, unfortunately, on the way to Thailand, the helicopter received a mission by radio to rescue a downed pilot in Quang Tri Province. As the aircraft went in to pick the pilot up, it was hit by North Vietnamese fire and crashed. Everyone on the aircraft was presumed to have perished, though remains of those on board were never recovered because the crash site was in enemy-held territory.

Bill Hanners stayed in close contact with the family of his friend after the war and frequently was a guest in their home. Bill said the tragedy was extremely difficult for the entire family but particularly for the mother. He said her life essentially stopped in 1972 when she first received word of her son's death.

When I was living in Bangkok, Bill wrote me a letter and asked me to investigate the case if I ever had an opportunity to do so. I answered and said that I would.

Bill also sent me a copy of BAT 21, a book written by the Air Force officer whom the search and rescue helicopter was attempting to rescue. The pilot was on an electronic emissions collection mission over central Vietnam when his aircraft was hit by a North Vietnamese missile. The aircraft had a crew of electronic warfare specialists aboard, but none were able to exit the aircraft and all perished in the crash. The pilot was the only member aboard able to exit the aircraft. "Bat 21," the radio call sign of the pilot, called for assistance, but the search and rescue aircraft sent to rescue him, the helicopter on which Bill Hanner's friend had caught a ride, was hit by enemy fire and crashed. Bat 21 watched in the distance as the helicopter went up in flames.

Bat 21 was caught in the middle of a major North Vietnamese offensive and unable to go anywhere. He was totally surrounded by enemy combat units, and the Air Force command deemed it too risky to send in another helicopter to try a second rescue. A second search and rescue aircraft would also likely have been shot down. Bat 21 stayed in hiding several weeks as an Air Force spotter aircraft flew overhead periodically and kept track of his situation.

Bat 21 was eventually rescued by special operations troops sent in to get him. They bravely infiltrated the area under the cover of darkness in a rubber boat on the Cam Lo River. As the special operations soldiers were intrepidly moving toward Bat 21's location, the spotter aircraft above passed instruction to Bat 21 on the ground where to meet them for the pick up.

To ensure the aircraft transmissions to Bat 21 were not being intercepted by enemy troops, the pilot of the spotter aircraft passed directions that consisted of a code based on Bat 21's knowledge of championship golf courses around the United States. Only Bat 21 and a close friend back at an Air Force headquarters knew the details about the golf courses, and the instructions to Bat 21 on the ground were indecipherable by the enemy. Upon linking up, Bat 21 and his rescuers exfiltrated the enemy-held area in the rubber boat.

The book BAT 21 was made into a movie by the same name, starring Gene Hackman. The movie was exciting, but took great liberties with the facts in the story. There were a number of changes the movie made to the real story, the most notable of which was the scene in which the search and rescue helicopter attempted to rescue Bat 21 and was shot down. The movie version was total fantasy. In the scene, the crew members survived the crash, but were all murdered by North Vietnamese forces. One of them had been forced to walk around in a mine field until he stepped on a mine and was killed.

When I found out my team was going to be operating in Thua Thien and Quang Tri Provinces during the Seventh Iteration, I researched the case involving Bill Hanner's friend and took all of the pertinent details along with me to Vietnam.

As I've already mentioned previously in this chapter, we had been in Dong Ha village a few weeks previously, back when the weather in the Ashau Valley had turned bad and we drove up to investigate a case. At that time, after we had concluded the investigation of the case on which we were working, Ho Xuan Dich came to my room at the Dong Ha guest house to talk to me. He told me the Quang Tri Province MIA investigative team wondered if we had a case they could be working on while we were in the Ashau Valley. The province team thought if we did, they would be able to do a preliminary investigation of the case and the joint team could stop back by Dong Ha before driving back to Hanoi. I retrieved the data sheet I had worked up and gave it to Dich for him to give it to the province investigative team.

So now the joint team was back in Dong Ha to see what the province investigative team had discovered about the case. The three province team members, all representatives from the Quang Tri Province People's Committee, told us they had located the crash site. They said that the actual site was about a half kilometer from the location I had provided on the data sheet I had given them. The province team members said they had also found some witnesses to the incident, though none had been to the crash site immediately after the helicopter went down. They had seen the crash only in the distance, just as Bat 21 had reported he had seen it. The witnesses were rice farmers fleeing the North Vietnamese offensive. They did not return to Cam Lo, the village where the crash occurred until after the North Vietnamese victory in 1975.

After the meeting the province team led the joint team to the helicopter crash site. There was little wreckage left at the crash site except for miscellaneous debris that local rice farmer had thrown in a pile over the years whenever they hit pieces with their plows. They had already salvaged the larger pieces and what remained were the remnants that one always finds at a crash site: small bits of rubber, plastic, and metal.

I had already read the book BAT 21, but I did not see the movie until I got back to Bangkok. As I walked around the crash site, I tried to visualize where Bat 21 may have been hiding when he saw the crash of the aircraft. The crash site is on the edge of a tiny hamlet, and all around the area are rice paddies. The Cam Lo River, on which Bat 21 was eventually able to exfiltrate to safety, is a hundred or so meters away.

The next morning, Dave Atherton, Ho Xuan Dich, and I travelled to the Cam Lo District Headquarters, where Dave and I interviewed three witnesses to the crash we were investigating. They were unable to give us too much information since they had been fleeing from the North Vietnamese Army at the time. But it was their belief, as was Bat 21's that the airmen on the aircraft all perished in the crash. They said the helicopter burned instantly upon impact and likely no one had been able to escape.

That night back at the Dong Ha guest house, a former South Vietnamese NCO came to my room to see me. He told me that his son was in a refugee camp in Hong Kong and he asked me if I would send him some American money that he would give me. I asked him why he didn't send the money himself, and he expressed that if he mailed it from Vietnam it would never get to him. I reluctantly agreed and the former ARVN gave me a one hundred dollar bill to give to his son. A month later, I found the man's son in a refugee camp in Hong Kong and gave him the money.

The next morning I told Dich that the former ARVN had come to see me. I was sure that he already knew about the visit from the local security snitches, and I figured if I mentioned it first, he wouldn't accuse me of conspiring with the enemy. He did, in fact, already know about it and told me that the hotel was doubling its security to ensure that we Americans weren't bothered again. It's too bad the Vietnamese economy isn't as efficient as the spy system.

Later back in Bangkok, I got a letter from the former ARVN and he said the next day after he had come to visit me, Dong Ha security officials ordered him to report to the local state security office. He said they gave him a warning about contacting Americans. In his letter he also requested assistance in leaving Vietnam, so I asked a friend of mine in the embassy refugee office to mail some standard forms to him.

After concluding the case in Cam Lo District, the joint team began the two-day return journey to Hanoi. On the evening of August 18, Team 2 reached Hanoi. Team 1 had already returned a few days before, and they had exotic tales of adventure just as we did. Both teams took the opportunity to celebrate by eating an American-style steak, french fries, salad, and onion soup at one of the private restaurants in the city. After almost three weeks of Vietnamese food, the meal was a welcome treat.

The next morning, August 19, the Americans were taken to the Noi Bai International Airport where we were met by LtCol Spurgeon, Jim's and my boss at the Liaison Office in Bangkok. He had flown in on the U.S. Air Force C-130 aircraft that had come to pick us up. On the flight back, Spurgeon informed Jim and me that we would be returning to Hanoi in a week with Harvey and him to attend a technical meeting. The purpose of the meeting was to prepare for a new series of investigations. Since we had finished up the "70-Name List," it was now time to put together a plan of how we were to proceed with the remainder of the discrepancy cases. Truthfully, Jim and I weren't overjoyed to hear that we would be returning to Vietnam again right away, but we expected it since the seventy cases on the original list had all been investigated, with mixed results.

Our return to Bangkok closed the chapter on the first year of joint U.S. and Vietnamese investigations of seventy discrepancy cases. And what a year it was! I participated in four of the seven iterations; Randy Nash, and David Atherton were on six; and Jim Coyle and Rick John went on all seven. We felt like we had done something historic, and indeed we had.

On August 28, Jim and I went back to Hanoi as members of Harvey's delegation, which flew from Bangkok to Hanoi in a U.S. Air Force C-12 aircraft. At the meeting in Hanoi, there was a lot of bickering back and forth among the two sides about how we were to proceed in investigating the additional compelling evidence cases. But one thing both sides were definitely able to agree on was that the Jeep Cherokees needed to be flown out of Vietnam for badly needed maintenance before we could start any more investigations. After having gone up and down Highway 1 many times and traversed some of the most rugged terrain in Southeast Asia, they seriously needed maintenance. They are unquestionably fine automobiles, but no vehicle can take that kind of abuse for long without repair. The Vietnamese agreed that U.S. Air Force transport aircraft could pick up five of the eight vehicles most in need of repair, carry them to a Jeep dealer in Guam for service, and then bring them back to Vietnam.

On August 30, Jim and I returned with Harvey and the other members of the delegation to Bangkok to await further developments in the search for MIAs in Vietnam. During the past month, Jim and I definitely had our rendezvous with destiny, but on the aircraft going back we weren't reflecting on that. We were just plain exhausted. Twenty days of investigations in Vietnam, plus preparation for and participation in the technical meeting, had worn us to a frazzle. Our "destiny" when we got back to Bangkok was to take off for a couple of days before the incredible grind began again.

CHAPTER 13

RECOVERY OPERATIONS

At the conclusion of the investigations of the "70-Name-List" during the Seventh Iteration in 1989, the Americans and the Vietnamese had a series of meetings in Hanoi and came to an agreement as to how the two sides would proceed through the remainder of the discrepancy cases in Vietnam. The agreement was by no means easily worked out and there was quite a bit of heated discussion from both sides.

The argument centered mainly around the formula for resolving cases. The U.S. wanted skeletal remains before resolving cases. The Vietnamese wanted cases to be resolved on the basis of preponderance of the evidence, not just remains. The Vietnamese argued that joint investigations had precisely determined the fate of a number of MIAs, but recovery of the remains was impossible due to the long passage of time and circumstance.

Eventually a compromise was worked out whereby the U.S. side would maintain its own internal resolution standards to satisfy U.S. legal requirements, but would close cases in Vietnam on the weight of the evidence.

With an agreement in place, several U.S.-Vietnamese investigations were conducted after the Seventh Iteration, but I didn't go on them. The American side was sending two teams into Vietnam each iteration, and Bill Bell and Jim Coyle were the team leaders. I was mainly involved in travelling to the refugee camps in Thailand, Hong Kong, and Macau. The mission of refugee interviewing was still ongoing, someone had to do that job, and I was chosen. I preferred being in Vietnam since that's where the action was; but getting information from the refugee camps for upcoming iterations was important also.

However, my luck changed and in February of 1990 I went back to Vietnam on an iteration. JCRC was fielding two investigative teams, and a remains recovery team. Bill Bell and Jim Coyle were to be the two investigative team chiefs, as usual, and my job was to provide Vietnamese linguistic support to a remains recovery operation.

Although I had headed a recovery team in Lang Son Province on the Chinese border in January of 1989, an agreement had been made since then between JRTC and CILHI that in investigative matters, JCRC would be in charge, and on recovery operations, a CILHI anthropologist would direct the effort.

I love being the guy in charge, but it was only fair that a CILHI representative run a recovery operation. He's the expert in recovering remains, and the person who potentially has his career on the line if things go sour. Also, he's subject to being subpoenaed in court cases contesting findings, which is never a pleasant experience. Usually in such cases, MIA families are mad about something in the identification process and take their anger out on CILHI through the legal system. In the past when this has happened, the CILHI anthropologist who worked on the case and the organization's commander, LTC Johnnie Webb, were run through the ringer several different ways.

Since Webb's organization potentially makes the final call in MIA cases, he ends up being the whipping boy for just about every group that has a legal ax to grind in the POW/MIA issue. In addition to legal hassles, Webb was once beaten up pretty badly during a so-called television MIA documentary. Webb knew the television directors were looking for sensationalism and he didn't want to participate, but was told to do so by his superiors in the Department of Defense. His bosses were concerned that it would look like the government was not cooperating if he refused to be interviewed. Webb did as he was told and fell victim to an egregious incident of television manipulation. The program was obviously designed to make it appear that the search for MIAs was being conducted by Keystone Cops.

Jason Ota, a Japanese-American anthropologist from CILHI, was in charge of the recovery operations that we were going to conduct in Son La Province. His recovery team members were Sergeant First Class Jack Robinson and Sergeant Scott Carpenter, both Army graves registration specialists from CILHI. A Vietnamese official from the Vietnamese Office for Seeking Missing Persons (VNOSMP), Nguyen Hung Manh, would be assisting us.

While Jason and I were involved in recovery operations, Bill Bell would be investigating cases in Hai Phong Province. Jim Coyle would be in Son La Province with Jason and me, but would be in the remote areas of the province investigating cases.

The game plan was that I would stay with the recovery team until the conclusion of the recovery, then I would travel to Hai Phong Province and work with Bill Bell. By this time I was pretty much considered the JCRC resident expert on cases that occurred in Hai Phong Province, because I had interviewed hundreds of refugees from there during my trips to Hong Kong and Macau.

In order to nail down the location of the remains of the pilot we were looking for in Son La Province, I interviewed three old soldiers who had been involved in the incident. Manh had brought them to Son La Town several days before. During the first years of the war before deploying to South Vietnam, they had been stationed in Son La. The three men were Captain (retired) Than Ai Quy of Son Tay, Hanoi; Former Senior Sergeant La Van Bot of Ba Na Liu Hamlet, Huy Ha Village, Phu Yen District, Son La Province (Bot was an ethnic Black Tai); and Captain (retired) Tran Nhu of Son Tay, Hanoi.

The three men had information about a pilot who had ejected safely over Son La after his aircraft had been hit by antiaircraft fire, but was killed by militia before landing. Quy and Bot had witnessed the incident, and all three men had seen the grave of the pilot.

At the time of the incident, Quy was senior sergeant (thuong si) who commanded a platoon designated as the 1st Sapper Platoon, 41st Reconnaissance Company, Northwest Military Region. Bot, the ethnic Black Tai witness, was a senior sergeant and squad leader of 1st Sapper Squad, which was commanded by Quy. Nhu, the third witness brought to Son La by Manh, was a senior sergeant and platoon leader of the 4th Sapper Platoon, 41st Reconnaissance Company. Nhu had not witnessed the shooting, but had investigated the case upon the order of the commander of the 41st Reconnaissance Company.

After obtaining detailed information about the death of the pilot, Jason Ota and I travelled with the witnesses to the hill on which the pilot was buried and asked them to stake out the grave site. Nhu was unable to because of the long period of time that had passed. Quy and Bot said they remembered the general area, but were hampered by the fact that during the war the area was covered with forest, which now was largely gone. Since they couldn't remember the specific location, they both staked out large squares that were about thirty meters apart from each other.

Then Jason staked out the area in between. The logic was that if we excavated the area identified by Quy and Bot, and also the area in the middle, hopefully we would be able to recover the remains of pilot.

I told Manh we needed a minimum of fifty workers to dig out the area identified by the witnesses. Manh had a meeting with local village leaders who agreed to supply our laborers. I watched in the distance as Manh bargained with them. The U.S. government paid thirty dollars a day for each laborer, but I don't have any idea how much Manh ended up paying the village, or what the village paid the laborers. Whatever was the final arrangement, the workers all seemed happy with it. Our workers, who were all ethnic Black Tai, were dressed in their traditional village garb.

I tried to take pictures of the excavation in progress, but the Black Tai female members in our work group didn't want their picture taken. The males didn't mind, but the women would giggle and turn away from the camera. However I did manage to get a few surreptitious shots that recorded for history the attempted excavation of the grave of an MIA pilot in Son La Province.

Bill Bell had attempted to excavate the grave in November of 1988, and I tried again in January 1989. Together we dug what amounted to large swimming pools. Jason was much more scientific and used a statistical equation to plan his digging operation. Jason directed, and I interpreted for him, that trenches be dug one meter wide by fifty meters long. Then he left a space one meter wide, which he called a "balk," and dug another trench. The result was a trench, balk, trench, balk, and so on. Jason said statistically, should remains be present, he would be ninety-five percent certain of finding the remains, and yet would only have to did up half of the area.

And to ensure that we tried everything possible, Jason also connected his trenches to the swimming-pool-sized holes that Bill Bell and I had dug previously in 1988 and 1989. At the time I thought Bill and I had done some pretty impressive digging; however, Jason's trenches made ours look tiny in comparison.

Colonel Tho, the province foreign affairs representative, had been an engineer during the Battle of Dien Bien Phu in the French war and in the last war with the Americans. As a captain in an engineer unit at Dien Bien Phu, he had supervised some of the trenching operations. During the American war, he was responsible for repairing roads and bridges in Son La Province that had been destroyed by U.S. bombs. Colonel Tho was definitely impressed with Jason and his ability to dig trenches. Tho sat down and sketched for Jason the trench system General Giap had masterminded during the battle.

After several days of supervising fifty Black Tai digging a vast trench system in miserable weather, Jason called off the dig. We had found nothing. I had now been to Son La three different times and had dug on the hillside three times. In my heart, I knew the pilot had to be buried somewhere on that hillside, but we had tried everything we knew to do and still were unable to recover the remains of the pilot.

We had been successful in that the evidence we obtained concerning the pilot's fate was overwhelmingly convincing; but we just didn't feel like the job was finished unless we were able to bring the pilot home.

One of my jobs in addition to interpreting was to verify expenses that the U.S. government had incurred at the excavation site. Manh and I negotiated for the total price the U.S. government would eventually be billed. Manh gave me his tally of the numbers of workers, supervisors, and vehicles that would be figured into the calculation. I had kept my own list and Manh and I resolved the differences between the two, which were minimal. Manh would be responsible for paying the province, and the U.S. government in turn would pay the Vietnamese government at the agreed-upon rate for each laborer, supervisor, and vehicle. Also, the U.S. government was charged for damage to the land as a result of Jason's vast trench system.

The next morning, Jason Ota's recovery team, Manh, and I departed Son La Town and drove east through the mountains to the town of Moc Chau, which is also in Son La Province. Jason, Manh, and I were going to meet up with Jim Coyle and Ngo Hoang at the Moc Chau guest house, before continuing on to Hanoi. The plan was that the next morning, I would accompany Jason and his recovery specialists to Hanoi, where they would catch a flight to Bangkok. From Hanoi, Manh and I would travel on to Hai Phong Province, where we would meet up with Bill Bell and David Atherton.

At the guest house, which was a dump even by Vietnamese standards, Jim and Ngo Hoang related to Jason, Manh, and me that their team had just investigated a crash incident that had occurred at the nearby Moc Chau Tea Plantation. The case had not been on their list to be investigated, but by happenstance, Ngo Hoang had picked up some leads that a crash had occurred at the plantation and two American had been buried there. In addition, Hoang had obtained a wartime document providing the names of the two dead crew members, the type of aircraft, and the date and time of death. The document appeared to have been originated by North Vietnamese Army troops stationed in the area of the tea plantation during the war.

Rick John, Jim's Air Force analyst, typed the names of the two Americans into his portable computer. When the corresponding case appeared on the computer screen, it became immediately evident that everything about the crash incident in the tea plantation correlated to a case that U.S. records say occurred in another province about fifty miles away. That particular case would have eventually been investigated by JCRC in an upcoming iteration, but had Ngo Hoang not obtained these chance leads at the tea plantation, JCRC would likely have been unsuccessful in resolving the case. The crash site would have been far away from where investigators would have been searching.

One of the problems in investigating crashes of high performance aircraft is that crash sites often aren't anywhere near the last known location of the aircraft. In a matter of minutes, a jet aircraft can easily travel miles from where it had run into difficulty.

Jim said that he and his team had visited the Moc Chau District People's Committee headquarters where they were introduced to Nguyen Van Dai, a sixty-seven year-old resident of the state tea plantation. Dai claimed he was the person who supervised the burial of the two pilots after the crash of the aircraft. Dai told Jim he believed he could point out the grave of the two Americans, but he recommended he do so surreptitiously. He said if local people saw where the graves were located, they would dig them up in the hopes of selling the remains. Dai said even his own son had asked him to dig up the remains and sell them.

Jason and I drove out with Jim and Ngo Hoang to Team 65, which is a workers' village on the grounds of the tea plantation. Jim and Hoang were going to pick up Dai, and he was going to show them the crash and grave sites.

The tea plantation is a lovely place. Within its vast domain are hundreds of acres of row after magnificent row of waist-high tea plants. Surrounding the plantation are karst mountains, which are jagged pieces of limestone that look like monstrous spikes sticking up out of the ground. The scenery is one of exotic wonder. The weather is crisp and cool year round because of the altitude. Frequently fog rolls in and obscures the karst, and when it burns off, the sun transforms the tea plantation into a paradise of verdant splendor.

Fidel Castro had been to Moc Chau back in the late seventies and had even stayed in the guest house where we were now staying. We had seen pictures of the bearded Cuban president with Vietnamese officials as they were touring the tea plantation. I wondered as I was walking through the plantation if Castro had decided to start tea production in Cuba, though I couldn't imagine macho Cubans drinking wimpy Vietnamese tea.

The tea produced at the Moc Chau Tea Plantation is a green-tea variety the Vietnamese love. Personally I didn't care for it; it was too bitter for my taste. The last time I had been to Son La, in January 1989, Colonel Tho had given me some to take back to my wife Betty in Bangkok. She and I brewed a pot one evening, and we ended up pouring it out. Bill and Xuan Bell like Moc Chau tea, and I gave them what we had left over.

At the tea plantation, Dai pointed out to us the various places connected with the incident: the crash site, the place where he had supervised the recovery of the remains, and the general vicinity of the graves. Dai explained that the remains were buried away from the tea plants because workers would have been reluctant to enter an area where they could potentially be confronted by angry American ghosts.

This may sound silly to American readers, but is something the Vietnamese in that part of Vietnam take seriously. The majority of the people in northwestern Vietnam are "Luong," which is a religion based on ancestor worship or reverence. The happiness and prosperity of the living depends on the appeasement of departed spirits. This includes the spirits of American pilots as well. A run of bad luck or a haunting would likely be the result of disrespect to a spirit.

During a previous iteration, my team obtained the remains of an American pilot that were being reverenced. In order to protect the privacy of the MIA family, I won't go into details, except to say the remains had been kept in a ceremonial urn.

Jason and I had gone to the grave site with Jim and Hoang to see the scenery. We still planned to leave the next day for Hanoi, and then I would be heading to Hai Phong with Manh. Should an excavation of the grave sites pointed out by Dai be warranted, it would have to wait for a future iteration.

However, something happened that made us change our minds. When we drove up to the vicinity of the grave sites where Dai would meet us, we came upon several young Vietnamese men who were in the process of digging holes all over the area. They obviously were looking for remains, with the likely motive of selling them. A public security officer from the plantation was with us and he questioned them. After determining they had found no remains, he ordered them to their homes.

At this point, Jason and I reasoned that if we were to leave the next day, remains hunters would attempt to excavate the site and we might never have a chance of repatriating the remains of the Americans. Jason and I decided to stay and conduct a completely unplanned excavation.

While Jason and I made preparations for another recovery, Jim and Ngo Hoang and their American and Vietnamese team members departed Moc Chau and travelled to a place called Phu Yen in northern Son La Province. Undoubtedly the investigation at Phu Yen was the most dangerous an investigative team had undertaken to date. The team was fortunate no one was killed. In cold wind and rain, they climbed up incredibly steep and slippery karst mountains to inspect a crash site and to interview ethnic minority witnesses. Jim told me later that never again would he take such risks. He said that in the future should he reach a decision point where he had to decide to abort the mission or to continue on, he was going to err on the side of caution.

I understood perfectly. Ho Xuan Dich and I faced the same decision in the Ashau Valley back in August of the previous year. But we were locked in to continue the mission because the route back would have been just as dangerous as moving forward.

The next day, February 25, 1990, Nguyen Van Dai, the witness to the burial, staked out for us an area in which he said he had ordered the bodies to be buried. Just like in Son La, the area staked out was large; because of the long passage of time he could not pinpoint the exact location of the graves. Jason began immediately roping off the site and precisely recording data with his technical instruments.

I told Manh I needed fifty workers and he went through the bargaining process with the tea plantation managers. Later back at the guest house I was joking with Manh and told him that I bet he paid the tea plantation two dollars for each worker and the Vietnamese government kept the twenty-eight additional dollars the American government was going to pay. I was just pulling Manh's leg, but he got red in the face, jumped up, and started telling me that wasn't true at all. Up until then I didn't believe it was true, but after seeing Manh's reaction I wondered if I had been closer to the truth than I thought. Whatever the reason for Manh's outburst, I had definitely struck a raw nerve.

The workers showed up in beat-up Russian trucks. Our laborers were mostly female, which was fine with me. Vietnamese men, as I've already mentioned, don't do too well at that type of labor.

The weather at Moc Chau was cold and rainy. Over the next few days as Jason, Manh, Jack Robinson, Scott Carpenter, and I stood out in the open supervising the operation, our feet got miserably cold. We had sufficient rain gear with us, but our boots got wet. We solved that problem partially by wrapping our feet in plastic before putting them in our boots. This kept our feet from getting wet, but when we walked our feet would slip and slide within the boots. Still, that was preferable to wet feet.

During the dig, the female workers flirted with the Americans and would giggle among themselves when we would walk by. They particularly liked teasing the young graves registration specialist, and I would end up interpreting the remarks back and forth.

Some of the women asked me why we were digging for remains (Tai sao cac anh dang dao len hai cot?). I jokingly replied that we were a family of grave diggers travelling around Vietnam digging up remains. I told them that Jack Robinson, a black, was my older brother; Jason, a Japanese-American, was my younger brother; and Scott Carpenter, a young white soldier, was my son. I thought I had said something really funny and was sure I would get a laugh in response, but the women just stared at me as if I were serious. Jason said, "I guess we all look alike to these people."

The supervisor of the women was a gruff Vietnamese male who obviously had years of supervising workers. He was a no-nonsense type of guy and when the workers slacked off, he was quick to bring them back in line. Just above where we were working was a little bluff, and two cute teenage Vietnamese girls came up one afternoon on bicycles to watch the work in progress. I reasoned they must have been daughters of senior plantation officials. They were dressed too nicely to be from a working family. They were giggling as they watched all the activity.

I asked them if they wanted jobs digging, to which they giggled and replied that the work was too dirty. They had on pretty, clean clothes and obviously had no intention of doing anything manual.

The work supervisor turned around and yelled in Vietnamese: "The man asked if you wanted to work. If you don't want to dig, then you get your young butts out of here!" The girls disappeared in a flash, colorful scarves and pointed Vietnamese hats flying in the wind.

At the excavation site, two Vietnamese males got in a fistfight. I'm not sure of the cause of the fray, but they were doing a pretty good job of pounding each other. One of the women said, "Where is the Public Security Service when you need it?"

We dug for two solid days and found absolutely nothing. I'm sure Dai was telling the truth about the burial, but he said that since the war, a road had been built through the depression where the bodies were buried, and that had thrown off his remembrance of how things had been arranged back then. Dai wanted us to continue on another hundred meters down the depression, but we already had an excavation site that rivaled the one Jason had dug at Son La Town, and Jason was adamant that we weren't going to dig further.

As we were finishing up at the excavation site, a tea worker named Vu Cong Phu came up to Manh and me and said the bodies had not been buried where Dai had indicated at all. He said that while it was true that Dai had given the order to bury the pilots, Dai had not observed the burial, but had departed after giving the order. Phu said that he and six other workers from the tea plantation had buried the bodies at another nearby location. He said the other workers who were in the burial party were now all deceased or had moved from the area. He said only one of the men was now still alive, and he was living at Son La Town. The man's name was Pham Cao.

Colonel Tho, the Son La Province foreign affairs representative, had driven up from Son La Town to see how things were going and was listening to me interview Phu about the burial.

Colonel Tho told me he knew Pham Cao and could bring him from Son La Town to Moc Chau for an interview if we would like. I told Colonel Tho that we might want to do that.

I asked Phu to stake out the area where he believed the graves to be. He staked out a square about seventy-five meters north of the area where we had been digging. Jason was standing firm that we were not going to dig. He said, "We can't dig every time some bozo comes up and claims he knows where someone is buried. A scientific excavation is exactly that: scientific. It's not a hit and miss thing." I told Jason I agreed, but I felt we were obligated to give it a try. Who knows, maybe the guy was telling the truth. Jason relented and agreed to try one more time, but he said this would be final. No more digging if this didn't work. We put our fifty workers to work and once again dug out a huge area. However, we found no remains nor any evidence of burial.

Colonel Tho approached Jason and me and said that he would be willing to send a vehicle back to Son La Town to pick up Pham Cao, the other individual whom Phu had identified as having been on the burial party.

Jason hit the roof. "No way! No more wild goose-chases!" Jason said he had enough. He voiced that in addition to digging a maze at Son La Town that would rival trench warfare in World War I, he exceeded his authority in conducting two additional excavations in Moc Chau. He said that he and his two graves registration specialists were not going to play. He stated that what needed to be done was to get all of these alleged witnesses together, find the site, and then he'd come out with a recovery team in a future iteration and do an orderly, scientific excavation. But he wouldn't tolerate any more Joe Blows being dragged out of the woodwork as witnesses.

I felt like we should bring the witness from Son La Town and dig if he could identify a spot. I argued that it was a matter of economics. The American taxpayers had spent incredible sums of money getting us there, we were already in place, and it would only take one more day. If an excavation team had to come back in the future, more money would have to be spent just to determine if some guy could actually remember where a grave was located—which we could do now. Even if we dug again, and the dig failed, at least we would know where the remains were not located, which was important too.

But Jason was firm and I had no choice but to go along. He owned the two graves registration specialist who were members of his organization. I had been told he was in charge of excavations and I was to provide linguistic and investigative support only. I reluctantly agreed and we shut down the operation.

The next morning at the Moc Chau guest house, just prior to our departure from Moc Chau, a worker in the building came to my room and told me there was a person visiting the guest house who would know about the case under investigation in the tea plantation. The worker left the room and a short time later returned with a person who identified himself as Nguyen Van Minh. Minh said he was the former director of the plantation. During the war, he was a cadre working in the plantation planning office. Minh expressed that he had seen the crash site and the recovery of the bodies, but had not seen the burial.

Minh said Nguyen Van Dai, as the work supervisor and militia commander of Team 65 of the plantation, was responsible for the disposition of the remains. He related that Dai's workers buried the remains. Minh voiced that he could not remember the names of any of the workers who participated in the burial, but he did remember seeing Doan Hai, the assistant director of the tea plantation at the crash site. Minh said Hai possibly may have stayed around and witnessed the burial. Minh related that Doan Hai now lives at a state farm in Lai Chau Province. Minh told me he had once been to Hai's house in Lai Chau Province, and could lead investigators there should someone wish to discuss the incident with him.

When I wrote the final joint U.S.- Vietnamese report on the Moc Chau dig, I included the names of the two potential witnesses: Pham Cao and Doan Hai. I don't know if they were ever contacted or not. Since I left JCRC I haven't had any word on the status on any of the cases on which I worked.

Early the next morning, Jason, Manh, the two graves registration specialists, and I departed for Hanoi. When we reached Hanoi, I tried to get flights for Jason and his team to fly back to Bangkok on Thai International, but none were available. Therefore, Jason and his team would have to wait until the arrival of our U.S. Air Force C-130, even though their mission was over. Air Vietnam had flights available, but Harvey had prohibited us from flying on that airline because of its safety record.

JCRC routinely used to fly on Air Vietnam until one of its aircraft crashed near Bangkok. During the investigation of the crash, it was discovered that the airline habitually flew from Hanoi to Bangkok with the minimum amount of fuel needed to make the trip, and then filled up in Bangkok for the return trip. Fuel shortages were chronic in Vietnam and the additional fuel obtained in this way was evidently being used to augment the refueling of Vietnamese aircraft. The ill-fated aircraft flying from Hanoi had run into bad weather and had to continue on because it didn't have enough fuel to bypass the storm. The aircraft was sucked into the ground by wind shear before it reached Bangkok.

Harvey, Bell, and Mather were waiting in Bangkok to take that particular flight back to Vietnam. That afternoon, Harvey ordered that JCRC personnel would no longer fly Air Vietnam.

And there were other horror stories as well about Air Vietnam. Employees assigned to the Orderly Departure Program in the American Embassy reported that Air Vietnam flights on more than one occasion loaded the aisles with passengers after running out of seats. One of the employees told me a few days before the crash in Bangkok that Air Vietnam was an accident just waiting to happen.

When I told one of the senior Vietnamese officials that Jason and his team couldn't get flights on Thai International and would have to stay in Hanoi several extra days, he smiled and said he would make arrangements for them to fly out on Air Vietnam. I politely declined his offer.

In Hanoi, I called LtCol Spurgeon at the Liaison Office in Bangkok. Using the Vietnamese government-run phone system is not AT&T or Sprint, and making an overseas call is an ordeal in socialist bureaucracy. I told Spurgeon the status of our recovery operation in Son La Province and that we had found nothing. I conveyed that I hadn't heard from Bill Bell and Dave Atherton and had no idea how their investigations were coming along. Spurgeon told me that he had a C-130 crew on standby to bring us back. All he needed was a call to set up the flight. I told him as soon as Bill and Dave showed up I'd call him with the information on when we would need the aircraft.

That evening Bill and Jim's teams arrived in Hanoi, and we all celebrated our return from the wilderness by going to our favorite capitalist-run restaurant in Hanoi. We had steak, salad, french fries, and Coca-Cola. The bill per person was about five dollars: an incredible bargain in any country in the world.

I knew that this might be the last time I would be in Vietnam. I had already made up my mind that I would be leaving JCRC when my tour was up—for purely personal reasons that had absolutely nothing to do with the job. Knowing that I might not ever be returning to Vietnam, I spent the next day nostalgically sightseeing and buying my last souvenirs at unbelievably low prices.

That evening and the following day, Bill Bell, Jim Coyle, and I finished up our joint reports with our Vietnamese counterparts and then the next morning drove out to Noi Bai International Airport to meet the C-130 that had flown in to pick us up. As usual LtCol Spurgeon had accompanied the aircraft from Bangkok.

I definitely felt a lump in my throat as I said goodbye to Vietnamese I had worked with for several years. With a few I had argued politics, economics, and religion; with others I had told jokes and had partied; with some I had shared dangerous adventures; and with one I had been in the same place during the Vietnam war, but on different sides of the wire.

I particularly was sad about saying goodbye to Ngo Hoang. I really liked that old man and was going to miss debating Marxist theory and Milton Friedman economics with him. I definitely was going to miss his hearty laugh which often was directed at himself.

I asked Hoang how much longer he would be at VNOSMP before he retired. He laughed and said his boss had told him he could retire when all the MIA cases had been resolved.

As I was saying goodbye I thought about the time Hoang and I were in a little dingy restaurant in the middle of absolutely nowhere, when a drunken Vietnamese army soldier started causing a ruckus in the place. I had asked Ngo Hoang what was going on, and with a solemn expression, he told me that something very serious was bothering the man. Seeing Hoang's sudden change in demeanor, I got somber myself and leaned over and asked him what the man's problem was. Bursting out in boisterous laughter that rocked the room, Hoang loudly retorted: "He's a drunkard!"

As the C-130 headed down the runway and rumbled aloft, I looked below at the rice fields knowing I might never again see the Vietnam I loved. The emotion was overwhelming.

Vietnamese women laborers at an excavation site in northwestern Vietnam. The weather was miserable.

A graves registration specialist recording technical data at a pilot's grave site.

Author and a Vietnamese Army Captain at the crash site of an F-4 Phantom fighter aircraft.

CHAPTER 14

DEATH OF THE GHOST

I returned to Bangkok knowing I had to make interview trips to refugee camps in Hong Kong and Thailand before I could start outprocessing from the Liaison Office. I would also have to train my replacement, my good friend Chief Warrant Officer James Webb, who would be arriving shortly. He had just graduated from a refresher Vietnamese course at the Defense Language Institute, in preparation for his up-coming assignment at the Liaison Office. From time to time throughout his language course, I had sent Jim job-specific vocabulary words and interview questions in Vietnamese for him to practice on during his language study.

LTC Harvey had called me months before Jim was identified as my replacement and asked me if I was going to stay on at JCRC. He said he needed to know my plans, so he could get a replacement for me in the mill should I decide to rotate. He told me that whoever would be replacing me would likely need Vietnamese language training at the Defense Language Institute; therefore, the requirement to identify someone months in advance was critical.

I told Harvey I would let him know as soon as I could. That evening, I gathered the family and we had a family vote. The vote was three to two: three for leaving and two to stay. My wife and I voted to leave; my youngest son voted to leave; and my oldest son and daughter voted to stay.

I left Joint Casualty Resolution Center for purely personal reasons: I didn't want my kids to grow up and leave the nest without getting to know their grandparents and other relatives. And it was just time to get back. Pure and simple, that was it. My wife and I gave up a lot to leave Bangkok; I had a job that I loved, and my wife's job at the International School in Bangkok was the most rewarding and best-paying she ever had.

Bill Bell told me I was an absolute fool to leave. He kept saying: "If it ain't broke don't fix it. If you're happy and everything is going good for you, don't make the change."

Bill Bell was absolutely right about the physical side of life: the money and the tangible things. But he was completely wrong about the abstract and personal. Bill, as clear-eyed and rational as he was about money, prestige, and power, did not always see the spiritual.

My family and I left Bangkok in mid-June of 1990 and took a month's leave to visit relatives and friends we hadn't seen for years. Then in July I signed in to my new unit, the Joint Readiness Training Center at Little Rock Air Force Base. I was to be an evaluator of prisoner of war interrogators and counterintelligence agents undergoing training at Ft. Chaffee, Arkansas, which was about 160 miles away.

During the first couple of weeks of August of 1990, a battalion of the 82nd Airborne Division was training at Ft. Chaffee, the training center for JRTC. While the exercise was in progress, Saddam Hussein launched his attack against Kuwait. Because the 82nd Airborne Division is always one of the first major units to be alerted in a national crisis, the exercise was called off and the airborne infantry battalion undergoing training was pulled out for deployment to Saudi Arabia. As a result I only spent one night in the field with the 82nd.

On August 23, 1990, I got a call informing me that I had been selected to participate in Desert Shield. I was told I would have to be at MacDill Air Force Base in Tampa, Florida, the next day. The individual who called was LTC Tom Hodge, who had been LTC Harvey's deputy when I first arrived at JCRC. I knew I was going to be in good hands. I got orders cut, obtained tickets to Tampa, drove the 160 miles to Ft. Chaffee, picked up my field gear, and caught a flight to MacDill out of Ft. Smith, Arkansas.

At MacDill I drew my desert gear and a pistol. LTC Hodge told me that my new unit was Special Operations Command Central (SOCCENT), and he was the J-1 (director for personnel and administration) for SOCCENT headquarters. Within a day most of the future SOCCENT headquarters had formed at MacDill, and we, including LTC Hodge, departed on a C-5A Galaxy en route to Saudi Arabia.

It was great working with Hodge again. Over the next half year, I popped in to see him in his office at SOCCENT headquarters at least once a day. He was always good for a cup of coffee and a laugh. Since he was in an administrative job, he was out of the loop concerning a lot of things going on in the intelligence arena, and I kept him up to date on the latest happenings. We swapped all kinds of JCRC stories, and I was able to give him insight into what JCRC had been doing in Laos and Vietnam since he had left the unit. He also gave me some JCRC gossip I had somehow missed out on during my three years in Bangkok.

Dave Atherton always liked Hodge, and I dropped Dave a note saying I was working with him. Dave wrote a letter back and enclosed a nice note to Hodge.

SOCCENT was one of five major commands organic to CENTCOM, General Norman Schwarzkoph's headquarters. The other commands in CENTCOM were ARCENT, which contained all Army forces; MARCENT, all ground Marine Corps forces; NAVCENT, all Persian Gulf Naval forces; and CENTAF, all Air Force units in the Kuwaiti theater of operations (KTO). SOCCENT had operational control (OPCON) of all SOF (special operations forces) assets in theater.

My job in SOCCENT was HUMINT Coordinator (human intelligence), which was fascinating. I was in constant contact with small intelligence teams at various places in Saudi Arabia that were collecting information from Kuwaiti refugees, Iraqi defectors, and later Iraqi prisoners of war. Also, SOCCENT had a team that became well-connected to elements of the Kuwaiti government in exile. This team was able to obtain information reported by the Kuwaiti Resistance from inside of occupied Kuwait, and occasionally even Iraq.

My job was to obtain information from the teams and disseminate it to various major headquarters in Saudi Arabia and to intelligence agencies back in the U.S. In addition, I was the primary POC (point of contact) for anything having to do with HUMINT on the SOCCENT staff.

The SOCCENT J-2 (intelligence director) was LTC Jack Grace. He had a SIGINT (signal intelligence) background and didn't have a clue what my job was supposed to be. His instructions to me were to do whatever needed to be done and keep him informed. I knew exactly what my function was, since in countless exercises all over the United States and overseas I had trained ad nauseam to do what I would be doing for the next six and a half months.

We worked unbelievably long hours: twelve, fourteen, and sixteen hour days were common. When we landed in Saudi Arabia, I started work and didn't have any time off for six weeks. When I finally was able to take a day off, I crashed and didn't move for an entire day. I had never been so mentally exhausted in my life—even when I came out of the Ashau Valley at the end of the Seventh Iteration.

When I had left JCRC, I was sure that I never again would have a job as interesting as the one I was leaving. It was hard to believe that within two months I would have a job that was every bit as good, and if I had not been living in the middle of a desert without my family, it would have been paradise.

I got to travel quite a bit around Saudi Arabia. Several times I went to King Khalid Military City, which we called "KKMC." In peace time, KKMC was a Saudi training base, and now it was being use as a support base for U.S. and Coalition Forces (Arab allies). If you ever want to see what billions of dollars of hard, cold cash look like in the middle of absolutely nowhere, then KKMC is the place you must see. The architecture is unreal and looks like a cross between Disney World and Hong Kong. A surrealistic mosque dominates the setting.

Several of our SOCCENT intelligence types stayed there, and they lived in style. They shared a suite that had two bathrooms and two balconies.

I had lunch several times in the officer club at KKMC, which looked more like a five-star hotel than a club on a military compound. I hadn't seen that much opulence since I visited the Oriental Hotel in Bangkok. The club even had luxurious suites for guests, and several of us were given one once to rest up before lunch.

Commanders of major units, which included Colonel Jesse Johnson, the SOCCENT commander, had the perk of being able to fly around in Lear jets, operated by an Air Force detachment. I had the opportunity to fly on his aircraft a couple of times: I went once to Riyadh with him and an intelligence officer when he had to brief General Schwarzkoph and once to KKMC.

I drove to Riyadh a number of times. It was a four- hour trip and we used to drive it at ninety miles an hour in Toyotas, given to us by the Japanese government. Saudis would pass us even at that speed. We never made the trip once that we didn't see the remains of at least one newly crashed automobile on the side of the highway being claimed by the desert sand.

When I visited Riyadh, I usually had business in the MODA Building (Ministry of Defense and Aviation), where General Norman Schwarzkoph was headquartered. I had never seen so much brass assembled in any one building in my life, with the exception of the Pentagon in Washington, D.C. Colonels, lieutenant colonels, and majors were a dime a dozen and were packed into offices like sardines.

My wife's brother was a senior executive in an oil exploration company in Saudi Arabia, and I visited him once. He lived well in a very nice compound in Dhaharan. One afternoon he and I went out to eat at a Mexican restaurant, of all places.

Being in SOCCENT was just like going to a high school reunion. I ran into old friends that I had known my entire Army career. Constantly former bosses and employees from the old days were stopping by to say hello. One of my former NCOs, Jim Justice, who was now an Army captain, heard through the grapevine that I was at SOCCENT and dropped by. We had a fine reunion. I was proud of Jim; he's a totally self-made guy who pulled himself up by his bootstraps. Jim had a poor family life when growing up: his father had been in prison, and Jim had run with gangs as a kid. But in the Army, Jim found his niche. In addition to receiving numerous awards for being an outstanding soldier, he graduated from college, and while in my section at Ft. Campbell, applied for OCS. Jim is a soldier's soldier and an Army success story.

I made so many friends at SOCCENT, it would be difficult to name them all. But one that comes readily to mind was a black Army officer, Captain Andrew Miller. He and I lived in a tiny trailer about the size of a camper. We were so lucky to have it. Most American soldiers were living in abject misery in tent cities, and not only did we have a trailer, but it had an air conditioner, shower, and a toilet as well. It wasn't the style of luxury offered at KKMC, but to us it was heaven.

Miller and I kept each other in stitches most of the time telling jokes and pulling pranks on each other. He was great at pranks, but I finally got him in one he couldn't top. One night during a SCUD attack, he was in the shower when the alarm sounded. I put on my protective mask and lay on the floor twitching like I had been poisoned with nerve agent. He came running out of the shower, saw me lying on the floor, and yelled as he started putting on his protective mask: "That's not funny, Chief!"

Miller was short, but had a powerful physique and was amazingly strong. I shook his hand one day like I was greeting him, and to be silly started squeezing his hand real hard. He started squeezing back and I thought my hand was in a vice. I dropped to one knee before he finally loosened his grip. I became fully aware that Andrew was not the guy to take on in a whimsical test of physical strength.

Another good friend I made was Major Bill Woodier (Air Force). Back during the war, Bill had been an enlisted man in a Marine ground reconnaissance unit. When people would refer to Bill as an "ex" Marine, he would correct them and say he was a "former" Marine. Bill had participated in countless hand-to-hand engagements with North Vietnamese soldiers and had even conducted ground reconnaissance in the Ashau Valley, one of the places where I had been on MIA investigations. Bill had been in just about every hot spot the United States had been involved in since Vietnam, to include Desert One and Grenada. (Desert One was the attempt to rescue the American hostages in Iran.) Just before the ground war, Bill was sent to MARCENT, the major Marine headquarters, as a liaison officer to SOCCENT.

The commander of SOCCENT, Colonel Jesse Johnson, or "J- Square" as he was known to the troops, was a wild man. He was a cigar-smoking, fireball of a Special Forces officer who had been in special operations units for years. During his career he had been involved in numerous special operations missions from Vietnam to Desert One. Just before the air war started, J-Square ordered that personnel working in SOCCENT headquarters be present for a formation that was to occur at midnight.

We all had a pretty good idea what he was going to tell us. January 15, The U.N. mandated deadline for Saddam Hussein to withdraw from Kuwait, had passed. We were expecting the war to start at any time. When J-Square entered the assembly room, we all stood at attention as he jumped up on a table to address us. With the American flag clearly visible behind him, be began his remarks.

He said majestically in his Arkansas twang: "Some people study history; some people watch history being made; and some people make history. And you ladies and gentlemen are the latter. For in exactly three hours and thirty-six minutes from now, U.S. and allied forces will start offensive air operations against enemy targets in Iraq and Kuwait." Then he told us that special operations aircraft would be firing the first shots of the war by putting out of action an Iraqi early-warning radar system.

At the conclusion of his grand speech, J-Square played a tape of Lee Greenwood's song, "I'm Proud to Be an American." It was all pure corn, but his performance and the music sent shivers down our spines. J-Square imparts the fervor of an old-fashioned revival preacher. At the closing notes of the song, J-Square saluted smartly, yelled "Hoo ah!," jumped off the table, and stormed out of the room. They just don't make them like that any more.

When the ground war started, the Marine Corps had the responsibility of advancing to Sixth Ring Road, which bounded the southern portion of Kuwait City. SOCCENT, in conjunction with Coalition Forces, had the mission of the liberation of the city in an operation called URBAN FREEDOM. The plan was that the Marines would take Kuwait City International Airport, and then SOCCENT elements would deploy to the airport, which would be used as a staging area for the SOCCENT and coalition assault on Kuwait City.

SOCCENT headquarter spent the first weeks of February 1991 planning for Operation Urban Freedom. LTC Grace had been medevac'ed back to the States for a desert-related ailment, and our new J-2, LTC Harvey Latson, was in charge of intelligence planning to support the operation.

At a meeting one evening, Latson said he couldn't take everybody to Kuwait City, since SOCCENT had to maintain a base in the rear. But he said he would take as many as he could and asked for volunteers to accompany SOCCENT Forward into the city. I didn't volunteer because I felt somebody had to stay back to run the HUMINT show in the rear. It's great having intelligence types up front gathering information, but the information doesn't go anywhere without support personnel pushing all of the right buttons to make it happen.

Latson asked me why I didn't put my name on his volunteer roster, and I told him. I said I would absolutely love to go, but I would be of better use to the operation as a support weenie in SOCCENT Rear. He told me he really wanted me to go forward with his element and asked me to volunteer. He didn't have to twist my arm; there was nothing I wanted to do more. Latson put me in charge of brainstorming a concept of a HUMINT intelligence organization that would support SOCCENT Forward in the liberation of Kuwait City.

Latson envisioned that SOCCENT and Coalition Forces would capture thousands of Iraqi prisoners, and SOCCENT would need some sort of intelligence organization to perform prisoner of war interrogations, conduct counterintelligence screenings, confiscate important documents, be on the look out for certain types of Iraqi equipment that U.S. intelligence agencies wanted, and collect evidence of Iraqi atrocities. The Special Forces units in SOCCENT had military intelligence detachments, but he felt the intelligence specialists in those units would be busy in providing intelligence support to their units. SOCCENT Forward would need its own intelligence unit to coordinate and exploit the massive number of prisoners that likely would be taken.

The magnitude of our problem was immense. There were an estimated 20,000 Iraqi soldiers in and around Kuwait City, and we anticipated that this number would swell to perhaps 40,000 as Iraqi units fell back to the city. In preparation for this eventuality we eventually put together an ad hoc intelligence unit composed of twenty-five American interrogators and counterintelligence agents, one lawyer for potential war crimes investigations, and fifteen English-speaking Kuwaiti soldiers on loan to the U.S. Army. The soldiers had been studying in the U.S. before the 2 August invasion.

We called our unit the Combined Intelligence Center, which I'm sure must have been the shortest-lived intelligence unit in the history of military intelligence. MAJ Bob Nugent (U.S. Army) was to be the commander of our small unit. He and I made plans that our organization would travel to Kuwait City by helicopter and vehicle as close as possible behind the lead SOCCENT combat elements.

When we got word that the Marines had taken Kuwait International Airport, LTC Latson flew to the airport with J-Square by helicopter to begin directing the initial phase of Operation Urban Freedom. At the same time, we were receiving information from our Kuwaiti Resistance sources in the city that the Iraqis were pulling out. It looked like SOCCENT and Coalition Forces might be able to enter the city unopposed. In any event, the operation was to continue as planned until the situation stabilized.

MAJ Nugent and I were the advance element of the Combined Intelligence Center. Just before dawn on the first morning after the Marine units took Kuwait City International Airport, we departed on five Air Force SOF helicopters to Kuwait. We flew to the Persian Gulf and then headed north over the water. At one point the aircraft launched flares as we entered an Iraqi missile zone along the coast that was thought to still be active. Afterward, all five helicopters refueled in flight from a special operations C-130 fuel tanker. Before we reached the city, the weather turned to soup, so we made a brief stop on an island just off Kuwait. As soon as the dense fog lifted we continued on. We flew north over the waters of the Persian Gulf until we were due east of Kuwait City, then made a sharp turn to the west, flew over the city, and landed at Kuwait City International Airport.

The airport clearly showed the marks of the battle that had occurred the previous day. In addition to widespread destruction, several buildings were still burning. Also there were hundreds of Iraqi prisoners under the guard of U.S. soldiers.

Although the morning weather was clear when we landed, during the early afternoon the winds shifted and we found ourselves in dense acrid smoke from burning oil wells that turned day into night. The resulting soot from the smoke left our skin and clothing grimy. Because of the air pollution, my face stayed red and raw the entire time I was in Kuwait.

SOCCENT had originally planned to set up a headquarters in the airport and weeks before had even constructed an elaborate model to delineate where all of the staff elements and units would initially be located. But the airport was severely damaged and the buildings that had not been destroyed had been trashed by the Iraqis and were filthy. Therefore, SOC-CENT headquarters and our ad hoc intelligence unit moved to a former Kuwaiti military complex located several kilometers to the east of the airport. A number of the buildings in the compound had been occupied by the Iraqis and were filthy, but we managed to find an old gym and a one-story barracks that were in fairly good shape and moved in.

The Iraqis had already pulled out of the city, but had left behind unbelievable amounts of equipment everywhere. Navy SEALS had accompanied our group and were acting like little kids in a candy shop. They were having a ball playing with all of the Iraqi weapons laying around. A couple of them started shooting off Iraqi antiaircraft weapons, which made all of SOCCENT Forward hit the ground. We thought for a brief moment we were under attack. The SOCCENT Headquarters Commandant came running out yelling that no one was to fire any more weapons.

The SEALs who were with us were equipped with special 9MM fully automatic weapons with silencers. One of them asked me if I wanted to hear what it sounded like. I said, "Sure, but the Headquarters Commandant just told us not to do any more shooting." He laughed and said, "Don't worry, he won't even hear it." The SEAL fired off a quick burst and sure enough the pops were barely audible.

That night was the coldest I had ever spent in my life, except for perhaps the week on the Chinese border in Lang Son Province, Vietnam. I was miserable. I had travelled light, and like the old military proverb says: "Travel light, freeze at night." The next morning I solved the cold problem by rummaging through Iraqi bunkers until I found two brand-new blankets, still in plastic wrappers. My guess is they probably had been looted from a Kuwaiti store.

Since the Iraqis had pulled out of Kuwait City, we no longer had an interrogation and counterintelligence function. We decided that the mission of The Combined Intelligence Center should be to search buildings, offices, and bunkers for Iraqi documents and evidence of atrocities. We spent the next few days combing the large compound where we were living, which had been occupied by an Iraqi infantry division and a Special Forces Brigade.

We broke up into teams and thoroughly searched the area. We confiscated truck loads of documents, most of which our troops didn't have any idea what they were. We just walked into abandoned Iraqi offices and cleaned out drawers of everything that had Arabic writing on it. Several of us had studied Arabic at DLI, and we also had fifteen Kuwaitis with us, so we were able to provide some guidance as to what was important, but mostly it was just a matter of collecting whatever was found.

A couple of the guys in the Combined Intelligence Center were really into souvenir hunting, and they had their pick of Iraqi equipment to rummage through. The Iraqi weapons were prohibited items, they couldn't keep those, but everything else was fair game under the laws of war. They collected uniforms, personal equipment, insignia, you name it. I found three oil paintings in a bunker that had obviously been looted from a wealthy Kuwaiti home. I kept them because I didn't know what else to do with them. They were too nice to leave for vandals to tear up.

We reasoned that the Iraqis must have been on reduced rations the last few weeks of the occupation. Everywhere we went we found piles of potatoes the Iraqis had been living on. I never thought about potatoes being plentiful in that part of the world, but they definitely had been in February 1991 in Kuwait City. Also, we found heads and legs of cattle that had been slaughtered. These animals likely were from herds of Kuwaiti dairy cattle that the Iraqis decimated when they ran out of food.

In going through areas where the Iraqis had lived, I was struck by how fast they must have pulled out. They left everything. I imagined their officers must have told them that they had ten minutes to get in their vehicles and leave. They fled with the clothes on their backs. They even left personal hygienic items such as tooth paste and shaving cream. We know now the Iraqis were totally fooled by the ruse that a Marine amphibious assault was underway. They saw themselves being trapped between an amphibious assault and a ground attack, hence the reason for their withdrawal in panic.

As I was going through the compound and observing abandoned Iraqi equipment and personal items everywhere, I saw a similarity to what I was witnessing and a story I once read in the Bible. In the story, two lepers were in city under siege by the Assyrians. They decided to leave the city and go to the Assyrian camp, since they believed they would die of starvation if they stayed, and perhaps they would fare better with the enemy.

When they reached the camp, they found it deserted because the terror of the Lord had come upon the Assyrians during the night. They had fled leaving everything. The two lepers returned to the city and reported the news, and the people in the city came out and spoiled what the Assyrian army had left behind.

As I walked around watching Americans and Kuwaitis sifting through the abundant spoils of war, left by an army that had fled in terror, I couldn't help but think of the parallel between the Bible story and what was going on around me.

We stayed in the former military compound a few more days, then eventually followed SOCCENT headquarters into the city. SOCCENT headquarters set up operations in the American Embassy, and we lived in former American Embassy housing. The house I stayed in had not been damaged, though a beautiful home next door had been totally trashed by the Iraqis and was inexpressibly filthy. The odor from inside the house was terrible since the Iraqis had been using it as a latrine.

Once in Kuwait City, I went over to the Hilton Hotel to look for a reporter who had some Iraqi documents he had found in a destroyed building. He had contacted SOCCENT in the American Embassy and said he wanted to turn them over to the U.S. government. When I got to the hotel, a television personality, whose face was familiar from weeks of international reporting, told me the newsman had just caught a vehicle to Saudi Arabia to cover a story. He said the reporter would drop by a U.S. Consulate in Saudi Arabia and turn them in there. Then the television journalist asked me if I wanted to call home on his international line. I said, Sure. He gave me the phone and I called my wife Betty. She said, "Where are you?" I told her I was in the Hilton Hotel in Kuwait City. Silence.

By this time, our Combined Intelligence Center had been considerably depleted in personnel, leaving us with only a half dozen or so American military intelligence specialists. A number of the intelligence specialists in our intelligence center had been borrowed from Special Forces intelligence detachments within SOCCENT, and they had gone back to their units. Two of them, SFC Bob Inscore and SSG Jay Funderburke, both Arabic linguists, had been members of my interrogation section some years before in the 311th MI Battalion, 101st Airborne Division at Ft. Campbell.

Also, we had given our fifteen Kuwaitis to the Document Exploitation Section of the 513th Military Intelligence Brigade. The brigade, which had mostly European linguists, was badly in need of Arabic speakers and was overjoyed to get our Kuwaitis.

For the next week those few of us who were left researched data to determine potential targets in Kuwait City for Kuwaiti and SOCCENT units to search for documents and evidence of atrocities. One of the targets was the former Kuwaiti Experimental Farm, commonly referred to as the "Dachau of Kuwait" because of the horrible atrocities that occurred there.

On one day I went with the remaining members of our now largely defunct intelligence center to the infamous "Highway to Hell" to search destroyed and abandoned vehicles for documents. The area was located northwest of Kuwait City. American aircraft and allied armored units operating parallel to the road had a field day in destroying Iraqi troop convoys that were fleeing Kuwait. It must have been like shooting fish in a barrel. Unable to get through a massive fireball and twisted wreckage that was blocking their escape route to Iraq, hundreds of vehicle attempted to bypass the blockage and escape through the desert. Some of the tactical military vehicles were able to make it around the conflagration and escape, but literally hundreds of non- military trucks and cars got stuck in the soft sand and were abandoned.

From news accounts, I had heard about the destruction, but nothing prepared me for the shock of seeing 1,000 destroyed Iraqi vehicles on a three-kilometer stretch of highway. Most of the Iraqi dead had already been picked up, though from time to time we did see bodies that the search parties had missed.

Next to one body I found a wallet in which was a laminated I.D. card with a photo of the dead man. I took the I.D. with the intention of eventually mailing it to the Iraqi Foreign Ministry with the details of what I knew about the incident. However, Lieutenant Commander Mike Williams (U.S. Navy), whom I had gotten to know very well in the past half year, thought it might be better to leave the I.D. with the body in the event that a search party came back through. I agreed and stuck the I.D. card in an armpit of the dead Iraqi.

We reasoned that retreating Iraqi units would likely have been carrying important documents with them in their attempted escape from Kuwait. We were right. Our search turned up truck loads of documents, which we delivered to the Document Exploitation Section of the 513th MI Brigade.

A day or so later, MAJ Nugent and I drove up another road just east of the Highway to Hell. We were looking for more convoys that had been shot up. On the road we saw destroyed vehicles and equipment everywhere, though the amount was not as great as on the main road of the Highway to Hell. Along this route the dead had not yet been policed up and bodies were everywhere. The scenes of death looked like something out of Dante's Inferno.

At one stop, we observed the charred remains of seven Iraqis who had died in agony in a flaming truck. As we walked around trying to visualize what happened, we were joined by a writer from the "New Republic" magazine. The writer recorded the terrible scene and our conversations in an article appropriately entitled "Highway to Hell," in the March 29, 1991, issue of the magazine.

At several places, packs of wild dogs were feasting on the dead, which made the gruesome spectacle so much worse. In the vicinity of one destroyed truck, I saw two human bones gnawed completely clean. Next to the bones was a cur that was wagging its tail in friendly greeting as we were walking up. I thought about shooting the dog with my Beretta pistol, but didn't. I couldn't really blame the dog for doing something that was just part of its nature, as repulsive as it was.

Occasionally, I'd begin to feel sorry for the dead Iraqis, and particularly for their families who didn't know where their loved ones were. But my feelings subsided when I'd see the dead lying in the middle of loot they had stolen from Kuwait City. Most of them were simply felons who had been caught leaving the scene of their crime.

After spending several weeks in Kuwait City, I flew back to Saudi Arabia. As I walked in the door of SOCCENT headquarters, one of the officers who had stayed behind asked me if I wanted to go home the next day. I said I did, but I just had too much to do before I left. He said, "Go!" He'd see that all of the loose ends were taken care of.

I spent the rest of the day and the next morning in finishing up as much as I could and then got Maj Nugent to take me to the airport to catch a C-141 transport aircraft back to the states.

While waiting at the airport, LtCdr Mike Williams drove up and said, "You didn't think

I'd let you get away without saying goodbye, did you?" He left Saudi Arabia a few week later, and since that time we've kept in touch. I've even had the opportunity to visit him and his lovely Vietnamese wife in Tampa, Florida. One evening she cooked us a delicious Vietnamese meal, the first Vietnamese food I had eaten since leaving Vietnam.

The aircraft rumbled aloft and my mind went back to the time I left Vietnam in November of 1972. Then, the exhilaration that was evident in the aircraft was contagious. This time the passengers were very quiet. I can't explain the difference.

Once we were over the Atlantic, the pilot let me call Betty and tell her I was en route.

The aircraft landed at MacGuire Air Force Base, New Jersey, and from there I went to Philadelphia and got a civilian flight to Little Rock.

I met Betty and the kids at the Little Rock airport. I was still wearing my desert "chocolate chip" fatigues and "boonie" hat. We attracted a lot of attention in the airport as we all embraced. Several passengers in the terminal started clapping when they saw us all hugging and kissing.

Even though I hated being gone from my family, I wouldn't have missed serving with SOCCENT for just about anything in the world. It felt great to have been part of a victorious Army, as opposed to participating in the debacle of Vietnam, which I had done years before. After Vietnam fell, I became a very embittered soldier. I left Kuwait with my head held high and proud to be an American.

Back at Little Rock Air Force Base, I put in my retirement papers and made plans to leave military service. I loved the Army and as a regular Army officer I could have stayed in for at least nine more years. But I felt I had done everything I could possibly do in my field and was ready to move on to something else.

The day before I was discharged, my family and I attended a special retirement ceremony for me held in the office of the commander of the Joint Readiness Training Center, Brigadier General Fisher. General Fisher decorated me with a Bronze Star Medal for service in Desert Storm, which made the fourth I had received in my military career. General Norman Schwarzkoph had signed the award.

In front of my family and friends I made a short farewell speech. I said: "Exactly one year ago today, I started inprocessing into the Joint Readiness Training Center here in this very building. In my wildest dreams, I never could have imagined that exactly 365 days later I would be awarded the Bronze Star Medal for having participated in a war.

"There are four people here this morning, my family, who deserve this medal more than I. While I was away having the time of my life, they had to stay behind and put their lives together after an overseas tour in Thailand. If something could go wrong, it did go wrong. I left them in a temporary, tiny apartment and a car sitting on a dock in New Orleans. But in all circumstances, they showed exemplary courage above and beyond the call of duty of a military family. I want them to know that I am proud of them and love them.

"I have just concluded twenty-one years of military service; I participated in two wars, Vietnam and Desert Storm; and I searched for MIAs in the jungles of Vietnam. I have come full circle. This is where I get off."

I stood at attention, saluted, and said, "Airborne!" I could feel the backbone of every soldier in the room, including the commanding general, stiffen with pride.

I signed out of the unit, my last official act before leaving the Army. As I walked out of the building with my family, I felt the ghost of Vietnam that was living within me had finally died. It had taken more than a quarter of a century, but I was finally free.

THE END

Destroyed vehicles on the "Highway to Hell" in Kuwait. The author, as a member of the Special Operations Command Central (SOCCENT) had the mission of searching these vehicles for documents and specialized equipment.

THE MIA ISSUE; AN ASSESSMENT

When folks learn I have some knowledge about the MIA issue, invariably I get asked, "Are Americans still being held captive in Indochina?" The answer I give has some qualifications to it. I generally say, "No American MIAs, excluding Bobby Garwood, and perhaps other deserters and/or so-called 'progressives,' were held in Indochina after the American withdrawal in 1973."

I'm not at all convinced there were American MIAs other than Garwood, who remained behind in Vietnam after the American withdrawal. However, some smart analysts have told me they believe that there were, and because I highly respect their analytical judgement, I am not ready to close the book yet on that particular chapter of the Vietnam War.

But as for American POWs being held after 1973 against their will—it just didn't happen. There's not a shred of proof that occurred. The majority of the better analysts at the Defense Intelligence Agency and the Joint Casualty Resolution Center could accept that statement with no mental reservation.

If I or others who have been involved in the MIA issue had concrete proof American POWs had been held in Indochina against their will, we would be standing on the street corners shouting it to anyone who would listen. No one could make anyone I know who had ever been part of the search for MIAs keep silent about such a thing. If there has been a cover-up to conceal that American POWs remained behind, then it has been the most cleverly devised conspiracy of misinformation the world has ever seen. Personally, I don't believe there is anyone in the U.S. government smart enough to concoct something like that.

But there have been several prominent individuals in and out of the federal government who believe strongly that American servicemen were held after the American withdrawal. One of them, Colonel Millard Peck, has gotten perhaps the most media attention. He was the former director of the Special Office of POW/MIA Affairs. He resigned his office in protest that the U.S. government was indeed involved in a cover-up of the alleged fact that the U.S. government had abandoned American MIAs in Southeast Asia. One of his comments upon his resignation was, "You can take it to the bank that Americans are being held in Vietnam."

I have no intention of attacking the integrity of Colonel Peck, who served his country with distinction over the years; however, I will say in response to his charge, that proof that Americans are being held doesn't exist in any of the intelligence files of the United States government. He may believe POWs were kept—and know it for certain with all of his heart—but that is not proof. And you definitely can not take it to the bank, as Colonel Peck said.

He accused the office he headed, the Special Office for POW/MIA Affairs of Defense Intelligence Agency, of perpetrating fraud in ignoring evidence that Americans are being held. He said that DIA analysts have a mind-set in which they automatically dismiss reports of live-sightings as fabrications.

Colonel Peck is correct that most of the live-sighting reports get dismissed by DIA, but they are not just looked at and discarded. Anytime a refugee reports a live-sighting, a detailed process is begun whereby the refugee's story is thoroughly checked out. The amount of effort and expense that goes into the investigation and evaluation of information provided by the source of a live-sighting is overwhelming. Often, investigators are required to work on cases that are obvious fabrications, just to make sure no one can say that the information wasn't checked out. Even Bunker Queer stories were handled seriously. JCRC and the Defense Intelligence Agency were charged with leaving no stone unturned in regard to the live-sighting issue. Unfortunately for those investigators who had to go out and check out some of the more ridiculous stories, that meant Bunker Queer, too.

There is another reason why Colonel Peck was wrong in his assessment of the way DIA analysts do their evaluations. Every analyst at the Defense Intelligence Agency, and at JCRC, would love to be the one who gets national attention for cracking the MIA issue wide open and showing the world American POWs do exist in Southeast Asia. The reason they have not done so is not because they are routinely dismissing important pieces of evidence about live- sightings; they haven't done so because the proof does not exist.

By the same token, every interviewer at JCRC, including myself when I was there, continuously searched for that one refugee who would have provided the proof that Americans POWs were held in Indochina after the withdrawal. Interviewers, including Bill Bell, who avidly believes Americans were held, have talked to thousand upon thousands of Vietnamese and Laotian refugees over many years, and not one has provided that missing piece of evidence. Again, I believe we didn't find that one refugee because he or she doesn't exist.

As I have mentioned several times already in this book, Bill Bell is a true-believer. I talked to him often about his theories of American POWs being held after the war. He can argue the point eloquently, and even convincingly. When he was called to testify as the Director of the POW/MIA Office in Hanoi before Senator Kerry's special POW/MIA committee, he strongly stated his belief that Americans POWs were held. However, when one of the senators asked if he had proof of their continued captivity, he had to say he had none.

I have studied in detail a number of books and articles about the MIA issue. Many of these, such as BOHICA (The title stands for: Bend Over Here It Comes Again) by Scott Barnes and KISS THE BOYS GOODBYE by Monika Jensen-Stevenson and her husband William Stevenson, allege that American POWs, perhaps large numbers of them, were held after the American withdrawal and continue to be held up until the present. In addition, the authors of the above books allege that the government is engaged in a conspiracy to cover up evidence that Americans POWs remained behind.

The author of BOHICA, Scott Barnes, has been discredited so frequently as a fraud that his book is probably not even worth talking about. In the MIA community, Barnes is often referred to as, "The-man-who-crossed-the-river-that-never- was." This goes back to one of Barnes' fabrications that he clandestinely crossed the river between Thailand and Cambodia. No such river exists. Barnes claims to have been a member of a CIA assassination team that was sent on a mission to kill American POWs so they would never surface and embarrass the U.S. government. Barnes alleges to have personally seen American POWs with his own eyes.

KISS THE BOYS GOODBYE was written with integrity and is not a fraud like BOHICA. It is an interesting and very readable book, but it's all done with smoke and mirrors; there's no substance whatsoever to authors' charges. The proof they offer is entirely circumstantial and flimsy at best.

Ross Perot, perhaps the most influential and the epitome of the true-believers, had extensive contact with Monika Jensen-Stevenson and William Stevenson while they were writing their book.

In all of the investigations and interviews I have conducted, and the government documents and civilian books I have read, I neither heard nor saw anything that convinced me there are living American POWs held against their will in Indochina. I'm not hard-headed and unwilling to look at the evidence; all I ask to see are a few facts that can be proven—and my belief is I haven't seen them because they don't exist.

As I mentioned at the first of this book, the week before I flew to Bangkok to start my job with JCRC-LNO, I saw a television special entitled "We Can Keep You Forever." The theme of the film was that Americans were kept in Vietnam as insurance, or as a bargaining chip. After watching what seemed to be a very well documented account of the MIA issue and presentations of supposedly concrete evidence, I went away a true-believer in every sense of the word. But after years of having seen the so-called evidence up close, and having talked to many alleged firsthand witnesses of live-sightings, I now give very little stock to the film at all. Everything brought out in the film, including the allegation that American POWs were taken to the Soviet Union, is based solely on opinion and speculation.

When Boris Yeltsin, the President of Russia, stated that American POWs were brought to the Soviet Union during the Vietnam War, the international news media went wild. Suddenly, here was the confirmation. What had been speculated about for years had actually occurred! The story, like so many other sensational MIA revelations the American public has been subjected to in recent years, died with barely a whimper.

Over the years I personally heard a lot of convincing stories from refugees who claimed to have seen and even talked to Americans in captivity in Indochina after the war. I got all excited in Hong Kong once when I stumbled onto a refugee who provided an incredible story about Americans who remained behind after the American withdrawal. Although the refugee seemed genuinely truthful, every claim he made eventually proved to be a total lie. That individual alone caused U.S. interviewers and analysts from several different U.S. government agencies to spend hundreds of hours of investigative time and incredible sums of money on a lead that went absolutely nowhere.

And the same was true of most of the other live-sighting stories about American POWs that have been reported over the years. Some of the refugees reporting such stories seemed very convincing, but one by one, most were shown to be deceptive.

I said that most of the live-sighting stories turned out to be deceptive. I did hear live-sighting stories that turned out to be true. However, all were eventually correlated to cases that analysts already knew about. Many of these concerned individuals who were unable to get out of South Vietnam in 1975 when the North Vietnamese Army overran the country. All of these cases have been resolved.

And I heard dozens upon dozens of stories about Bobby Garwood, who remained in Vietnam until 1979. Hundreds of Vietnamese saw and talked to Bobby Garwood in Vietnam, and they frequently report this information to interviewers. The stories usually follow along the lines of: "I know about an American who was at Yen Bai Re-education camp after the war, who went by the Vietnamese name of 'Nam.' He operated the electric generators in the camp, and sometimes ran a movie projector to show propaganda films."

When I was assigned to the Liaison Office in Bangkok, visitors would frequently show up at the JCRC Liaison Office with some sort of story of living American prisoners of war somewhere in Indochina. Regardless of how high-minded or altruistic the visitors seemed to be, sooner or later the bottom line of how much it was going to cost the U.S. government to get them out of Laos, Cambodia, or Vietnam reared its ugly head. The price tag was always high.

Once I interviewed a refugee who claimed to have seen and talked with living American POWs in Vietnam. At the end of the interview the refugee said that another person in camp had also seen and talked to the Americans at the same time. Being an old Army interrogator, my antenna went right up. I love it when I have two sources who claim to have witnessed the same incident. I immediately called in the other refugee and interviewed him separately. The live-sighting had supposedly occurred a few months before, and should have still been fresh in their memories, if true. In comparing the two stories, word for word, it was obvious they had fabricated the incident. The stories were so out of kilter with each other to indicate at least one witness, and likely both, was lying.

Although Laotian, Cambodian, and Vietnamese refugees can and have been excellent sources of information about what happened to American MIAs, there are a multitude of unscrupulous opportunists in the camps who see the MIA issue as a potential pot of gold. These people are the lowest form of humanity who would commit any type of crime if the opportunity presented itself. With the intention of obtaining money for their information, they prey on the feelings of MIA family members who often are susceptible to their lies and hoaxes.

I believe the best circumstantial proof that Americans were not kept after the American withdrawal is the "discrepancy" or "compelling evidence" cases. These were incidents where compelling evidence exists that living American servicemen came under the control of wartime enemy forces and never came home. Should Americans have been held in Indochina, they likely would be the MIAs who make up these cases. The majority of the other cases have elements about them that would cause a prudent person to conclude the serviceman did not survive. A wartime incident of an aircraft going down with no chutes observed would be typical of many of them.

But many of the compelling evidence cases have been troubling. Examples of these cases are parachutes seen descending into a populated area, search and rescue personnel talking to a downed pilot, and wartime pictures of an American POW in a communist newspaper. Compelling evidence cases comprise roughly ten percent of the more than 2,000 unresolved cases of missing Americans from the war in the countries that make up what was once known as Indochina.

In recent years, JCRC investigative teams have routinely been going into Vietnam and Laos to investigate compelling evidence cases. Most have now been investigated and many have been resolved with remains repatriated. Not one iota of evidence has been obtained by the teams that would indicate any Americans from compelling evidence cases were held in Vietnam after the American withdrawal.

I believe another example of circumstantial proof that Americans were not held exists in a document published by JCRC called "Refugee Reports By Location." This is a document that I was able to get the data processing section in the JCRC headquarters to put together shortly after my arrival at the Liaison Office in Bangkok. I'm proud of this document and believe this to have been one of my best contributions to the MIA issue during the three years I spent in Bangkok.

This document, as the title suggests, lists by location every refugee report ever published by JCRC. The locations are identified by military coordinates. JCRC has published literally thousands of refugees reports, and each report contains the location of where the reported incident occurred.

Below is an example of the way JCRC reports are listed in "Refugee Reports By Location." Each line represents a JCRC report and provides the incident location, the type of incident, the date the incident occurred, the name of the source providing the information, the country in which the refugee was located when he gave the information, the year he was interviewed, and report number. The example is as follows:

Location	Incident	Date	Source	Report
XD 765432	Crash Site	1966	Nguyen Van Minh	H90-173
XD 766431	Capture of pilot	1967	Tran Hung Trinh	P89-023
XD 800343	Grave of pilot	1969	Ho Xuan Cao	M87-006
XD 813444	Remains recovered	1974	Pham Thi Linh	S83-442
XD 945331	Hearsay of capture	1988	Quang Thi Linh	I91-116

Under the heading "Location" are military coordinates that identify where the incident occurred. The "XD" signifies a specific grid zone on a military map somewhere in Vietnam. The six numbers to the right of the "XD" delineate a specific spot within the grid, thereby pinpointing the location of the incident, as described by the refugee to the interviewer. Under the heading of "Incident" are the types of incidents reported. Under the heading of "Date" are the dates the incidents occurred. Under the heading of "Source" are the names of the Vietnamese refugees who reported the incidents. Under the heading of "Report" are the countries where the refugees were interviewed by JCRC. In the example, "H" is Hong Kong; "M" is Malaysia; "P" is the Philippines; "S" is Singapore; and "I" is Indonesia. The two numbers to the right of the letter designating the country are the year the refugee reported the incident. The three numbers that follow the year represent the number of the report.

The JCRC reports in "Refugee Reports" by Location are listed by incident location; therefore, it's easy to determine at a glance all of the incidents reported by refugees that occurred within a certain locality.

This is important because many incidents reported to JCRC interviewers are told over and over again. For instance, if an aircraft crashed near a populated village, many local villagers likely witnessed the crash or knew about it. As a result, JCRC interviewers often write multiple reports about the same incident, all reported by different refugees. Multiple reporting of the same incident in the "Refugee Reports By Location," generally will have the same location, the same date, and the same type of incident. As an example, reports by refugees who saw the same incident might appear as follows:

Location	Incident	Date	Source	Report
YD 865432	Crash of Aircraft	1966	Nguyen Thi Anh	H86-003
YD 865432	Crash of Aircraft	1966	Lam Hu Cao	P83-079
YD 865432	Crash of Aircraft	1966	Tran Ai Tam	M85-101
YD 865432	Crash of Aircraft	1966	Nhu Minh Hung	S90-103
YD 865432	Crash of Aircraft	1966	Tranh Minh Ta	I91-113

The example shows that the identical incident, which occurred in 1966, has been reported by five different sources in refugee camps, in five different countries: Hong Kong, the Philippines, Malaysia, Singapore, and Indonesia. The incidents were reported in five different years.

In a nutshell, incidents that really happened and are not fabrications are frequently reported over and over again, because many refugees are aware of the incident. If an incident, such as a crash and death of a pilot, is reported only one time, it may indicate three things: the incident is a fabrication; the incident actually happened, but was in an isolated area and only a few people were aware of it; the incident happened, but few refugees are in the refugee camps from the particular area of the country where the incident occurred.

There are a number of live-sighting incidents contained in JCRC reports, but most are reported only once, and in my mind that most likely indicates they are fabrications.

But in the JCRC "Refugee Reports By Location," there are, in fact, live-sighting incidents that are reported over and over. This indicates that the live-sightings likely really occurred and are not fabrications. As an illustration, the coordinates for the Yen Bai Re-education Camp, where Bobby Garwood was held, are listed line after line, page after page, in "Refugee Reports by Location." The reason they are listed together in this way means that many refugees saw Bobby Garwood at the camp and reported him to JCRC interviewers over and over again.

In addition to Bobby Garwood, there are other live-sighting incidents reported multiple times, but they correlate to cases analysts already know about, such as American citizens who were picked up after the fall of the South, etc.

My question is: If Americans POWs were held after 1973, why don't we see page after page of sightings all listed together by location like we do with the live-sightings of Bobby Garwood and others that correlate to resolved incidents? I believe the answer is: We don't see them because they didn't happen.

I presented the above argument to Bill Bell and he countered that American POWs who were held were kept in isolated conditions and were never seen except by a handful of security people.

I argued in return that JCRC had interviewed a number of refugees who held sensitive public security jobs for long periods of time, and surely they would have seen or known about American POWs who were being held. If they were aware of such live-sighting incidents, they would have reported them, and a pattern of locations in the "Refugee Reports By Location" would have become evident.

Two important facts: secrets don't remain secret long in Vietnam, and Vietnamese are the nosiest people in the world. Should large numbers of Americans have been kept after 1973, or even small numbers, everybody in the country would eventually know about it—and JCRC interviewers would have the locations and circumstances pinpointed in no time. In addition, a pattern would become immediately evident when the JCRC reports were printed out by incident location in the "Refugee Reports By Location."

There is one final reason why I don't believe POWs were held against their will in Southeast Asia after 1973. This is because some outstanding senior analysts at the Defense Intelligence Agency, such as Wick Tourison and Bob Destatte, don't believe it. Wick and Bob, who are both combat veterans of Vietnam, are reasonable men with character. They spent years sifting through intelligence reports and have not been able to find one scintilla of convincing proof that any were held. Had they ever seen proof that American POWs remained behind, they would be screaming their heads off.

I once had a one-on-one conversation in Bangkok with General John Vessey, Special Envoy for Presidents Reagan and Bush on the POW/MIA issue. General Vessey wanted to talk personally with an MIA investigative team leader who had participated in the iterations in Vietnam. Bill Bell and Jim Coyle were both away on refugee interview trips at the time, so I was elected to sit down with the general and answer his questions. General Vessey had been in Hanoi meeting with Foreign Minister Nguyen Co Thach, and stopped over in Bangkok at the American Embassy before returning to Washington to brief senior members of the Bush administration about his talks.

During our meeting, Vessey asked me what I thought of the live-sighting reports that interviewers would submit from time to time. Before I could answer, he said: "Most of these reports are pure baloney, aren't they?"

I answered: "Sir, they are all baloney. No Americans POWs are being held in Southeast Asia."

Vessey said nothing, but sat silently staring at me with his arms folded. I had no idea what he was thinking, but there was absolutely no way he could say something like that because of his official position and the potential political fallout that would occur as a result of his comments.

Vessey told me that Foreign Minister Thach said in their meeting that he would swear on a Bible, or anything else Vessey wanted him to swear on, that no Americans were being held in Vietnam, nor were any remains being "warehoused."

Warehousing was a sensitive issue within the U.S. government. There had been undeniable evidence—real proof—that remains had been warehoused by the Vietnamese government in past years.

However, Foreign Minister Thach may have been telling Vessey the truth. I had heard good analysts at JCRC say they believed all the warehoused remains had been turned over to the United States in a spectacular series of remains repatriations that had occurred in the few months prior to Vessey's trip to Vietnam.

Nothing made Bill Bell angrier than hearing evidence about the warehousing of the remains of MIAs. Bill expressed that to keep American families guessing about the fate of their loved ones, when their remains were being stored in Hanoi in anticipation of the right political moment, was a crime beyond belief.

Bill and I don't agree on whether American POWs were held after the American withdrawal, but there's one thing we do agree on one hundred percent: whoever in the Vietnamese government was responsible for the warehousing of MIA remains should burn in Hell.

Vessey asked me very pointed questions, such as, "Are the Vietnamese cooperating in the search for MIAs?" I told the general that I believed they were—at least at the level at which I worked, down where the rubber meets the road. I personally heard a senior Vietnamese official say once in defense of whether or not Vietnam was cooperating, that for American investigators to be able to travel at will through Vietnam was unheard of and unprecedented in socialist countries and was proof of Hanoi's genuine interest in resolving the MIA issue.

Even Bill Bell, who was always suspicious of Vietnamese motives, grudgingly admitted to me once that our Vietnamese team members were cooperating and doing what they could to help us resolve cases, at least at the local level.

Ngo Hoang, a senior official in the Foreign Ministry, and frequently my counterpart on investigations, asked me once on an investigation: "Am I cooperating?"

Surprised, I said,"Yes, Mr. Hoang, I think you probably are."

Then he said, "But do you feel certain that I am cooperating?"

"Why, yes, Mr. Hoang, I feel that you are."

"Is there anything else I can do in this investigation to make you sure that I'm cooperating with you."

"Well, no, Mr. Hoang, I can't think of anything right now, but if I do I'll let you know."

Hoang then told me that his superiors in the Foreign Ministry had ordered all officials of the Vietnamese Office for Seeking Missing Persons (VNOSMP) to cooperate to the fullest extent in the search for MIAs, and they were to assist American investigators in any way possible.

The overwhelming majority of leaders in our government have come to the conclusion that Americans are not being held in Southeast Asia, but unfortunately all it takes to keep the MIA issue from being put behind us is a tiny minority, such as Colonel Peck and Bill Bell, who stand up and say they believe Americans are being held in Southeast Asia. As a result, the American public is confused because they see these officials as experts who have been in the system and should know what they are talking about.

When Colonel Peck, former head of the Special Office of POW/MIA Affairs in the Department of Defense, resigns in protest over the handling of the MIA issue, the public sits up and takes notice. When Bill Bell, who had spent years working in the MIA issue, and was later the Director of the POW/MIA Office in Hanoi, says American POWs were held in Vietnam after the withdrawal, people assume they must indeed have evidence. Little does the public realize that Colonel Peck and Bill Bell operate at the gut level and allow their prejudices and feelings to guide their actions.

While I was at JCRC, we debated among ourselves whether or not live-sighting reports should be released to the public. I always said they should not because the news media would sensationalize them, and the American public would be even more confused about the MIA issue. I'm afraid my prediction proved true. Live-sighting reports, such as a story about an underground prison in Hanoi holding American POWs, have been released, and unfortunately sensationalized by the press.

I didn't interview the refugee who gave the information about the underground prison, but I knew the interviewer who did, and I talked with the refugee who gave the information a time or two myself. The refugee has been proved to be a fabricator, but unfortunately his garbage is now not only spread around JCRC and DIA, but the American people now get to smell it. The problem with that is the American public becomes confused as to what is the truth and ends up giving credence to conspiracy theories that have no basis in fact whatsoever.

I believe what a future administration needs to do, but likely won't be able to, is to declare that no Americans POWs were held against their will after the U.S. withdrawal. Afterward, the huge bureaucracy that has been created to research and investigate these cases should be dismantled and cut back to minimal levels.

In a brief few years, the POW/MIA bureaucracy has grown from four interviewers stationed in Bangkok and small research centers at JCRC headquarters and the Defense Intelligence Agency, to a vast army of analysts and an MIA task force headed by a U.S. Army general. The bureaucracy that has been created will undoubtedly perpetuate itself, which will mean the issue will never come to a head.

During my three years at JCRC-LNO I wish I could have found information that would prove American MIAs were still alive in Indochina. It would be thrilling for MIA families to have their loved ones come home. But unfortunately it's not to be. It's extremely sad to see MIA families taken in by MIA scams and sensational reports of live-sightings, only to have their hopes cruelly dashed once again.

Politically it would be very difficult to declare the MIA issue settled and start a new era of relations with the Vietnamese government, but I believe it's time to do just exactly that. It is time to move on and get the Vietnam War and the MIA issue behind us.

Postscript

As this book is going to press, there have been significant new revelations in the MIA issue in regard to the Vietnamese turn-over of POW/MIA archival records to a delegation composed of General John Vessey, Senator McCain, and Ann Mills Griffiths. The records, which were kept in the People's Army Central Museum in Hanoi, show that during the war, North Vietnam maintained meticulous documentation of servicemen who were downed, captured, or found dead in areas under the control of North Vietnamese forces.

This came as no surprise to those of us who had been JCRC interviewers. We knew that records of captured or killed American servicemen must exist somewhere. While on MIA investigations in Vietnam or interview trips at Vietnamese refugee camps, we heard witnesses say on numerous occasions that whenever an American serviceman was captured or killed, he, or his body, was searched thoroughly for identification documentation and papers. Also, interviewers heard that photographs frequently were taken of captured or dead Americans and a report describing the incident was made. These were forwarded along with documents found in the search. JCRC interviewers and analysts reasoned that these had to have been stored in a central repository, likely in Hanoi.

As the cold, dead hands of the old guard in Vietnam have been slowly pried from the controls of power over the communist bureaucracy, and moderates have gradually taken control, more and more information has, and will, come out about MIAs. Now that the moderates have become dominant in the government, a reasonable accounting of the MIA issue is possible and at hand.

The recent extensive turn-over of critical documents reiterates in my mind the extent of Vietnamese cooperation in the MIA issue in recent years. I personally know many senior officials in the Vietnamese government, undoubtedly ultimately responsible for the turn-over of the records, who want to see the MIA issue resolved and relations develop between the two countries. So do I. The war is over and it is time to move on.

The author and former Viet Cong Lieutenant Colonel Cu Pang stop on a battlefield in the Ashau Valley to salute the war dead. SFC Jim William has his back to the camera.

The author on an overnight hike in the Ashau Valley.

MIA search team en route to crash site.

JCRC MISSION STATEMENT

The Joint Casualty Resolution Center (JCRC) is the only government organization which has as its sole mission resolving the status of U.S. military and civilian personnel who remain unaccounted for as a result of the Southeast Asian conflict. The JCRC was established by the Joint Chiefs of Staff in January of 1973 and is under the operational control of the Commander in Chief, U.S. Pacific Command.

From its headquarters at Naval Air Station, Barbers Point, Hawaii, and a liaison office at the American Embassy, Bangkok, Thailand, the JCRC staff of 26 personnel performs specialized functions which are fundamental to achieving the fullest possible accounting of Americans missing in Southeast Asia. The JCRC headquarters staff consists of casualty data, negotiation assistance and operations specialists. Linguists who are fluent in one or more Southeast Asian languages also serve on the Headquarters and the Liaison Office staffs.

JCRC linguists take the first steps toward casualty resolution by obtaining information on unaccounted for personnel from refugees who have fled Vietnam, Laos, and Cambodia. The linguists are skilled interviewers who visit refugee camps in Thailand, Malaysia, Indonesia, the Philippines, Singapore, Hong Kong, and Macau. They prepare over 900 initial interview reports annually. Casualty data analysts identify crash and grave sites of missing Americans and attempt to determine whether Americans are still held captive in Southeast Asia by correlating the refugee reports with data contained in case files of unaccounted for personnel.

The Commander, JRCCRC meets several times each year with officials of the Socialist Republic of Vietnam (SRV) in a technical exchange of POW/MIA information and analyses. The technical meetings are devoted solely to discussing issues concerning unaccounted for Americans. Discussion materials are prepared by JCRC for coordination and approval by the POW/MIA Interagency Group. Since September 1988, the meetings have provided a forum for obtaining greater SRV cooperation and evaluating the results of JCRC investigations throughout Vietnam.

The investigators, accompanied by SRV officials, gather information from Vietnamese officials and citizens who may have knowledge of unaccounted for Americans. These ongoing investigations are an important step toward resolving the status of Americans unaccounted for in Vietnam. Team members also survey potential crash and grave sites for future remains-recovery operations.

With regard to recovery efforts in Laos, the Lao agreed in January 1989 to a year-round program of cooperation. By mid-1989, JCRC and CILHI experts had conducted two recovery operations at helicopter crash sites bringing to six the number of joint recovery efforts since the first operation in February 1985. The JCRC hopes to expand cooperative efforts through additional recoveries and investigations of unresolved cases in Laos.

JCRC operations personnel plan and direct the recovery operations and investigations in Laos and Vietnam. These activities require special airlift, field communications, explosive ordinance disposal, medical, and logistics support. All recovery operations are conducted in close coordination with, and support from, the U.S. Army Central Identification Laboratory. JCRC is also the primary agency for repatriating to U.S. soil remains recovered in Southeast Asia. As part of each such event, JCRC personnel plan and conduct ceremonies to honor appropriately those who died serving our nation.

Achieving the fullest possible accounting of missing Americans will continue to require the concerted efforts of all involved agencies. The JCRC will continue to play a central role in this effort by collecting and analyzing POW/MIA data, engaging in technical discussions with Southeast Asian governments, and conducting field investigations and recovery operations.

Department of Defense
POW/MIA Fact Book
July 1989

MORE GOOD BOOKS
FROM HONORIBUS PRESS

THIS IS YOUR ORDER FORM JUST CLIP and MAIL

________ VALLEY OF THE SHADOW $4.95
Ed. Y. Hall
The Vietnam War. A young army officer's combat tour as
an Advisor with the South Vietnamese Army. Introduction
by Gen. William C. Westmoreland. 1966-67.

________ FLYING WITH THE HELL'S ANGELS $5.95
Samuel P. Fleming as told to Ed. Y. Hall.
Memoirs of an Eighth Air Force Navigator's 30 missions
over Fortress Europe with the 303rd Bombardment Group.
1943-1944.

________ UNPUBLISHED ACTIVITIES OF WORLD WAR II $16.95
Earl J. Roberts. Hard Cover.
Frontline duty with the infantry in Europe during
World War II with the 187th Infantry Regiment. 1944-1945.

________ FATED TO SURVIVE $7.50
William P. Maher, Edited by Ed. Y. Hall.
Memoirs of an Eighth Air Force B-17 Pilot / POW.
401st Bomb Group. 1943-1945.

________ THE SEARCH FOR MIAs $12.95
Garry L. Smith, Edited by Ed. Y. Hall.
Answers to the question of "What happened to our Vietnam
War unaccounted for POWs and MIAs?"
Soft Cover.

________ HARRIET QUIMBY – $12.95
AMERICA'S FIRST LADY OF THE AIR
Ed. Y. Hall. The tragic life of America's first licensed
woman pilot, and the first woman to pilot an aircraft across
the English Channel. 1875-1912. Soft Cover.

(TURN PAGE FOR ORDER FORM)

TO ORDER

Please check the space next to the book(s) you want, send this order form together with your check or money order, include the price of the book(s) and add $1.75 each for handling and mailing to:

HONORIBUS PRESS
P.O. BOX 4872
SPARTANBURG, SC 29305

I have enclosed $ _________________ Check _________________ or money order as payment in full. Please no COD's.

Name ____

Address____

City____

State _______________________________ Zip _______________

Please allow 2-3 weeks for delivery.